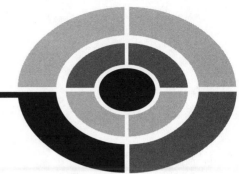

MANAGEMENT ACCOUNTING
DEMYSTIFIED

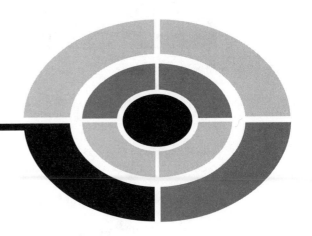

MANAGEMENT ACCOUNTING DEMYSTIFIED

LEONARD EUGENE BERRY,
PhD, CIA

McGraw-Hill

New York   Chicago   San Francisco   Lisbon   London
Madrid   Mexico City   Milan   New Delhi   San Juan
Seoul   Singapore   Sydney   Toronto

The McGraw·Hill Companies

McGraw-Hill
2100 Powell Street, 10th Floor
Emeryville, California 94608
U.S.A.

To arrange bulk purchase discounts for sales promotions, premiums, or fund-raisers, please contact **McGraw-Hill** at the above address.

Management Accounting Demystified

 234567890 FGR FGR 019876

ISBN 0-07-145961-8

Acquisitions Editor
  Margie McAneny

Project Editor
  Samik Roy Chowdhury (Sam)

Acquisitions Coordinator
  Agatha Kim

Technical Editor
  Kermit Natho

Copy Editor
  Argosy Publishing

Proofreader
  Chris Andreasen

Indexer
  WordCo Indexing Services

Composition
  International Typesetting
  and Composition

Illustration
  International Typesetting
  and Composition

Cover Series Design
  Margaret Webster-Shapiro

Cover Illustration
  Lance Lekander

This book was composed with Adobe® InDesign® CS Mac.

To Rebecca for her encouragement all through this project and for reading the manuscript and checking all those computations.

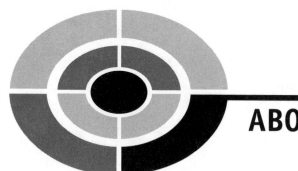

ABOUT THE AUTHOR

Leonard Eugene Berry, PhD, CIA, is Professor Emeritus and Director Emeritus in the School of Accountancy, Georgia State University. He is a retired CPA in the State of Georgia.

CONTENTS AT A GLANCE

CONTENTS

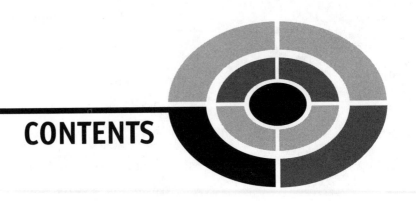

CONTENTS

INTRODUCTION

Management accounting is "where the action is" in the field of accounting. It is located at the intersection of where accounting information meets decision making. Management needs the right kind of information to make decisions and management accounting must be able to provide that information in a relevant and timely form.

What kinds of decisions do business managers make? They include decisions such as planning the future course of the business, pricing products or services so as to cover costs and make a profit, planning and allocating capital resources, acquiring and evaluating human resources, and evaluating the business segments and its managers. To be effective, the management accountant must not only have a good understanding of accounting but a have a basic understanding of the principles of management, human behavior, and basic microeconomics. Likewise, the manager must have a basic understanding of management accounting in order to use the information effectively: its origins, its strengths and weaknesses, and its terminology and procedures.

Thus, this book is written to be useful to both managers and management accountants. Specifically, it is designed to be most useful to:

- Managers who have little or no knowledge of management accounting or who once had a good knowledge but need a review.
- Accountants who need:
  - A review of the fundamental concepts and procedures of management accounting as a refresher course or to study for a professional examination.
  - An understanding of the basics for an entry-level position in management accounting.
- Students who do not have a basic knowledge of management accounting or who need help in preparing for a test to improve their performance. This book could be useful as a supplement to an MBA casebook or as a way of reviewing the basics when using a more difficult book on management accounting.

As the title implies, this book is written to take the mystery out of management accounting. It is written to provide the major accounting concepts and procedures in a concise form. Often in a "bullet" format, key terms, concepts, and procedures are always identified in bold type. Each term and concept is followed by examples and each procedure is followed by a problem illustration with solutions, where applicable. With the exception of Chapter 1, each chapter ends with additional practice problems and solutions. At the end of the book there is a comprehensive final examination covering the major concepts and procedures in the book.

If you have taken a course in management accounting before and think you know the material in any of the chapters, answer all questions and problems at the end of the chapter as a pretest. If you can answer all questions correctly, then you can probably skip that chapter. But it could be valuable to review the concepts and procedures anyway.

When studying a specific subject, you should spend as much time on a topic as is necessary to master it. Always answer the questions and problems after each section, and make sure you answer them before you look at the answers! When you finish a chapter, answer all questions and work on all problems. If you can answer at least 90 percent of them, then you can assume that you have successfully learned the material. Always spend more time reviewing the chapter material pertaining to the questions or problems that you missed.

The author would appreciate receiving e-mail regarding any errors in the book or any suggestions for improvement. Please send them to accleb@yahoo.com.

Thanks and good luck!

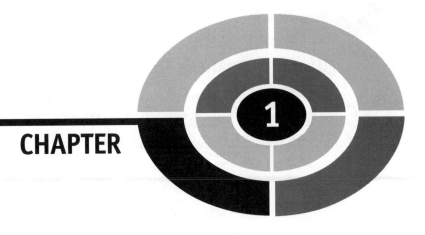

What Is Management Accounting?

Information for Decision Making

Every day, all around the world, managers in companies of all sizes make important decisions that will affect the ultimate success of their businesses. Often these managers look to the management accountant to provide the necessary information they need to make these decisions. The decisions managers are faced with relate to the following categories:

Strategic Analysis Information

Strategy involves scanning the business environment (potential markets, customers, products/services, and competitors) for opportunities and making decisions relating to:

- What kind of business should the company engage in?
- What products or services should the company produce and/or sell?
- What markets should the company compete in?
- Should the company merge or acquire another company?
- How much should be spent on research and development over the long run?
- What capital assets should be acquired and how will they be financed?

Strategic analysis involves developing measures and a feedback system to evaluate the success of the strategies developed by the company.

The management accountant assists management in setting strategic planning and analysis by giving input on projected sales and costs of various strategic opportunities, creating benchmarks to evaluate strategies, assisting on due diligence of various strategic alternatives, and providing input on the effectiveness of business policies.

Planning Information

Planning involves long- and short-term decisions about the future course of the business.

- **Long-term planning** involves developing the broad steps to achieve the business's strategic growth goals. Long-term planning and strategic planning are very closely linked and may be used interchangeably. The long-range planning process involves deciding on such things as what capital assets and human resources are required to meet the strategic goals of the company; how these resources will be financed; and what processes will be employed to meet the customers' satisfaction effectively and efficiently.
- **Short-term planning** involves breaking down the long-range plans into smaller steps for the coming year or the coming quarter. This will require such decisions as setting prices for the coming year, estimating costs, and preparing a master budget. Management accountants assist management in planning by providing analysis of long-term investments, financial projections for long-term budgets, and master budgets for the coming period.

Organizing and Directing Information

To implement plans and operations, management must be organized to achieve the business goals effectively and efficiently. This involves such things as dividing responsibilities, creating an organization structure, and setting up an information system that provides information for all parts of the organization. In addition, management must oversee continuing operations, and keep the organization running smoothly. This requires motivating, directing, and communicating with all personnel within the organization. In a word, it has to do with *leadership* by top and middle managers.

The management accountant assists management in organizing and directing by providing input on organizational structure, information systems, internal controls, and compensation plans that motivate managers to achieve company goals.

Performance Evaluation Information

Evaluating Business Unit Performance

Each major business unit should be evaluated to determine whether it is competing effectively in the market to which it has been assigned. This evaluation involves:

- Using business unit financial reports to evaluate current operations; that is, is that unit profitable?

- Assessing whether a business unit is making a satisfactory return on investment.

- Deciding whether the business should close a business unit; for example, should Bank of America close a branch?

Evaluating Managers' Performance

Managerial evaluation involves evaluating the personal performance of a segment manager, rather than evaluating the unit itself. Evaluating the manager involves:

- Reviewing cost reports or budget reports to determine whether the manager met the assigned budget.

- Using specialized reporting to evaluate the manager's effectiveness in carrying out the strategy goals. Typical reports involve special measurement techniques such as Balanced Score Card, Return on

Investment, Residual Income, and Economic Value Added (EVA) discussed in Chapter 14.

- Developing information to structure compensation plans.

The management accountant's role in organizational and management evaluation is critical since he or she will provide the key measures of performance, financial reports of responsibility center performance, reports of variance from budgets and standards, and other key pieces of information that help evaluate the success of the business.

The Key Accounting and Finance Players in a Large Business

Who provides the information for making the major decisions discussed above? The key players who are responsible for this role are:

- The **Chief Financial Officer (CFO)**, the senior executive who is responsible for all the financing and accounting functions of the business.

- The **Controller**, the chief accounting officer of the business responsible for all accounting functions in the corporation. The Controller normally reports to the CFO. In some businesses, the title "Comptroller" is used instead of "Controller." When used in a corporation, it has the same meaning as "Controller." The information generated by the Controller includes financial information for both internal managers and external users of financial statements. Persons providing the information for internal users making the decisions discussed in the previous section, and who report to the Controller, are known as management accountants.

- The **Treasurer**, responsible for cash and other financial resources of the company, such as maintaining bank relations, managing investments, handling cash receipts and similar operations. The Treasurer normally reports to the CFO.

- The **Internal Auditor**, who performs financial, compliance, and management audits for internal management. The InternalAuditor provides independent appraisal of the organization's internal control system. Often, the Internal Auditor performs consulting services to internal management, and can report to the board of directors, the CEO, or the CFO, depending on the policy set by the board of directors or the CEO. The Internal Auditor may be a CPA and/or a **Certified Internal Auditor (CIA)**. To be certified, candidates must pass a written examination, possess a specified level of experience, and hold a college degree. A CIA is certified by the Institute of Internal Auditors.

Changing Roles of the Controller and Management Accountant

The roles of the Controller and the management accountant have changed dramatically during the past decade. The Controller and modern management accountants go beyond the role of just providing the numbers for management, often becoming directly involved in the decision making process as consultants to management. Moreover, many Controllers are adding value to their function by developing a partnership role with operating management. The notion of adding value means taking the perspective of the customer—the users of Controller services—and providing innovative products and services that incorporate but go beyond traditional transaction processing, financial reporting, and control. Further, Controllers add value by being members of the business leadership team. By sitting at the table where strategic and tactical decisions are made, a Controller provides an important contribution and perspective in shaping corporate decisions and positively influencing their outcomes.

All of this means that the management accountants of the future must include in their skills not only traditional areas of accounting but microeconomics, management, and finance as well. The modern management accountant will be more of a consultant than a mere scorekeeper. This means that accountants may be able to finally shed the "green eye shade" persona that has always been attributed to their role in the corporation.

What Does "certified" Mean Anyway?

The term "certified" means that an individual has met a minimum of education and experience requirements set by a government entity or professional organization, has passed a rigorous examination, and agreed to follow a set of established standards and body of ethics. Only the CPA is licensed by a state to independently attest to a company's financial statements. There are also Certified Management Accountants (CMA) and Certified Internal Auditors (CIA). The CMA is certified by the Institute of Management Accounting and the CIA is certified by the Institute of Internal Auditors. The certification by these two latter groups simply means that these individuals have met minimum education requirements and have passed a rigorous examination.

The Profession of Accounting

There are several types of accountants who specialize in the various subfields of accounting. The most familiar of these is the **Certified Public Accountant (CPA)**, who is often referred to as an external auditor (that is, external to the business). (See the sidebar for more information on certification.) There are also internal accountants, tax accountants, internal auditors, and governmental accountants.

A **Certified Management Accountant (CMA)** is granted a certificate from the Institute of Management Accountants (IMA) after passing a rigorous four-part examination and meeting practical experience requirements. A CMA generally provides services directly to an employer rather than to the public. This book is directed primarily toward management accountants who work internally for a business. To be employed as a management accountant, one does not have to be certified. However, many are certified as CMAs or CPAs to attest to their education and experience in accounting and to enhance their professional status. The sidebar contains more information on what it means to be certified.

While the management accountant does not have to be certified, he or she must have a sound knowledge of Generally Accepted Accounting Principles (GAAP). As stated above, since many management accountants act as consultants to management, they should have a good knowledge of behavioral science, management techniques, and microeconomics. This book does not cover these topics, except as they relate to the management accountant's role and to practice problem situations.

Management Accounting Compared to Financial Accounting

Accounting in a business is often divided into management accounting and financial accounting. The following is a brief comparison of the two.

Financial accounting has the following characteristics:

- It is primarily for external users of the corporation such as stockholders, prospective investors, lending institutions, and regulatory agencies.

- It must follow GAAP set by the Financial Accounting Standards Board and the regulatory requirements of the Securities and Exchange Commission, and may be influenced by professional organizations such as the American Institute of Certified Public Accountants.

- Its numbers are historical in nature and may contain estimates.
- Its numbers are primarily monetary.
- Its reporting entity is usually the entire corporation.
- Its reporting frequency is usually quarterly and annually.

Management Accounting has the following characteristics:

- Its primary role is to provide information and advice to internal managers in order to assist them in their management responsibilities.
- It may or may not use GAAP in the preparation of its information, depending on the purpose of this information. Management techniques, human behavioral considerations, and economics heavily influence the preparation of accounting information for management decision making. Thus, the management accountant must have a good knowledge of economics, behavioral science, statistics, and management.
- It may be historical in nature but usually is future oriented, as in the preparation of a budget.
- It may have a monetary focus but other nonmonetary metrics may be used. Some examples of nonmonetary metrics are number of customer complaints, market share of a business, and setup time in a manufacturing operation.
- Its reporting entities are usually responsibility centers such as business units, profit centers, and cost centers.
- Its reporting frequency is as needed but in some cases it can be on a specified cycle: daily, weekly, monthly, or annually. Examples of the latter are cost reports and business unit financial reports.

Summary

Today's management accountant has an exciting role of contributing to the success of a business. This new role must not only perform the traditional function of providing the "numbers" for financial statements and management reports, but must also involve the development and distribution of information to key managers for strategic decision making, planning, and evaluation and control of the business.

The management accountant will likely become more actively involved in the design of information systems that can effectively provide needed decision making support. The management accountant will become a more valuable member of the business team.

Those who choose management accounting as a career or use management accounting information in the performance of their responsibilities will find the remainder of this book very useful. It is hoped that you find it valuable in achieving your business career goals.

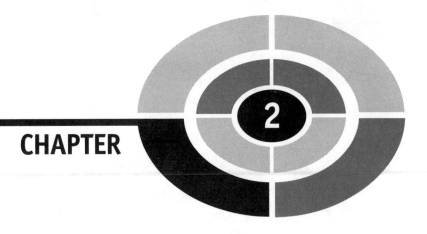

CHAPTER 2

Basic Cost Terms and Concepts

In this chapter the following topics are presented: definitions of concepts and terms that will be used throughout this book; three types of business organizations that impact management accounting; how costs flow through a manufacturing operation; and the preparation of financial statements in a merchandising and manufacturing operation.

In order to effectively prepare and use management accounting information, the preparer and the user must understand the language that is used to transmit this information. There are many terms and concepts that make up the language of management accounting, and we need to carefully define many of them before we attempt to learn how management accounting works. First, consider the term *cost*. There are many ways to define this elusive term, which often results in its misuse. The broad economic definition of **cost** is that it is a sacrifice of resources for a specific purpose. However, for management accountants this is too vague, therefore they attempt to define it more concretely. Likewise, the term **expense** is often misused and sometimes even used interchangeably with *cost*. It is defined technically

as the expenditure of resources to generate revenue during a specific period of time. The following are the most common definitions of *cost* and *expense* based on the type of business involved or the purpose for the cost.

Cost as an Asset or Expense

Costs That Become Assets

Asset Costs

These costs are expended resources or the incurring of liabilities to acquire assets. The resources expended are normally in a monetary form. The asset acquired may be tangible (such as a piece of equipment) or intangible (such as goodwill in a merger) or it may be in the form of a prepayment (such as prepaid insurance). After this expenditure is entered into the business accounts, it is sometimes referred to as an **unexpired cost**. An asset is reported on the balance sheet. A **capitalized cost** is the present value of a uniform series of periodic costs that continue for a long time.

Inventoriable Costs

These include all costs of purchasing or manufacturing items of inventory. In a merchandising company, inventoriable costs would be all costs associated with the purchase and receipt of merchandise. All purchased items are inventoriable costs until they are sold, at which time they become cost of goods sold and are included on the income statement.

Product Costs

These are inventoriable costs that are incurred by a company to manufacture a product. They include costs of raw materials, labor, and overhead that are put into production. If items in production were unfinished at the end of the period, their costs would be included in Work in Process Inventory. Raw materials acquired to manufacture a product that have not yet been issued to production would be included in Raw Materials Inventory. All such inventories are included on the balance sheet.

Costs That Become Expenses

Expenses

This is a general term and includes all costs that have expired, been consumed, or been used up in the generation of income during a particular period. Because they are usually charged on the income statement for a given period, expenses are usually called **period expenses**. Expenses may have once been an asset or costs that never became an asset, such as wages. Assets that have a long useful life, such as buildings, require an estimate of how much they have been used up during a period. This estimated amount is called **depreciation**, which is then charged against income generated by the business during the same period.

Selling and **general administrative expenses** are the most common categories of expenses that occur in any type of organizations. They are expended in the general administration of a company and in the marketing, advertising, and distribution of products or services sold to customers. Expenses are charged to the income statement of the period in which they were incurred in generating revenue.

Identification of Costs and Expenses in Three Types of Businesses

Manufacturing Company

A helpful way of distinguishing between product costs and period expenses in a manufacturing company, such as Mohawk Industries, is to think of all costs expended for use *inside* a factory as manufacturing or product costs, which are always part of inventoriable costs until they are sold. After their sale, they become the cost of goods sold. As stated above, product costs can usually be divided into three major categories: raw materials, direct labor, and manufacturing overhead.

All costs expended *outside* of the factory and not used in the manufacture of a product but used to generate income are called *period expenses* and are included on the income statement. These expenses are also called **nonmanufacturing expenses** and are broken down into **administrative expenses** and **selling expenses**, as stated above. Figure 2-1 depicts the flow of manufacturing and nonmanufacturing costs in a manufacturing company (direct and indirect costs are discussed below).

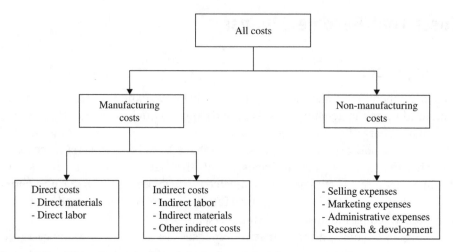

Figure 2-1 Flow of costs in a manufacturing company.

Merchandising Company

In a merchandising company, such as Macy's, all products are purchased in a finished state and are charged directly to cost of goods sold when they are sold. All expenses incurred in generating revenue for a given period are identified as administrative or selling expenses and are charged to the income statement. Figure 2-2 depicts the flow of costs in a merchandising company.

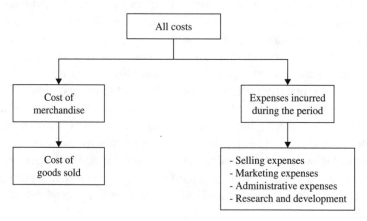

Figure 2-2 Flow of costs in a merchandising company.

Service Company

In a service company, such as an advertising or accounting firm, there is no merchandising inventory. All costs incurred during the period are normally identified as administrative and selling expenses. The income statement would include only sales, less all expenses.

Tracing Costs to Cost Objects

Cost Objects

A concept that is helpful for identifying and tracing costs is that of **cost object**. A cost object helps answer the question, "How much did something cost?" Sometimes that is a hard question to answer because costs are accumulated and moved around (aggregated and re-aggregated) for different purposes. Thus, it is very important that the accountant specify the purpose (cost object) for which the cost is being collected or aggregated. Some examples of cost objects are costs of a specific product or service, costs incurred at a specific responsibility center, costs incurred in a specific operation or activity, and costs incurred for a specific contract.

Direct Costs

Once the cost object is specified, the accountant asks, "What cost can be directly traced to that cost object?" Costs that are directly traceable to a cost object are called *direct costs*. The top part of Figure 2-3 graphically depicts the tracing of

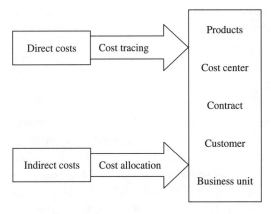

Figure 2-3   Tracking costs to cost objects.

direct costs to a cost object. In a manufacturing company, for example, the most common types of direct costs are **direct material** and **direct labor** costs, which are sometimes referred to as **prime costs**.

Materiality and Cost Tracing

Sometimes management has to decide if it is economically worthwhile to determine whether a cost is direct or indirect. That is, the expense of tracing the cost to a cost object might be greater than the benefit of having a more accurate figure for that cost object. In making the decision on what direct costs to trace to the cost object, management might ask some of the following questions: (1) What is the significance (materiality) of the costs? For example, small screws could be traced to a piece of furniture, but this process would be "precision overkill" by being too costly. Management would probably collect all costs of screws as indirect and allocate these costs to the pieces of furniture. (2) How expensive is it to trace the costs? New technology over the years has facilitated the identification of more indirect costs as direct costs. An example of such technology is the use of bar codes on raw material items, which are scanned as they are placed into production to help associate the costs with a specific batch of products. Another example of such technology use is software on photocopying machines that can identify the number of copies produced for a particular project (cost object).

As an illustration of cost tracing, consider General Motors. A cost object for General Motors is an automobile. A direct material cost for an automobile is radiator costs, since each automobile requires one radiator and the cost of this radiator can be easily traced to each automobile. The associated costs of purchasing and receiving the radiators are part of direct material cost for each automobile. Similarly, the wages of assembly workers working directly on a given automobile could be traced directly to each automobile as direct labor. Today, as industries move to more automated equipment such as robots (a fixed cost), the total direct labor costs of a product are declining.

Indirect Costs

Costs that cannot be traced directly to a cost object are identified as indirect costs. These costs are tracked to the cost object as shown in the bottom part of Figure 2-3. Using the product as the cost object, these costs are usually called **manufacturing overhead**. Basically, indirect costs are all costs that are not directly traceable to the cost object. See the sidebar on materiality for more information on the economics of cost tracing. Some examples of indirect costs, again using the automobile example, are depreciation costs of building and equipment, the cost of a supervisor of an assembly line, heating and electricity bills for the building, etc. These costs are indirectly traced to the product using a procedure called **cost allocation**, which is covered in Chapter 4 in much more detail.

What are Conversion Costs?

These are costs to convert the raw materials put into production into a finished product: direct labor and manufacturing overhead. Hence, conversion costs = direct labor + manufacturing overhead.

The preceding example used the product as an example of cost object. Another example of a cost object could be a cost center. In this case all direct costs are directly traceable to that center and would be aggregated for some purpose such as the evaluation of costs related to the cost center manager.

Illustration of Cost Classifications

Identify each of the following cost items as a direct (D) or indirect (I) cost, assuming that the product or service produced is the final cost object unless otherwise specified. Also, identify whether each item is a product cost (PC) or a period expense (PE) and whether it is an inventoriable cost (INV) or a noninventoriable cost (NI). Identify any item that does not apply to a category as "not applicable" (N/A).

1. Glue used to produce a computer desk in a factory.
2. Hours that a lawyer spends on a case for a client in a large law firm.
3. Wood that is used to manufacture a computer desk in a factory.
4. Salesperson's salary for a specific sales district.
5. Cost to advertise the desks for sale.
6. Insurance on the factory that produces the desks.
7. Salary of the factory production foreman.
8. Wages of person sanding desks for staining in the factory.
9. Salary of the business president.
10. Electricity for the building in which the accounting department is housed.

The solution to the practice problem is shown in Exhibit 2-1.

Exhibit 2-1.	Classification of Costs (Cost Object = Final Product)		
COST ITEM	**D OR I** (D = Direct Cost) (I = Indirect Cost)	**PC OR PE** (PC = Product Cost) (PE = Period Expense)	**INV OR NI** (INV = Inventoriable cost) (NI = Noninventoriable Cost)
1	I	PC	INV
2	D (cost object = case)	PE	NI
3	D	PC	INV
4	D (cost object = sales district)	PE	NI
5	N/A	PE	NI
6	I	PC	INV
7	I	PC	INV
8	D	PC	INV
9	N/A	PE	NI
10	N/A	PE	NI

Costs Based on Cost Behavior

Managers often require costs to be aggregated based on **cost behavior**, which may be aggregated as variable, fixed, mixed (semi-variable), or stepped fixed costs. A good knowledge of cost behavior aids managers in more accurately determining the cost of products, in performing cost-volume-profit analysis, budgeting, pricing products or services, and in evaluating performance.

Total Variable Costs

Costs that vary in direct proportion to changes in the level of some measure of activity are aggregated as *total* variable costs. This measure of activity is also called a **cost driver** in that it is assumed to cause the change in total variable costs. The measure of activity could be the production volume, machine hour volume, sales volume of the finished product, or some other measure of volume or activity. Two examples of variable costs are (1) raw materials costs that vary in direct proportion to production and (2) sales commissions that vary based on changes in sales volume. Figure 2-4A is a graph view of these costs.

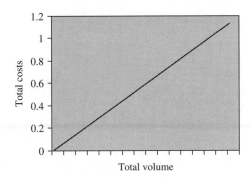

Figure 2-4A   Total variable costs.

Relevant Range

The total variable costs relationship between cost and volume is assumed to occur within what is called the *relevant range*. The relevant range is the range of activity for a specified period in which the proportional relationship between the levels of activity and the total costs is assumed to remain relatively constant. For example, if a company wanted to budget a department's variable costs for the coming year, it would project that department's relevant range of production based on the overall range of the sales forecast. Then the total variable costs would be computed based on this relevant range.

Total Fixed Costs

Those costs that do not vary with changes in some level of activity are *total* fixed costs. Fixed costs relate to the capacity to produce or to sell the product or services of the business. Two examples of fixed costs are building and equipment costs, and executive salaries. Figure 2-4B is a graph view of total fixed costs.

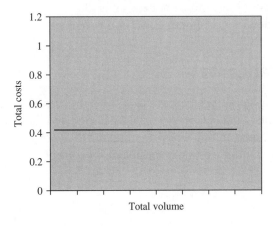

Figure 2-4B   Total fixed costs.

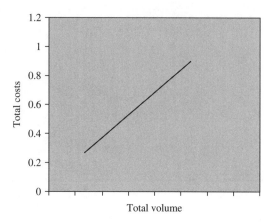

Figure 2-4C   Total mixed costs.

Mixed Variable Costs

Many costs are not true variable or true fixed costs and are referred to as *mixed* or *semi-variable* costs. In fact, it can be said that *most* costs are not true variable or fixed costs. An example of a mixed cost is electricity that has a flat rate of $1,000 per month plus $0.25 per kWh used. Figure 2-4C shows a chart of mixed costs.

Stepped Fixed Costs

Another type of costs that is not a true variable or fixed cost is a stepped fixed cost. An example is the cost of a supervisor of an assembly line in a factory. In this case, all supervisors' salary would be fixed within the capacity of a given range. When the company decides to add another assembly line because of an increase in sales, another supervisor will have to be added. Thus, the fixed cost would be increased to a new level or new "step." Figure 2-4D shows a chart of stepped fixed costs.

Unit vs. Total Costs

It should be emphasized that when one uses the term *variable cost* or *fixed cost* it is assumed to be a total concept, unless otherwise specified. However, a unit variable or unit fixed cost can be computed by dividing the total costs by the related volume, which is useful in costing a product for inventory control.

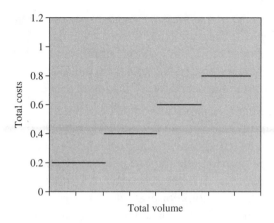

Figure 2-4D Total stepped costs.

Cost Definitions for Decision Making

In making decisions that affect the future of the business, managers are always faced with the problem of choice. That is, in defining a problem and seeking data to analyze in making an informed decision, the manager is always faced with different alternatives. This type of analysis and related decisions are sometimes referred to as *alternative-choice decision making*. For example, in deciding whether to replace a piece of equipment, the manager is faced with at least two alternatives: to purchase the piece of equipment or not to purchase the new piece of equipment. There could be more alternatives if there are different brands of equipment with different capabilities to consider. The management accountant's job is to assist the manager by clearly identifying the alternatives and projecting the relevant costs and revenues for each of the alternatives.

- **Differential Costs.** A very important concept in aggregating the costs for alternatives is that of **differential costs and revenues**. The latter may also be referred to as **incremental costs or revenues**. A differential cost/revenue simply means the cost that differs between two alternatives. Differential costs are aggregated by the management accountant for a particular problem facing management and are not included in the accounting records under this name.

- **Opportunity Costs.** A concept closely related to differential costs/revenues is that of opportunity costs, which is defined as the potential benefit (cost savings or profit) that is foregone by selecting one alternative over another. Opportunity costs are identified in a decision situation and are not included in the accounting records. Consider an example for an individual: A person has $10,000 to invest and faces the decision of depositing it into an interest bearing account and receiving 5% interest. Alternatively, that person could invest it in a stock with a *projected* rate of return of 8%. If this person decides to accept the risk and invest in a stock then the 5% interest lost would be an opportunity cost to the alternative of having invested in the stock.

- **Sunk Cost.** Finally, another important decision making cost is that of **sunk cost**. This simply means that in considering new alternatives any past costs that might relate to either alternative has already been incurred and is not relevant to the decision relating to the *future*. A sunk cost is the book value of an asset and is found in the accounting records as cost of an asset less its accumulated depreciation. For example, a business in January 2006 decides to purchase a more efficient machine. Six months later a breakthrough improvement in the machine is developed by another company. Should the purchasing company acquire the new machine, having purchased a new one only six months ago? Of course, it depends on the benefits and costs of the new machine that becomes available six months later. However, the cost (actually the book value) of the machine purchased six months earlier would *not* be relevant, regardless of any costs and benefits of the new machine. It is a sunk cost and management can do nothing to change that; only future costs matter in decision making.

Summary of Cost Definitions

In summary, it is important to remember that costs can be aggregated and reaggregated or classified or re-classified for many different purposes. Therefore, it is very important for the management accountant and manager to specify the purpose for which the cost is to be classified or aggregated. A summary of the classifications that we have covered is shown in Exhibit 2-2.

Exhibit 2-2. Summary of Cost Classifications	
Purpose of Costing	**Classification of Cost**
Based on cost object	Direct or indirect cost
Based on type of business	Manufacturing (product) or nonmanufacturing cost
Based on behavior of cost driver	Variable, fixed, or semi-variable cost
Based on aggregation	Total or unit cost
Based on financial statement preparation	Capitalized (asset) or inventoriable cost or an expense
Based on decision making	Incremental, opportunity, or sunk cost

Illustration of Costs for Decision Making

The Kings Book Store sells used books and compact disks and operates a coffee bar where customers can purchase coffee and rolls. Customers often purchase coffee and drink it as they peruse the bookshelves or the CDs on display. The monthly costs for Kings Book Store are shown in Exhibit 2-3. Identify each item as a variable cost, a fixed cost, an opportunity cost, or a sunk cost by placing an "X" in the appropriate column.

Exhibit 2-3. Identifying Costs for Decision Making					
Cost Description	**Variable Cost (VC)**	**Fixed Cost (FC)**	**Opportunity Cost (OC)**	**Sunk Cost (SC)**	**Differential Cost (DC)**
1. CDs that are purchased for $12 each for sale to customers; purchases per month total $36,000, including shipping costs.					
2. Books that cost $9.00 per book including shipping charges; purchases per month usually total $27,000.					
3. Cost of leasing of computers totals $250 per month.					
4. Cost of coffee and rolls is usually $2,200 per month.					
5. Cost of insurance policy on the store and its contents is $1,200 per month.					
6. Cost to provide free Internet service for customers to access e-mail costs $90 per month.					
7. Depreciation charge on the building is $4,000 per month.					
8. The owner is considering closing the coffee shop and using the space to expand the CD section. He estimates that he presently makes a monthly profit of $250 on the coffee shop. What kind of cost is the $250?					

Cost Description	Variable Cost (VC)	Fixed Cost (FC)	Opportunity Cost (OC)	Sunk Cost (SC)	Differential Cost (DC)
Exhibit 2-3. *(Continued)*					
9. The owner is torn between closing the coffee shop and keeping it open because he purchased a new espresso machine last year for $2,000 and believes that he will not be able to sell the machine for any amount. Classify the cost of the expresso machine.					
10. The owner subscribes to ten magazines for customers to read while sitting in the coffee shop and enjoying their espresso coffee and rolls. They cost $300 per year.					
11. The owner estimates that the difference in cost between closing the coffee shop and using the space to sell CDs is $400. Classify the $400.					
12. Utilities for the bookstore costs $350 per month.					

SOLUTION: *1. VC, 2. VC, 3. FC, 4. VC, 5. FC, 6. FC, 7. FC, 8. OC, 9. SC, 10. FC, 11. DC, 12. FC*

Cost Flows in a Manufacturing Business

Cost flows in a manufacturing company can be summarized in Figure 2-5. When a manufacturing business enters into cost transactions, these are entered into the accounting records. When a product is put into production all related costs are transferred to work in process. This transfer can occur at the beginning of the process, during it, or at its end.

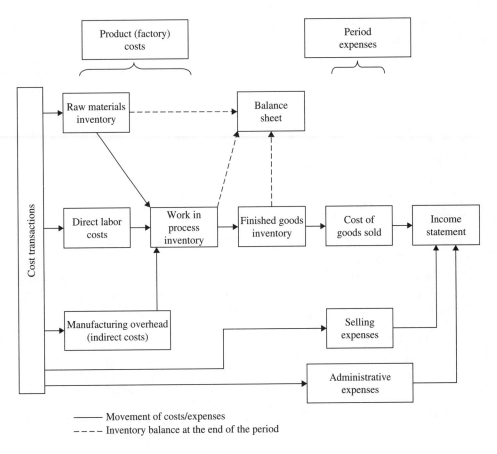

Figure 2-5   Cost flows in a manufacturing company.

- Raw materials are issued from a stock room and labor is collected as the product moves through the production process.
- Direct labor is collected as the products move through the production process and charged to Work in Process.
- Manufacturing overhead is collected into an overhead account and allocated to Work in Process, usually when production has been completed.

When products are completed, all related costs are transferred to Finished Goods Inventory from the Work in Process Inventory. As products move through the process, the accounting records are updated to reflect the stage of the product completion. Later, when the item is sold, the related costs are transferred to Cost of

Goods Sold, which are included on the Income Statement. All Raw Materials Inventory, Work in Process Inventory, and Finished Good Inventory on hand at the end of the period are assets and are included on the balance sheet.

All expenditures for selling and administrative expenses are charged directly to an expense account and are included on the income statement at the end of the period.

Preparation of Financial Statements

The Balance Sheet

The balance sheet is a statement of financial position of a business at a specific point in time. It includes all of the assets, liabilities, and stockholder equities owned or owed by the business. The balance sheet of a merchandising company would include an account for Merchandising Inventory. That of a manufacturing company would include three inventory accounts: Raw Materials, Work in Process, and Finished Goods.

The Income Statement

The income statement in a *merchandising company* has the following relationships:

> **SALES – COST OF GOODS SOLD = GROSS MARGIN – SELLING AND ADMINISTRATIVE EXPENSES = NET INCOME**

The "cost of goods sold" section of the income statement in a merchandising company is computed as follows:

> **BEGINNING MERCHANDISING INVENTORY + PURCHASES – ENDING INVENTORY = COST OF GOODS SOLD**

The income statement in a manufacturing company has the same basic relationships as shown in the first box above. However, the "cost of goods sold" section is considerably different and has the following relationships:

> **BEGINNING FINISHED GOODS INVENTORY + COST OF GOODS MANUFACTURED – ENDING FINISHED GOODS INVENTORY = COST OF GOODS SOLD**

The "cost of goods manufactured" section of the "cost of goods sold" section is more complicated and is computed as follows:

> **BEGINNING RAW MATERIALS INVENTORY + PURCHASES OF RAW MATERIALS**

– ENDING RAW MATERIALS INVENTORY
= RAW MATERIALS USED
+ DIRECT LABOR
+ MANUFACTURING OVERHEAD
= TOTAL MANUFACTURING COSTS
+ BEGINNING WORK IN PROCESS INVENTORY
– ENDING WORK IN PROCESS INVENTORY
= COST OF GOODS MANUFACTURED

Illustration of Preparation of Income Statement and Statement of Cost of Goods Manufactured:

The Cherry Desk Company manufactures fine executive desks, which are sold to various office supply companies. The company's accounting period is for the calendar year. Exhibit 2-4 is a list of account balances at the beginning and ending of the accounting period, December 31, 20XX. Using this data, prepare an Income Statement and a Statement of Cost of Goods Manufactured for 20XX.

Exhibit 2-4.
CHERRY DESK COMPANY
Schedule of Selected Accounts
January 1, 20XX and December 31, 20XX

	Jan. 1, 20XX	Dec. 31, 20XX
Raw Materials Inventory	$50,000	$60,000
Work in Process Inventory	75,000	80,000
Finished Goods Inventory	200,000	250,000
Raw Materials Purchased		250,000
Direct Labor Used in Production		200,000
Depreciation, Factory		150,000
Taxes for Factory Building		12,000
Maintenance, Factory		9,000
Utilities, Factory		10,000
Supplies Used in Factory		3,000
Indirect Labor, Factory		100,000
Sales		2,100,000
Selling Expenses		100,000
Administrative Expenses		650,000

The solution to the illustration is shown in Exhibits 2-4A and 2-4B.

Exhibit 2-4A. CHERRY DESK COMPANY Schedule of Cost of Goods Manufactured for the Period Ending December 31, 20XX		
Direct materials:		
Raw materials inventory, beginning	$50,000	
Add: Purchases of raw materials	250,000	
Raw materials available for use	$300,000	
Deduct: Raw materials inventory, ending	60,000	
Raw materials used in production		$240,000
Direct labor		200,000
Manufacturing factory overhead:		
Depreciation in Factory	$150,000	
Taxes for Factory Building	12,000	
Maintenance, Factory	9,000	
Utilities for Factory	10,000	
Supplies for Factory	3,000	
Indirect Labor	100,000	
Total overhead costs		284,000
Total manufacturing costs		$724,000
Add: Work in process inventory, beginning		75,000
		$799,000
Deduct: Work in process inventory, ending		80,000
Cost of goods manufactured		$719,000

Summary

How much something costs is an ambiguous concept, because "cost" can have many meanings and is best described when it has a qualifying adjective.

A *cost object* is the purpose for which a cost is measured. A *direct cost* is directly traceable to a cost object. All other costs are indirect costs.

A *variable cost* is defined as a cost that changes in direct relation to the ratio of change in costs in terms of activity or volume, within a given relevant range. Fixed costs do not change in relation to some activity or volume, within a given relevant range.

Opportunity cost is some potential benefit given up when one alternative is chosen over another in a given decision situation. It is an estimate, and therefore not

Exhibit 2-4B.
CHERRY DESK COMPANY
Income Statement
for the Period Ending December 31, 20XX

Sales		$2,100,000
Less cost of goods sold:		
Finished goods inventory, beginning	$200,000	
Add: Cost of goods manufactured	719,000	
Goods available for sale	$919,000	
Less: Finished goods inventory, ending	250,000	669,000
Gross margin		$1,431,000
Less operating expenses:		
Selling expenses	$100,000	
Administrative expenses	650,000	750,000
Net operating income		$681,000

recorded in the accounting records. *Sunk costs* are those costs incurred that cannot be changed by any decision.

Presentation of financial statements for a manufacturing company is significantly different than those for a merchandising or service company. Statements must account for cost of goods manufactured (raw materials, labor, overhead, work in process, and finished goods). The balance sheet will reflect raw materials inventory, work in process inventory, and finished goods inventory.

A merchandising company will present costs of goods sold based on the purchase of a ready-made product, along with selling and administrative expenses. The balance sheet will present only a merchandise inventory. A service company will present costs relating to labor (services provided) along with selling and administrative expenses. There are no inventories in a service company, with the exception of a supplies account, usually with a small balance.

Practice Problems

2-1 (a) What is the difference between a merchandising company, a manufacturing company, and a service company in terms of acquiring, producing, and selling goods and services? (b) How do these differences affect the balance sheet and income statement?

2-2 Listed below are various costs for the specified business. Identify each item as a selling expense (S) or an administrative expense (A), as a product cost (P), as a variable cost (V), or as a fixed cost (F), by placing an "X" in the appropriate box. An item may have more than one "X".

Name of Cost	Selling Expense (S)	Administrative Expense (A)	Product (P)	Variable Cost (VC)	Fixed Cost (FC)
1. Interest expense on Home Depot's long-term debt.					
2. Salesperson's commissions at HP for selling storage software.					
3. Insurance cost on General Electric's plant used to manufacture light bulbs.					
4. Costs of shipping furniture from Denmark Teak Company to customer.					
5. Depreciation of Borders display cases used for CDs.					
6. Cost of electricity used to light Kroger's store retail area.					
7. Costs of turn signal switches used in Lexus automobiles.					
8. Salary costs of Georgia Pacific executives.					
9. Costs of padding used in Simmons mattresses.					
10. Cost of leasing an 800 telephone line for taking customer orders at Amazon.com. Charges are based on number of minutes used.					

2-3 Schedule of Cost of Goods Sold and Cost of Goods Manufactured

Listed below are balances from the XYZ Manufacturing Company. Prepare a "cost of goods manufactured statement" and a "cost of goods sold statement."

XYZ MANUFACTURING COMPANY Schedule of Selected Accounts January 1, 20XX and December 31, 20XX		
	Jan 1, 20XX	Dec 31, 20XX
Raw Materials Inventory	44,000	31,000
Work in Process Inventory	30,000	36,000
Finished Goods Inventory	40,000	43,000
Raw Materials Purchased		75,000
Direct Labor		38,000
Depreciation, Factory Building		21,000
Depreciation, Plant Equipment		17,000
Property Taxes, Factory		4,000
Repairs and Maintenance, Factory		15,000
Utilities, Factory		16,000
Indirect Factory Labor		20,000
Indirect Materials Used in Factory		9,000
Sales		400,000
Selling Expenses		42,000
Administrative Expenses		38,000

2-4 Classifying Product Costs and Period Expenses

Motherboard Manufacturing Company manufactures motherboard circuits for personal computers. The company's accountant who prepares the financial statements suddenly resigned from the company. The company has temporarily moved another person into his job but the person does not have a strong accounting background. He has called you, the company's CPA, to help him figure out which costs should be charged to the income statement as an expense and which should go into product costs for inventory purposes. You have taken the items in question and prepared a schedule, which is shown below. Please indicate which item is a product cost and which is a period cost by placing an "X" in the appropriate columns.

	Costs	Product (Inventoriable) Cost (PC)	Period Expense (PE)
1.	The President's salary		
2.	Plant heating costs		
3.	Plant equipment maintenance and repair costs		
4.	Training costs for new sales personnel		
5.	The cost of the board material that is used in assembling the motherboard		
6.	The travel costs of the company's salespersons		
7.	Wages and salaries of factory security personnel		
8.	The cost of air conditioning for executive offices		
9.	Wages and salaries for billing personnel		
10.	Depreciation on the equipment in the break room for factory workers		
11.	Telephone expenses incurred by factory management		
12.	The costs of shipping completed motherboards to customers		
13.	The wages of the workers who assemble the motherboards		
14.	The cost of the memory chips used in the motherboards		
15.	Health insurance premiums for factory personnel		

2-5 The insurance on the manufacturing plant building would be a

A. Conversion cost but not a prime cost.

B. A prime cost but not a conversion cost.

C. Both a prime cost and a conversion cost.

D. Neither a prime cost nor a conversion cost.

2-6 Which of the following would probably be included in manufacturing overhead used in the production of a sofa?

A. The wages of a worker who stitches the sofa fabric

B. The cost of the foam for the sofa seats

C. The cost of the factory supervisor overseeing the production

D. The cloth that is part of the soft production

2-7 Which of the following type of costs best describes an inventoriable cost?

A. Fixed costs in the factory

B. Product costs

C. Prime costs

D. All of the above

2-8 Place an "X" in against each item below that should not be entered into the accounting records.

1. A sunk cost
2. A direct cost
3. An indirect cost
4. An opportunity cost
5. A prime cost

2-9 Consider the items of costs listed below.

1. Raw materials used in the factory (RM)	$40,000
2. Direct labor used in the factory (DL)	$35,000
3. Manufacturing overhead (OH)	$60,000
4. Selling expenses (S)	$25,000
5. Research and development expenses (R&D)	$20,000

From the table above, compute the following.

A. The amount of prime costs would be_____.

B. The amount of conversion costs would be_____.

C. The amount of product costs would be_____.

D. The amount of period expenses would be_____.

E. If the product was the cost object the amount of direct costs would be_____.

F. If the product was the cost object, the amount of indirect costs would be_____.

2-10 During the past year a manufacturing company had the following balances.

Beginning finished goods inventory	$80,000
Ending finished goods inventory	$70,000
Sales	$400,000
Gross margin	$70,000

What was the cost of goods manufactured for the month?

A. $320,000

B. $330,000

C. $400,000

D. None of the above

Solutions to Practice Problems

2-1A Differences in types of companies are shown below.

2-1

TYPE OF COMPANY	MAJOR DIFFERENCES
1. Merchandising company	Purchases merchandise products in their finished state and resells them to customers. Examples: Sears, Wal-Mart, and Macy's.
2. Manufacturing company	Purchases raw materials and inputs them into a production process, produces a finished product, and sells them to businesses or individual customers. Examples: Dow Chemical, General Motors, and Intel.
3. Service company	Sells services of an intangible nature to businesses or individual customers. Examples: Bank of America, Deloitte & Touche, and Accenture.

2-1B The effect of the nature of the company on the preparation of financial statements is shown below.

2-2 1. A., F.; 2. S, V; 3. P, F; 4. S,V; 5. S, F; 6. S, F (assuming lights are left on most of time); 7. P, V; 8. A, F; 9. P, V; 10. S, V.

2-3 The solution is shown below.

TYPE OF COMPANY	MAJOR DIFFERENCES IN FINANCIAL STATEMENTS
1. Merchandising company	*a. The **Balance Sheet** includes a Merchandising Inventory account.*
	*b. The **Income Statement** includes a Cost of Goods Sold section but no Cost of Goods Manufactured section.*
2. Manufacturing company	*a. The **Balance Sheet** includes three inventory accounts: Raw Materials Inventory, Work In Process Inventory and Finished Goods Inventory.*
	*b. The **Income Statement** includes a Cost of Goods Statement, which includes the Cost of Goods Manufactured section. The latter may be included as a separate statement.*
3. Service company	*a. The **Balance Sheet** does not include a major account for inventories.*
	*b. The **Income Statement** does not include a Cost of Goods Sold section.*

XYZ MANUFACTURING COMPANY

Schedule of Cost of Goods Manufactured

for the Period Ending December 31, 20XX

Direct materials:		
Raw materials inventory, beginning	$44,000	
Add: Purchases of raw materials	75,000	
Raw materials available for use	119,000	
Deduct: Raw materials inventory, ending	31,000	
Raw materials used in production		$88,000
Direct labor		38,000
Manufacturing factory overhead:		
Depreciation, factory building	21,000	
Depreciation, plant equipment	17,000	
Property taxes, factory	4,000	
Repairs and maintenance, factory	15,000	
Utilities for factory	16,000	
Indirect materials used in factory	9,000	
Indirect labor used in factory	20,000	
Total overhead costs		102,000
Total manufacturing costs		$228,000
Add: Work in process inventory, beginning		30,000
		$258,000
Deduct: Work in process inventory, ending		36,000
Cost of goods manufactured		$222,000

XYZ MANUFACTURING COMPANY Income Statement January 1 – December 31, 20XX		
Sales		$400,000
Less cost of goods sold:		
Finished goods inventory, beginning	$40,000	
Add: Cost of goods manufactured	222,000	
Goods available for sale	$262,000	
Finished goods inventory, ending	43,000	219,000
Gross margin		$181,000
Less operating expenses:		
Selling expenses	42,000	
Administrative expenses	38,000	80,000
Net operating income		$101,000

2-4 1. PE, 2. PC, 3. PC, 4. PE, 5. PC, 6. PE, 7. PC, 8. PE, 9. PE, 10. PC, 11. PC, 12. PE, 13. PC, 14. PC, 15. PC

2-5 A

2-6 C

2-7 D

2-8 Items 1 and 4 would not be entered in the accounting records. Item 1 has already been entered in the accounting records and is considered sunk. Item 4 is never entered into the accounting records.

2-9 A. $75,000 (RM + DL)

B. $95,000 (DL + OH)

C. $135,000 (DM + DL + OH)

D. $45,000 (S + A)

E. $75,000 (RM + DL)

F. $60,000 (OH)

2-10 The solution can be computed by using the relationships in an income statement for a manufacturing company. Insert the numbers that are given in the problem and then "back into" the answer, as follows:

First, compute Cost of Goods Sold (CGS):

Sales – CGS = GM; 400,000 – CGS = 70,000; CGS = 330,000
Then, Beginning FG + CGM – CGS = Ending FG
$80,000 + CGM – $330,000 = $70,000
CGM = $320,000

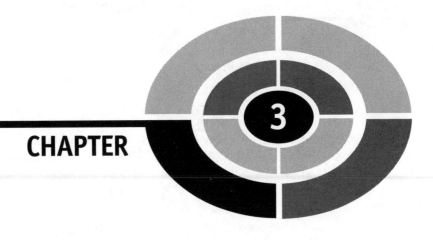

Job Order Cost Systems

This chapter introduces the concept of cost systems and presents the concept of a job order cost system, its accounting components, and the major steps involved in designing the system itself.

Factors in Designing a Cost System

The primary focus of a cost system design should be the purposes and needs of the user. As we discussed in Chapter 2, cost information is used for many purposes and the system must be seamlessly integrated to provide information for these purposes. Thus, a business cost system should be capable of providing information for:

- Inventory valuation
- The financial statements of external users
- Planning and decision making

In deciding on a new or revised system, the company should always perform a cost-benefit analysis. The reason for this is that managers often want to buy the newest system with all the latest advances in technology. But the expense of the newest system might surpass the benefits derived from it. For example, when the client-server systems were developed in the 1990s, they were widely popular. However, studies showed that mainframe, legacy systems that companies already had installed were just as effective and cost less to operate.

The most important factor in selecting and designing a cost system is to consider the type of business in which the company engages and its underlying operations, including the production process. In a **service company**, such as a law firm or an accounting firm, the service provided is client focused. Therefore, the cost system should collect the cost expended on each client case so that the company can effectively plan and control costs for a given case.

In a **manufacturing company**, the type of product and the production process usually dictate the type of system needed. For example, a company that produces batches of furniture to order would require a different system from a company that produces a single item on an assembly line, like refrigerators.

In this chapter we will cover one of the most widely used cost systems in business: a job order cost system. Two other systems that are used in businesses are process costing and activity based costing, which are covered in Chapters 5 and 6.

Job Order Cost System

A job order cost system is widely used in both service and manufacturing companies and has the following characteristics:

- The company produces several different (heterogeneous) products or services—usually simultaneously—each period.
- The cost object is usually a small quantity of a distinct product or service that is produced as one unit, a batch, or a lot.
- The products are often custom-made for a customer, such as furniture, a printing job, or a cruise ship.

Some examples of projects using job order costing are:

- The completion of a building construction project, which is a single item but with a high unit cost.
- The production of a movie, which is also a single item with a high unit cost.
- The completion of a client's tax return by a public accounting firm.
- The completion of a batch or lot of products in a manufacturing company, such as a batch of sofas having the same or similar design.

We will focus primarily on the manufacturing application of job order costing, since it is the most complicated. Service company users would generally follow the same steps in their application of this system, but we will present such variances from the manufacturing example when appropriate, along with a related practice problem.

To fully understand the accounting components, you should review the cost flows in a manufacturing company depicted in Figure 2-5 in Chapter 2. As shown there, after raw materials, labor, and overhead are acquired, they flow into work in process to initiate the production of new products. After these products are completed, the related costs flow into finished goods. Finally, when the products are sold, the related costs are moved to cost of goods sold.

The physical flow of costs is the same for most manufacturing cost systems and the major control accounts in the general ledger are very similar: Raw Materials Control, Wages Payable Control, Manufacturing Overhead Control, Work in Process Control, and Finished Goods Control. However, there are differences in the source documents and the subsidiary ledgers using the job order costing system, as we will see in the next section.

The Accounting Components of a Job Order Costing System

Source Documents Used in the System

Our first consideration in designing a job order system is the various **source documents** used for acquiring and transferring costs through the system. A source document is the original record of a transaction event that supports a journal entry into the accounting records of an organization. It is part of the audit trail that results in an entry on one of the financial statements issued by an organization.

The audit trail goes like this. Before the beginning of the production process, raw materials are acquired from vendors and stored in a stock room. As materials are required, the production center requisitions the material through a requisitioning system from the stock room. The requisition must state the job order number so that the cost can be traced to the cost center and the job. An example of a **material requisition form** is shown in Figure 3-1. Companies that use a standard cost system (to be discussed later) would requisition a bill of materials for the number of products to be produced.

As the jobs are worked on in each production center, each worker keeps a record of his or her time on a specific job and posts that information to the employee time sheet (the recording may be done using a computer terminal in the factory). An example of an **employee time sheet** is shown in Figure 3-2.

In a service company where labor is the major cost of doing business, the major source document is the time report form. For example, in a law or accounting firm employees would carefully track on a time report form their time spent servicing a client as well as other direct costs, such as travel and other direct expenses. Returning to the manufacturing case, the most important source document is probably the **job cost record** itself. As raw materials are requisitioned and time sheets are completed, their contents are entered into the computer at the end of the day or on a real-time basis, which updates the job cost sheet. All indirect costs (overhead) are usually pooled into one or more accounts and allocated to the job on a timely basis.

XYZ Manufacturing Company

Materials Requisition Form

Requisition No._____   Date_____

Cost Center_____   Job Number_____

Authorized by_____   Issued by_____

Authorized Receiver's Signature _____

Item Number	Stock Number	Description of Item(s)	Unit of Measure	Quantity Requested	Quantity Issued	Quantity Back Ordered	Unit Cost	Total Cost

Figure 3-1 Materials requisition form.

XYC Manufacturing Company

Employee Time Sheet

Date_____   For the Period Ending_____

Cost Center_____

Employee Name_____

Employee Badge Number_____

Employee's Signature_____

Work Code	Work Description	Job Number	Unit of Measure	Start Time	Stop Time	Day(s) of the Week	Total Hours

Figure 3-2   Employee time sheet.

How this is done is covered later in this chapter and in more detail in Chapter 4. An illustration of a job order cost record is shown in Figure 3-3.

The General Ledger and Subsidiary Ledgers

The **second major** accounting component in a job order cost system is the **general ledger** along with its **subsidiary ledgers**. The control and subsidiary accounts that are unique to the job order cost systems are summarized in Figure 3-4 along with the flow of costs through work in process. These relationships are based on Figure 2-5, which gives a complete picture of the flow of costs. Note that in a job order cost system as depicted in Figure 3-4, the Work in Process Control account in the general ledger has as a subsidiary all of the Job Cost Records that are presently in process. (In a service company the control account may be labeled as Jobs in Process Control with the individual jobs or cases as its subsidiary.) The Figure 3-4 illustration shows only two jobs in process for illustrative purposes but in a real company there likely would be many jobs in process.

XYZ Manufacturing Company
Job Cost Record

Job Order Number _____   Customer_____

Date Started _____   Date Completed _____

Name of Product or Project _____

Name of Production Department _____ Cost Center No. _____

Units Completed _____

Direct Materials

Date Received	Requisition Number	Stock Number	Quantity Used	Unit Cost	Total Cost

Total Direct Material Costs (1) _____

Direct Labor

Date	Employee Badge Number	Operation Performed	Hourly Rate	Hours Used	Total Costs

Total Direct Labor Costs (2) _____

Overhead

Date	Cost Pool to Be Allocated	Allocation Base	Allocation Base Units	Allocation Base Rate	Total Cost

Total Overhead Costs (3) _____

Total Job Costs: (1) + (2) + (3) ========

Total Units Produced _____
Cost per Unit _____

Figure 3-3   Job cost record.

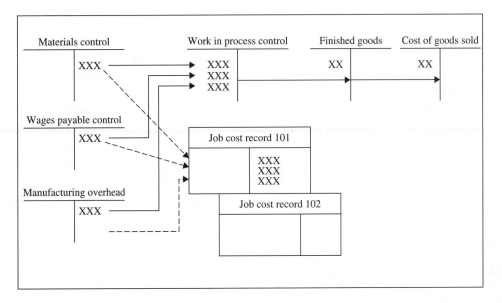

Figure 3-4   Flow of costs to work in process control account and subsidiary ledger.

From studying Figure 3-4, one should see that there are two entries required each time that costs are moved to work in process in a job order cost system. The total costs of raw materials for all jobs requisitioned from the stock room during a period are debited (see sidebar for a review of debits and credits) to the Work in Process Control and credited to Materials Control. This entry is represented by the solid line. The second entry is to debit the individual Job Cost Record (Job 101) for the raw materials issued for that specific job. This entry is made when the raw material is issued or no later than when the job is completed. This entry is represented by the dashed line.

Do You Remember Your Debits and Credits?

A quick review of the rules of debits and credits might be helpful. These rules are based on the accounting equation: Assets = Liabilities + Stockholders Equity. On the left side of the equation, all debits to an asset account *increase* that account (debits are always on the left side of any account). All credits to an asset account *decrease* that account (credits are always on the right side of any account). On the right side of the equation, all debits to liabilities and stockholders' equity accounts *decrease* the account. All credits have the opposite effect. For expense (cost) accounts (which are temporary accounts and can be thought of as subsidiary to the stockholders' equity section) all debits *increase* these accounts and all credits *decrease* these accounts. For revenue accounts, credits *increase* these accounts and debits *decrease* these accounts.

The costs for direct labor and manufacturing overhead also have two entries. For direct labor, the total labor costs are debited to Work in Process Control in total when the payroll is completed or at the end of the period, whichever comes first. The time spent on each job and its related costs are recorded on the employee time sheet (Figure 3-2) and are posted to the job record at the end of the day or when the worker finishes the job. The individual job records may be updated at the end of the day or no later than when the job is completed.

For illustrative purposes, the discussion has assumed that the accounting records are updated manually by individuals. However, in fact, most companies have sophisticated software that updates the general ledger and the subsidiary ledgers on a continuous basis. It should be noted that the timing of posting to records will vary from company to company.

The Major Steps in Designing a Job Order Cost System

Now that we have discussed the major components of a job order cost system, we will discuss the major procedural steps in the system. We will cover the major steps first and then provide an extended illustration to further explain these steps.

Step 1: Identify the Cost Objects in the System. As discussed in Chapter 1, a cost object accumulates costs for a specific purpose. Since there are several different types of user needs for information in a business, there may be several cost objects within a cost system to collect these different types of information. For example, in a manufacturing company, management will need costs collected to evaluate managers and cost centers. In addition, it will need costs collected to determine the cost of the product for inventory purposes. To accommodate these two different needs, the system will have what are called intermediate and final cost objects. First, costs may be traced or allocated to the departmental level and, second, they would then be traced or allocated to the product itself. As we will see in Chapter 6, there could be further intermediate cost objects identified as activities.

Step 2: Identify Direct and Indirect Costs. Once the cost objects have been considered and identified, the system designer will need to identify all direct costs that can be traced directly to the intermediate cost object and the final objects. For example, in a Toyota Service Department the cost object would be the customer work order and the direct costs would be the parts required and the labor of the service technician working on a specific automobile. In the King and Spaulding law firm the cost object would be the client's case and the direct costs would be the hours each lawyer and paralegal spent on the case times their average salary rate per hour, along with any related travel, supplies, and miscellaneous costs that can be directly traced to that client or job. All other costs would be identified as indirect costs and would be allocated to the cost objects as discussed in step 4.

Step 3: Trace All Direct Costs to the Cost Object and Post to the General Ledger and Subsidiary Accounts. This would entail the collection of costs from requisitions, time sheets, and other relevant documents and input them into the system. The system is programmed with software to update the relevant general ledge and subsidiary accounts, such as Work in Process Control, Job Order Cost Sheets, and Finished Goods, as discussed above.

Step 4: Allocate Indirect Costs (Manufacturing Overhead) to Intermediate and Final Cost Objects. To cover this step we need to briefly discuss the allocation procedure. Our discussion will be limited, leaving more details to Chapter 4. The allocation of manufacturing overhead can be a difficult and complex process in larger companies. This complexity is due to the fact that there can be many cost objects and still more cost centers, each using varying degrees of an overhead cost. Also, the fact that indirect costs by their very nature cannot be directly traced to cost objects makes it very difficult to determine how much of an overhead item should be allocated. For example, in a manufacturing plant it is impossible to determine the exact amount of a building depreciation cost that should be allocated to a particular job or product. The only way to allocate manufacturing overhead is to allocate these costs using a predefined, systematic process that will result in the computation of an overhead rate. The following procedures show how to compute the overhead rate:

1. **Identify the Cost Pools.** At this point we will assume that there is only one cost pool of overhead, i.e., a company-wide cost pool where all overhead or indirect costs are grouped into one pool. In Chapter 4, we will see that there can be multiple pools of overhead costs that are used to develop more accurate allocation of these costs.

2. **Identify All Indirect Costs.** Most manufacturing companies will have an Overhead Control Account with a subsidiary ledger that contains all of the individual overhead costs. Figure 3-5 illustrates a manufacturing

| | | XYZ Manufacturing Company
Manufacturing Overhead
For the Month of _____ | | | | |
Date	Indirect Materials and Supplies Issued	Supervision and Other Indirect Factory Labor	Factory Depreciation	Equipment Depreciation	Factory Utilities	Property Taxes and Insurance

Figure 3-5   Manufacturing overhead subsidiary ledger.

overhead subsidiary ledger. It assumes there is only one overhead account, but companies may have overhead accounts for each cost pool such as a department.

3. **Choose the Allocation Base or Cost Driver.** The cost allocation base is a measure of activity that helps link the indirect cost to the cost object. In choosing this base there should be a cause-and-effect relationship between the base and the consumption of indirect costs. In other words, as the base increases or decreases it is assumed that the consumption of indirect costs also increases or decreases. Thus, the base is often called a **cost driver** as defined in Chapter 1. The most common plant-wide allocation base is a form of direct labor, e.g., direct labor hours or total direct labor costs. The assumption for using direct labor hours as the base is that as they increase there is an increase in factory production that uses up more of the indirect costs. This is particularly true for higher paid workers. In other words, the assumption is that higher paid workers have a higher influence on the rise of indirect costs than lower paid workers do. Other allocation bases or cost drivers will be discussed in Chapter 4.

4. **Decide Whether to Use an Actual Overhead Rate or a Predetermined Overhead Rate.** We have assumed thus far that we would use an actual overhead rate. However, very few companies use

an actual rate. Why? Because to compute an actual rate the company must wait until the end of the period in order to collect the actual costs and the actual units of the allocation base. In a job order cost system this means that when a job is completed before the end of the period, there would be no way to compute the costs of the job at the time of completion. This has obvious problems such as not being able to value inventory, prepare interim financial statements, and evaluate the costs of a particular job on a timely basis. To overcome this problem companies use a **predetermined overhead rate** as described next.

5. **Compute the Overhead Rate.** Once the decision is made to use an actual manufacturing overhead rate or a predetermined one, the next step is to compute the rate itself. For our purposes we will use the predetermined rate, since it is the preferred approach as stated above. (An actual overhead rate would be computed the same way, except the actual units of the base and the actual overhead costs would be used.) At the beginning of the period the budgeted manufacturing costs are aggregated from the company's manufacturing budget. At the same time the budgeted units of the allocation base are determined. For example, if direct labor hours are used as the base then these hours are taken from the manufacturing budget. Finally, the total manufactured overhead costs are divided by the budgeted units of the allocation base to give the predetermined manufacturing overhead rate.

Once the overhead rate is determined, it is used to compute how much overhead should be allocated to each job, by multiplying it by the actual units of the allocation base—that is, direct labor hours. This is done when the job is completed or at the end of an accounting period for financial statement preparation. Note that many companies prefer the verb "applying" overhead than "allocating" overhead. For our purposes, these two terms are essentially the same.

In a service company, such as law or accounting firms with professional labor involved, there are normally three different types of rates computed: (1) a direct professional labor rate based on actual or budgeted professional labor. This rate is used to charge partner and paraprofessional direct labor to a client's job. The computation of a professional labor rate is necessary because partners and paraprofessionals will be paid different salaries and there must be a way of determining how much of partners' salaries should be charged to a given client. (2) A predetermined rate for charging indirect costs to a client's job. (3) A billable rate that is determined at the beginning of the year. This rate contains two components: (a) professional labor and (b) a markup to cover profit and overhead.

Step 5: Compute the Total Cost of the Job. When each job is completed and all direct costs have been charged to the job and the indirect costs (manufacturing overhead) have been charged using the allocation process, all of the cost elements are totaled. This total is divided by the number of units produced for that job to arrive at a total unit cost. The unit cost is used in inventory management and pricing. (See Figure 3-3 for a job cost record in a manufacturing company.)

Step 6: Transfer Costs from Work in Process Control to Finished Goods Control. The completed job cost record becomes the basis to make a journal entry to transfer the related costs to finished goods. It also is the basis for updating the subsidiary finished goods records for units being transferred to the warehouse, if these items are not shipped. These journal entries will be illustrated in the extended exhibits that follow.

Service companies use an account labeled jobs in process control instead of work in process control. As jobs are completed for clients the related costs are normally transferred to an account labeled cost of jobs billed, which is analogous to cost of goods sold in a manufacturing or merchandising company.

Disposition of Overallocated or Underallocated Overhead

When a business uses the predetermined overhead rate, the actual amounts of the allocation base and the overhead costs rarely match the estimates of the beginning of the period. Thus the business will have overallocated or underallocated overhead in the overhead control account, resulting in a credit or debit balance. Since the overhead account is a temporary one, this balance must be closed at the end of the accounting period. There are two methods for closing out this account:

- **Close the account to cost of goods sold.** For example, assume that there is a $10,000 credit balance in the overhead account, which means that overhead was overallocated during the period. The entry to close this account would be:

Manufacturing Overhead	10,000	
Cost of Goods Sold		10,000

- **Prorate between accounts.** The preceding method of disposing of overhead is not accurate because the related overhead costs that were allocated during the period may be found in the Work in Process, Finished Goods, and Cost of Goods Sold accounts. Therefore, a more accurate method would be to prorate the overhead balance to these three accounts in proportion to their ending inventories. Assume the following inventories at the end of the period:

Work in Process	$ 300,000	
Finished Goods	200,000	
Cost of Goods Sold	500,000	
The computations for allocating the overhead are:		
Overhead allocated in Work in Process inventory	$ 300,000	30%
Overhead allocated in Finished Goods inventory	200,000	20%
Overhead allocated in Cost of Goods Sold	500,000	50%
Total overhead allocated	$1,000,000	100%

The adjustment to the overhead account credit balance of $10,000 using the above percentages is:

Manufacturing Overhead	10,000	
Work in Process (30% x $10,000)		3,000
Finished Goods (20% x $10,000)		2,000
Cost of Goods Sold (50% x $10,000)		5,000

Illustration of a job order cost system in a manufacturing company:
The Pine Manufacturing Company uses a job order cost system and all production is in a single production department. The company had the following balances at the beginning of January 20XX:

Raw materials	$80,000
Work in process	30,000
Finished goods	60,000
Factory supplies inventory	5,000

The company allocates overhead on the basis of direct labor hours worked in the factory. It uses a predetermined overhead rate that is based on the production budget. The company budgeted 7,000 direct labor hours at the beginning of the year and

$287,000 of overhead. The following data apply to the company operations during 20XX but do not necessarily contain all transactions for this period:

1. Purchases of raw materials during the year were $500,000.
2. Total payrolls for the company employees were:
    a. Employees working directly on the products produced were paid $300,000 or $40 per hour on average.
    b. Supervisory and service employees in the factory were paid $150,000.
    c. Executives and support staff employees were paid $600,000.
    d. Sales staff employees were paid $200,000.
3. Factory building depreciation costs were $60,000.
4. Factory equipment depreciation was $30,000.
5. Factory taxes and insurance were $10,000.
6. Factory supplies used were $5,000.
7. Sales and administrative expenses other than payroll were $25,000.
8. Raw materials issued into production were $525,000.
9. Overhead costs were allocated to the product (see computations under item 5a in "Required.")
10. Products costing $950,000 were completed during the year.

Required

1. Identify the cost object and direct and indirect factory costs in the above data.
2. Compute the predetermined overhead rate.
3. Prepare all relevant journal entries based on the above transactions.
4. Post the entries to T-accounts, including the beginning balances.
5. Allocate overhead and close out the manufacturing overhead account for the year.

Solution

1. The cost object is the product produced and the direct costs (steps 1 and 2) are items labeled 2a and 8 above. All factory indirect costs (manufacturing overhead) are items 2b, 3, 4, 5, and 6. Items 2c, 2d, and 7 are not factory costs and are charged as period expenses.

2. The predetermined overhead rate (POR) is computed as follows:

   POR = Total budgeted manufacturing overhead ÷ Total direct labor hours

   POR = $287,000 ÷ 7,000 = $41 per direct labor hour (DLH)

3. The journal entries are:

(1)	Raw Materials Control	500,000	
	Accounts Payable		500,000
(2)(a)	Work in Process Control	300,000	
	Salaries and Wages Payable		300,000

NOTE: *Each individual job cost record would be updated for the amount of labor spent on each job during a given day. The total labor entered on the job cost records must equal the total payroll paid during the period.*

(2)(b)	Manufacturing Overhead Control	150,000	
	Salaries and Wages Payable		150,000

NOTE: *The job cost records would not be updated for actual manufacturing overhead costs acquired. Overhead costs would be allocated to each job as they are completed and entered on the individual job cost record. At the end of the period each job in process would be charged with the amount of overhead used to that point.*

(2)(c)	Administrative Salaries Expense	600,000	
	Salaries and Wages Payable		600,000
(2)(d)	Sales Salaries Expense	200,000	
	Salaries and Wages Payable		200,000
(3)	Manufacturing Overhead Control	60,000	
	Accumulated Building Depreciation		60,000
(4)	Manufacturing Overhead Control	30,000	
	Accumulated Equipment Depreciation		30,000
(5)	Manufacturing Overhead Control	10,000	
	Accounts Payable		10,000
(6)	Manufacturing Overhead Control	5,000	
	Factory Supplies Inventory		5,000
(7)	Sales and Administrative Expenses	25,000	
	Accounts Payable		25,000
(8)	Work in Process Control	525,000	
	Raw Materials Control		525,000

> **NOTE:** *Similar to direct labor, each individual job cost record would be charged for the amount of raw materials requisitioned for that job when the raw materials are issued to production by the stock room.*

(9)	See item 5 below.		
(10)	Finished Goods Control	950,000	
	Work in Process Control		950,000

4. T-Accounts and related postings for the above journal entries are shown in Exhibits 3-1 through 3-13:

Exhibit 3-1.

Raw Materials Control

Dr.	Cr.
1/1 80,000	(8) 525,000
(1) 500,000	

Exhibit 3-2.

Work in Process Control

Dr.	Cr.
1/1 30,000	(10) 950,000
(2a) 300,000	
(8) 525,000	
(9) 307,000	

Exhibit 3-3.

Accounts Payable

Dr.	Cr.
	(1) 500,000
	(5) 10,000
	(7) 25,000

Exhibit 3-4.

Manufacturing Overhead Control

Dr.	Cr.
(2b) 150,000	(10)
(3) 60,000	307,000
(4) 30,000	
(5) 10,000	
(6) 5,000	

Exhibit 3-5.

Factory Supplies Inventory

Dr.	Cr.
1/1 15,000	(6) 5,000

Exhibit 3-6.

Salaries and Wages Payable

Dr.	Cr.
	(2a) 300,000
	(2b) 150,000
	(2c) 600,000
	(2d) 200,000
	(7) 25,000

Exhibit 3-7.

Finished Goods Control

Dr.	Cr.
1/1 60,000	
(10) 950,000	

Exhibit 3-8.

Sales Salaries Expense

Dr.	Cr.
(2d) 200,000	
(7) 25,000	

Exhibit 3-9.

Accumulated Building Depreciation

Dr.	Cr.
	(3) 60,000

Exhibit 3-10.

Administrative Salaries Expense

Dr.	Cr.
(2c) 600,000	

Exhibit 3-11.

Sales and Administrative Expense

Dr.	Cr.
(7) 25,000	

Exhibit 3-12.

Accumulated Equipment Depreciation

Dr.	Cr.
	(4) 30,000

Exhibit 3-13.

Manufacturing Overhead Control

Dr.	Cr.
(2b) 150,000	(9) 307,000
(3) 60,000	
(4) 30,000	
(5) 10,000	
(6) 5,000	
255,000	307,000

5a. Factory overhead would be allocated as follows:

Since employees working directly on the product were paid a total of $300,000 (see 2.a above) at an average rate of $40 per hour, they worked 7,500 direct labor hours (300,000 ÷ 40 = 7,500). Therefore, the amount allocated to work in process would be DLH × POR or 7,500 × $41 = 307,000. The journal entry is:

Work in Process Control	307,000	
Manufacturing Overhead Control		307,000

5b. The overallocated or underallocated overhead would be determined as follows:

The factory overhead control account has the balances shown in Exhibit 3-13 at the end of the year.

After allocating manufacturing overhead to work in process, the manufacturing overhead account has a credit balance of $52,000 ($307,000 – 255,000).

This means that overhead was overallocated to work in process based on the budgeted DLH and manufacturing overhead costs. To close out this account the following entry should be made:

Manufacturing Overhead Control	52,000	
Cost of Goods Sold		52,000

Alternatively, the overallocated could be allocated between Work in Process, Finished Goods, and Cost of Sold in proportion to the ending inventory balances in those accounts.

Illustration of a job order costing system in a service organization: A.B. Jones and Sons is a CPA firm with five partners and three support administrative staff. There are no paraprofessionals. Jones uses a job order cost system with each client being a specific job. The senior partner has decided to use a budgeted overhead rate in allocating any support overhead. All direct costs that can be associated with a client, such as travel and supplies, are charged (debited) to Jobs in Process Control and to the individual client job sheet.

The partner's actual salaries are debited to Direct Professional Labor Control and the number of hours worked on the client's job is charged to the individual client job cost sheet. When the job is completed, or at the end of the period, the professional labor is allocated to the Cost of Jobs Billed based on the number of hours worked for the client during the period multiplied by the budgeted professional labor rate. This rate was determined at the beginning of the period.

Total actual indirect costs (supplies, depreciation, and other indirect costs) are debited to Overhead Control and allocated to Jobs in Process Control based on direct professional billable hours. The allocation rate is determined at the beginning of the period by dividing total budgeted indirect costs by budgeted billable hours.

In addition, Jones uses an estimated billable rate to bill clients. This rate is estimated to be $150 per partner hour for 20XX. This estimation was based on the going rate for other similar CPA firms in the market area. There are three entries made when billing a client: (1) The Fees Earned account is credited for the number of billable hours times the $150 per hour rate, and the corresponding debit is to accounts receivable. (2) The Cost of Jobs Billed is debited for the cost of the professional labor, which is the number of billable hours times the professional labor rate and the corresponding credit is made to Jobs in Process Control. The Cost of Jobs Billed account is similar to Cost of Goods Sold in a manufacturing or merchandising company. (3) The Cost of Jobs Billed is debited for the transfer of indirect support cost based on the budget overhead rate and the Overhead Control account is credited for the same amount.

The only inventory accounts maintained in this firm is a Supplies account and Jobs in Process Control.

The data below are projected for 20XX:

1.	Partner salaries and benefits	$600,000
2.	Partner billable hours	8,000
3.	Support staff salaries	90,000
4.	Lease on building	60,000
5.	Equipment depreciation	15,000
6.	Indirect supplies	3,000
7.	Other indirect costs	8,000

The transactions below occurred during the year 20XX:

1. Travel to service clients	$15,000
2. Supplies used on specific clients	12,000
3. Entertainment expenses for specific clients	15,000
4. Billings of client fee (8,100 partner hours were charged): the Cost of Jobs Billed is charged for partner labor when the billing is made to a client	1,215,000
5. Total costs of jobs billed, other than professional labor	190,000
6. Supplies used but not charged to a specific client	3,500
7. Actual support staff salaries for 20XX	91,000
8. Actual lease payments	60,000
9. Equipment depreciation	15,000
10. Property taxes	2,500
11. Other indirect costs consumed	8,200
12. Actual salaries and benefits paid to partners	595,000
13. Indirect costs (overhead) allocated for the year	?

Required

(Note: The reader may find it helpful to create T-accounts to track the costs in this problem.)

1. Compute (a) the budgeted direct professional labor rate and (b) the budgeted overhead rate for the year 20XX.

2. Prepare journal entries for the transactions occurring during 20XX.

3. Determine (a) the overallocated or underallocated overhead during the year and (b) the amount of overallocated or underallocated direct professional labor for the year. Assume that these amounts are charged to Cost of Jobs Billed.

4. Compute operating income for A.B. Jones and Sons for 20XX.

5. Joe Simpson is a wealthy tax client of A.B. Jones. His case was assigned job number T-114, which was completed during the year, and the following work and costs were incurred on services provided to this client. One partner spent 40 hours working on the 20XX tax return for this client. The partner spent $2,500 on travel costs traveling to visit the client in a nearby city. In addition, $300 entertainment expenses were spent taking the client to dinners and lunches. Compute the total costs charged to Job Number T-114.

Solution

1a. Computation of the budgeted professional labor rate is: $600,000 ÷ 8,000 DL hours = $75.00

1b. Computation of budgeted overhead rate:

Total overhead costs budgeted (90,000 + 60,000 + 15,000 + 3,000 + 8,000 = 176,000)

Total budgeted overhead costs ÷ Total budgeted partner billable hours = Budgeted Rate

$176,000 ÷ 8,000 = $22.00

2. The journal entries for 20XX transactions are:

Account	Debit	Credit
(1) Jobs in Process Control	15,000	
Accounts Payable		15,000
(2) Jobs in Process Control	12,000	
Supplies Inventory		12,000
(3) Jobs in Process Control	15,000	
Accounts Payable		15,000
(4a) Accounts Receivable	1,215,000	
Fees Earned		1,215,000
(8,100 billable hours x $150)		
(4b) Costs of Job Billed	607,500	
Direct Professional Labor Control		607,500
(8,100 billable hours x $75)		
(5) Costs of Job Billed	190,000	
Jobs in Process Control		190,000
(6) Overhead Control	3,500	
Accounts Payable		3,500
(7) Overhead Control	91,000	
Wages Payable		91,000
(8) Overhead Control	60,000	
Leases Payable		60,000
(9) Overhead Control	15,000	
Accumulated Equipment Depreciation		15,000
(10) Overhead Control	2,500	
Taxes Payable		2,500
(11) Overhead Control	8,200	
Accounts Payable		8,200
(12) Direct Professional Labor	595,000	
Salaries Payable		595,000
(13) Jobs in Process	178,200	
Overhead Control		178,200

Computation: (8,100 actual partner hours x $22 Budgeted Rate = 178,200)

3a. The under-applied overhead is computed as follows:

Actual overhead = (3,500 + 91,000 + 60,000 + 15,000 + 2,500 + 8,200) = 180,200

Allocated overhead	178,200
Minus Actual Overhead	180,200
Underallocated overhead	2,000

The journal entry to close the overhead account is:

Cost of Jobs Billed	2,000	
Overhead Control		2,000

3b. The overallocated or underallocated professional labor is computed as follows:

Actual professional labor (journal entry 12)	595,000
Allocated professional labor (journal entry 4b)	607,500
Overallocated professional labor	12,500

The journal entry to close the Direct Professional Labor Control account is:

Direct Professional Labor	12,500	
Costs of Jobs Billed		12,500

4. Operating income is computed as follows:

Fees Earned	$1,215,000
Cost of Jobs (607,500 + 190,000 + 2,000 – 12,500)	787,000
Operating Income	$428,000

5. The cost of Job Number T-114 is computed as follows:

Direct costs:		
Partner labor	(40 chargeable hours x $75/hour)	$3,000
Partner travel costs		2,500
Partner entertainment expenses		300
Total Direct Costs		$5,800
Indirect Costs: Overhead	(40 chargeable hours x $22/hour)	880
Total costs for job T-114		$6,680

Summary

The job order cost system is used when the company produces several different (heterogeneous) products or services—usually simultaneously—each period. The products are usually produced in batches or small quantities. It is often used in special order situations.

The accounting components of a job order system are the source documents and the general ledger accounts. The cost flow is from raw materials, labor, and overhead accounts into work in process account and then into the finished goods account. The uniqueness of the job order system is that the work in process has several subsidiary ledgers to account for each job as it moves through the production processes.

In review, the major steps in designing a job order system presented are as follows:

- Identify the cost objects in the system
- Identify direct and indirect costs
- Trace all direct costs to the cost object and post to general ledger and subsidiary accounts
- Allocate indirect costs to intermediate and final cost objects
- Compute the total cost of the job
- Transfer costs from Work in Process Control to Finished Goods Control

The overallocated or underallocated overhead is closed to cost of goods sold or prorated to work in process, finished goods, and cost of goods sold based on the ending balances in these accounts.

Practice Problems

3-1 Salvo Company uses a predetermined overhead rate based on direct labor to apply overhead. The data below were taken from the manufacturing budget and accounting records:

On September 1, the estimates for the month were:	
Manufacturing overhead	$20,000
Direct labor hours	10,000
During September, the actual results were:	
Manufacturing overhead	$21,000
Direct labor hours	11,000

The Overhead Allocated account for September will show:

A. Overallocated overhead of $1,000

B. Underallocated overhead of $1,000

C. Overallocated overhead of $2,500

D. Underallocated overhead of $2,500

Questions 3-2 and 3-3 are based on the following information:

Stewart and Peters Law Firm employs three full-time attorneys and five paraprofessionals. The firm provides corporate services to medium-sized corporations. The firm allocates both direct professional labor and indirect costs using a predetermined rate. The 20XX budget for Stewart and Peters is listed below:

Attorneys' salaries	$225,000
Paraprofessionals' salaries	100,000
Budgeted labor hours for attorneys and paraprofessionals	25,000
Indirect costs	$125,000

The actual costs for 20XX are shown below:

Attorneys' salaries	$240,000
Paraprofessionals' salaries	112,500
Actual labor hours for attorneys and paraprofessionals	30,000
Indirect costs	$150,000

3-2 Job A-100 required 1,000 professional labor hours for 20XX. The total direct professional labor and indirect costs charged to Job A-100 for billing purposes using a predetermined direct and indirect cost rate would be:

A. $20,025

B. $18,000

C. $16,750

D. $13,626

3-3 When 200 professional labor hours are used, the total costs of a job (client) for billing purposes, using an actual direct and actual indirect costs rate would be:

A. $6,425

B. $5,250

C. $4,200

D. $3,350

3-4 The Hope Manufacturing Company uses a job order costing system. The following transactions or events occurred during January 20XX:

1. The payroll data showed direct labor incurred was $51,000 and indirect labor incurred was $19,000.

2. Raw materials purchased on account were $190,000

3. Raw materials issued into production were $175,000.

4. Miscellaneous materials issued into production were $24,000. None of these could be directly traced to a job.

5. Taxes on the plant building were $7,000.

6. Depreciation recorded on the plant building was $150,000.

7. Depreciation recorded on the plant equipment was $79,000.

8. Other overhead costs were $67,000 and all were purchased on account.

9. The company allocates manufacturing overhead to production on the basis of a predetermined overhead rate of $4 per machine hour. There were 75,000 machine hours recorded during January 20XX.

10. Production orders showed that 52 jobs were completed during January and the total related costs were $510,000.

For each transaction, prepare journal entries for recording into the accounts.

3-5 For each journal entry in problem 3-4 give the source document that most likely authorized the transaction and indicate the necessary posting to the subsidiary ledger, if one is required.

3-6 The Peterson Printing Company uses a predetermined overhead rate based on direct labor hours to apply manufacturing overhead to jobs. Listed below is a segment of the budget for the year 20XX:

Direct materials	$16,000
Direct labor	25,000
Rent on factory building	15,000
Sales salaries	20,000
Depreciation on factory equipment	8,000
Indirect labor	11,000
Production supervisor's salary	16,000

Peterman budgeted 25,000 direct labor hours for the year. The predetermined overhead rate (POR) per hour will be:

A. $2.00

B. $2.79

C. $3.00

D. $4.00

3-7 After making all entries into the accounting system at the end of the month, the Lambers Company accountant found that the overhead account showed underallocated overhead of $12,000. The entry to close out this balance to Cost of Goods Sold would be:

A. Cost of Goods Sold	12,000	
Manufacturing Overhead Control		12,000
B. Manufacturing Overhead Control	12,000	
Cost of Goods Sold		12,000
C. Work in Process	12,000	
Cost of Goods Sold		12,000
D. Finished Goods	12,000	
Cost of Goods Sold		12,000

3-8 Sampson Company allocates overhead cost to jobs on the basis of 50% of direct labor cost. If Job 101 shows $30,000 of manufacturing overhead allocated, the direct labor cost on the job was:

A. $60,000

B. $45,000

C. $15,000

D. None of the above

Problems 3-9 and 3-10 are based on the following information:
Jameson Company uses a job-order cost system in costing its inventory. Direct material and direct labor are charged directly to the job using requisitions and time sheets, respectively. Jameson uses a predetermined overhead rate (POR) based on direct labor hours to allocate manufacturing overhead to jobs. Manufacturing overhead cost and direct labor hours were budgeted at $112,000 and 44,800 hours, respectively, for the year.

In July, Job 301 was completed at a cost of $4,400 in direct materials and $3,600 in direct labor. The labor rate paid to factory workers was $6 per hour. By the end of the year, Jameson had worked a total of 46,000 direct labor hours and had incurred $109,000 actual manufacturing overhead cost.

3-9 If Job 301 contained 200 units, the unit cost on the completed job cost sheet would be:

A. $37.00

B. $47.50

C. $41.90

D. $39.50

3-10 Jameson's manufacturing overhead for the year was:

A. $3,000 underallocated

B. $6,000 overallocated

C. $6,000 underallocated

D. $3,000 overallocated

Solutions to Practice Problems

3-1 A.
$$POR = \left(\frac{\$20,000}{\$10,000}\right) = \$2; \text{Allocated overhead} = 11,000 \times \$2 = \$22,000$$

actual – allocated overhead = overallocated or underallocated overhead

$21,000 – $22,000 = $1,000 overallocated overhead

3-2 B.
Direct professional labor predetermined rate = $\left(\dfrac{(\$225,000 + 100,000)}{25,000 \text{ hours}}\right) =$ $13.00

$$\text{Indirect cost predetermined rate} = \left(\frac{\$125,000}{25,000 \text{ hours}}\right) = \$5.00$$

Total costs allocated to job = ($13 × 1,000) + ($5 × 1,000) = $18,000

3-3 D.

$$\text{Direct professional labor actual rate} = \left(\frac{(\$240,000 + 112,500)}{30,000}\right) = \$11.75$$

$$\text{Indirect cost actual rate} = \left(\frac{\$150,000}{30,000}\right) = \$5$$

Total costs allocated to job = ($11.75 × 200) + ($5 × 200) = $3,350

3-4 Answers for this problem are shown below:

Account	Debit	Credit
1. Work in Process Control	51,000	
Overhead Control	19,000	
Wages Payable		70,000
2. Raw Materials Control	190,000	
Accounts Payable		190,000
3. Work in Process Control	175,000	
Raw Materials Control		175,000
4. Overhead Control	24,000	
Raw Materials Control		24,000
5. Overhead Control	7,000	
Taxes Payable		7,000
6. Overhead Control	150,000	
Accumulated Depreciation Buildings		150,000
7. Overhead Control	79,000	
Accumulated Depreciation Equipment		79,000
8. Overhead Control	67,000	
Accounts Payable		67,000
9. Work in Process Control	300,000	
Overhead Control		300,000
(Computation: 75,000 × $4 = $300,000)		
10. Finished Goods Control	510,000	
Work in Process Control		510,000

3-5 Answers for this problem are shown below:

1. a. Summary of individual time sheets for the direct labor and the payroll summary for the indirect costs.

   b. Debit job cost records for the direct cost and debit the indirect labor column of the department overhead ledger.

2. a. Approved invoice.

   b. Materials record received column.

3. a. Materials requisitions.

   b. Debit job cost records materials column.

   Credit Materials record, "issued" column.

4. a. Materials requisitions.

   b. Debit Department Overhead indirect materials column.

   Credit Materials record issued column.

5. a. Approved tax invoice statement.

   b. Debit department overhead taxes (or miscellaneous) column.

6. a. Approved authorization form.

   b. Debit department overhead depreciation column.

7. a. Approved authorization form.

   b. Debit department overhead depreciation column.

8. a. Approved invoices.

   b. Debit department overhead miscellaneous costs column.

9. a. Approved document reflecting computation of overhead charged using predetermined overhead rate.

   b. Debit individual job cost records overhead section.

10. a. Completed job cost records.

    b. Debit finished goods warehouse records.

    Credit job cost records.

3-6 A.

Computations: $15,000 + 8,000 + 11,000 + 16,000 = $50,000 = Total Budgeted Overhead Costs

POR = 50,000 ÷ 25,000 = $2.

3-7 A.

3-8 A.

Let X = amount of DL. Therefore, 0.50X = $30,000
X = $60,000

3-9 B.

The predetermined overhead rate (POR) is computed as:

$112,000 ÷ 44,800 = $2.50 per DLH

Hence, the overhead charged to the job is: 600 DLH × $2.50 = $1,500

The total cost charged to Job 301 is:
There is incomplete data to compute the amount of overhead charged to Job 301, that is, the number of direct labor hours (DLH) worked on the job is not given. To compute DLH:

$3,600 of direct labor cost was charged to the job at a rate of $6 per hour. Therefore, $3,600 ÷ $6 = 600 DLH

Direct Materials	$4,400
Direct Labor	$3,600
Overhead (600 × $2.50)	$1,500
Total	$9,500

The unit cost of Job 200 is:

$9,500 ÷ 200 units completed = $47.50

3-10 B.

The amount of overhead allocated for the year is: 46,000 × $2.50 = $115,000, which would be credited to the overhead account. The actual overhead was $109,000, which was debited to the overhead account. Thus, the overhead account had a credit balance of $6,000 ($115,000 − 109,000) at the end of the period, meaning that overhead was overallocated for the year.

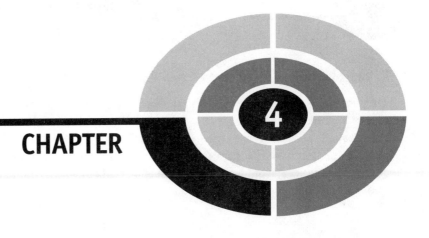

CHAPTER 4

Cost Allocation Systems

In Chapter 3 we introduced cost allocation as a system used by businesses to assign indirect costs to cost objects. It this chapter we will discuss the concept of cost allocation in more detail, examine why cost allocation is necessary, raise issues that must be addressed before implementing a cost allocation system, present graphs showing the flow of costs in an allocation system, and present the methods for allocating support and indirect costs to departments and then to products.

As we described in Chapter 2, indirect costs are those costs that cannot be directly traced to a cost object but need to be assigned to one anyway in order to determine the specific object's **full cost** (both direct and indirect costs). For example, if Lockheed has a contract to build an aircraft for the U.S. Air Force and the price is set to reimburse Lockheed its full cost (see sidebar) plus a profit, it must be able to determine how much of the indirect costs should be assigned to the contract. The purpose of this chapter is to explore the nature of cost allocation more fully, to discuss the various purposes of cost allocation, and to cover the various allocation bases and methods used in cost allocation.

What Is "full" Cost?

The term *full cost* can have different meanings, depending on its usage. In manufacturing it means the full production cost of a finished product, direct and indirect. The latter is sometimes called *full absorption costing*. In pricing, the term *full cost* refers to the total costs of manufacture plus a share of administrative and selling expenses. Therefore, in the Lockheed contract example, it would include all costs: manufacturing, administrative, and selling. So, to determine meaning one must evaluate its context.

It should be pointed out that while we will be using the manufacturing sector in many of our examples, cost allocation applies to all types of businesses where the company wants to trace all costs to particular cost objects in order to obtain more accurate cost information. Further, allocation can apply to all types of organizations: service, nonprofit (such as hospitals), and governmental organizations. The concepts and procedures that we discuss can be adapted for any of these organizations.

Why Allocate Indirect Costs?

There are many situations in which cost allocation is necessary in a business. The following are the more common ones.

- **Tax and financial reporting.** Both tax regulations and generally accepted accounting principles require allocation of costs to units produced by a manufacturing company. This is necessary to obtaining the full costs of a unit for costing of inventory.

- **Business decision making.** When managers are choosing between two or more alternatives, they need to know the full cost information for each alternative. For example, if a company is deciding whether to make a part for a finished product or buy it from another manufacturer, it needs to know the total costs for the "make or buy" alternatives. Another decision process that may require cost allocation is that of long range pricing. Businesses will need to know the full cost of a product in order to determine whether they can sell at the market price and make a profit in the long run.

- **Contract reimbursement.** As stated above, some businesses sell goods and services on a contractual basis. The contract usually stipulates that the firm will be paid full cost plus a reasonable profit. Identifying and assigning all costs (product, administrative, and selling) is critical in this case. Defense contractors are examples of companies that receive payments on this basis.

- **Motivate the manager of the cost object:** The objective of top management is to motivate lower managers to use resources effectively and efficiently. Therefore, an allocation system must help guard against the overutilization and underutilization of costs. The control for the *overutilization* of costs allocated from support centers or from the corporate headquarters is most effective when there is a cause-and-effect relationship between the cost base, or cost driver, and the usage of the costs involved. For example, a computer center's services are often allocated on the basis of usage (activity) by other cost centers in the company. In this situation, the cost center manager has control over the amount of usage and should be responsible for efficient use of computer costs through a budget and cost reports.

Often there is no cause-and-effect relationship in allocating costs, particularly those involving fixed costs. Theoretically, these are noncontrollable costs and should not be allocated to a cost object for control purposes. However, many companies may do so anyway. The reasoning is that the using manager may have some influence over the cost by persuading the support center manager to exert better control. But this is not common and may actually have the opposite effect by causing ill will, particularly if the using manager perceives that the manager upstream is doing a poor job of controlling support center costs and simply passing on inefficiencies to the receiving cost center.

On the other hand, underutilization of a supporting department's services may be a problem. Management may want to allocate costs to motivate lower managers to make use of these services. A good example is the reluctance of corporate managers to use the consulting services of the internal audit department because they are afraid the auditor will find a discrepancy in their operations and report it back to senior management. But if a manager knows a charge will be made anyway, he or she may decide to go ahead and use these services.

Nature of Cost Allocation

As described above, cost allocation simply means allocating a proportional amount of indirect costs to cost objects. By its nature, cost allocation is arbitrary in that there is no "best" way to allocate indirect costs. For example, there is no way to determine exactly how much use of a machine should be allocated to a product being made by that machine. The management accountant needs to use good judgment in developing a reasonable, systematic method to allocate these costs, as difficult as it may be to apply fairness and equity in a measurement scheme.

The criterion most often used to allocate indirect costs is that of **cause and effect**. That is, the base used to allocate indirect costs should be related to the indirect

Are Allocated Indirect Costs the Same as Common Costs?

Another term that is similar to indirect costs is that of *common costs*. This term refers to a cost that is shared by two or more cost objects. It can be thought of as a special type of indirect cost. For example, two departments hold an awards dinner to honor outstanding employees. The managers agree to share the costs of the dinner on a 50-50 basis. The costs are usually shared on a proportional basis, by allocating to the primary user the costs that would have been incurred by a stand-alone user, and charging to the secondary user the additional or incremental amounts.

costs that are being allocated. For example, direct labor hours are most often used for accounting in situations where the manufacturing operation is labor intensive. The rationale is that if labor hours increase, then it is assumed that the indirect costs—are being consumed in comparative proportion to this increase. In machine-intensive operations, it is machine hours that are most often used for the base. Bases meeting the cause-and-effect criterion are often called *cost drivers*.

When the cause-and-effect relationship cannot be determined, other criteria must be used to allocate indirect costs. One such criterion is **benefits received**. The theory supporting this approach is that the cost object should receive a proportional share of indirect costs based on benefits received. An example is using square footage as a base for allocating building depreciation to a production department since the department is a major beneficiary of the building costs.

A further refinement of indirect costs is the concept of common costs, which is discussed in the sidebar.

Issues to Address in Cost Allocation

- **Should a budgeted or actual rate be used?** This was discussed in Chapter 3, where we emphasized that a budgeted rate allocation rate is preferable to an actual one. Very few companies compute an actual rate. The principal reason is that a budgeted rate allows the company to compute the cost of products in advance for pricing and inventory valuation purposes. Otherwise, it must wait until the end of the period to make this computation, which may be long after the product or service has been sold.

- **Which time period should be used?** Most management accountants will choose a longer period, usually one year, over a quarterly or monthly period in computing the budgeted rate. There are two reasons: First, the longer period tends to eliminate seasonal and other erratic patterns when costs are either much higher or lower. The longer period averages the costs over a year and gives a more realistic value of the costs allocated. For example, property taxes may be incurred during one quarter of the year but should be spread over the entire year. The second reason for a long period is that in shorter periods of time the base or cost driver may fluctuate over the year, therefore giving greatly changing rates within a single year.

- **How many pools should be used?** To obtain the most accurate data for a cost object indirect costs should be grouped into **homogeneous** cost pools. That is, in a cause-and-effect relationship costs with a similar relationship to the cost driver (base) should be grouped together. For example, building depreciation, building insurance, building taxes, utilities, and similar occupancy costs could be grouped into one pool. Again, costs and benefits should be evaluated. As will be discussed in the next section, pools can be further refined and split into variable cost pools and fixed cost pools.

- **Should a plant-wide rate or departmental rates be used?** This is closely related to the previous discussion on how many pools of indirect costs a company should use. Many companies will use a plant-wide rate because of the costs involved in collecting data for individual departments. However, the information from plant-wide rates may prove misleading for product valuation and for decisions such as pricing. That is, the allocation system may assign more costs to one department than those it actually used, or it may assign fewer costs to a department that used more. This discrepancy is normally caused by using the departmental bases or cost drivers rather than the single base used for a plant-wide rate. Thus, the management accountant should give careful consideration to using department rates in order to give more accurate information.

- **Should the company use dual rates?** That is, should the company separate common overheads costs into their variable and fixed components and compute an allocation rate for each? As stated above, the company will usually compute the dual rates for indirect costs to motivate lower managers to make good decisions when they have some control over the incurrence of the variable costs involved. This is more effectively achieved by separating the portion of fixed indirect costs that represents **capacity** (see sidebar), and a portion that represents actual usage, a variable. For example, a company leases computers based on a fixed charge for renting the equipment and a variable charge for operation of the computers.

  Using dual rates may require some mixed costs—costs having both variable and fixed components—to be separated into fixed and variable pools. The methodology for doing this is discussed in Chapter 7. Problem 4-1 illustrates the use of dual rates in allocating common overhead costs.

Production Capacity

Capacity is the ability of the firm's productive assets—capital, human, and other assets—to create a product or service (see Chapter 12 for different definitions of *capacity* in a manufacturing operation).

- **What cost allocation bases (cost drivers) should be used?** As stated above, the two criteria normally used to select an allocation base are cause and effect and benefits received, with cause and effect being the best criterion if it can be determined. Some common examples of allocation bases for indirect costs in a manufacturing company are shown in Exhibit 4-1. Some common examples of allocation bases for assigning common corporate costs to other cost objects are shown in Exhibit 4-2.

Exhibit 4-1.   Typical Allocation Bases for a Manufacturing Plant

Type of Cost	Typical Allocation Base(s)
Building rental/depreciation	Space occupied
Building taxes and insurance	Value of buildings
Building utilities and maintenance	Space occupied
Equipment rental/depreciation	Machine hours
Equipment taxes and insurance	Taxable value of machines
Equipment repair and maintenance	Charges from work order or machine hours
Factory supervision	Number of employees or payroll dollars
Factory cafeteria	Number of factory employees
Stockroom costs	Value of requisitions from departments or number of requisitions
Buildings and grounds maintenance	Space occupied

Exhibit 4-2.   Typical Allocation Bases for Corporate Common Costs

Type of Cost	Typical Allocation Base(s)
Corporate administrative costs	Revenues in division or business center or dollar value of assets used
Corporate human resources costs	Dollar value of salary and/or labor costs in divisions or business centers
Accounting activities	Number of documents processed for divisions or business centers or estimated usage by divisions
Purchasing activities	Number of purchase orders, dollar value of purchase orders submitted by division or business center
Property taxes	Real estate valuation or square feet occupied by division or business center

An Overview of Cost Flows in a Manufacturing Cost Allocation System

In larger manufacturing operations there are two types of departments: support and production. As the term implies, the **support department** is responsible for providing support to the production department. An example is the repair and maintenance department, which provides service to the production departments. A complication in this scheme is that some service departments provide reciprocal services to one another. For example, the plant cafeteria provides service to all departments; at the same time, the repair and maintenance department provides support to the cafeteria.

The graph in Figure 4-1 is an overview of the cost flows in a manufacturing company.

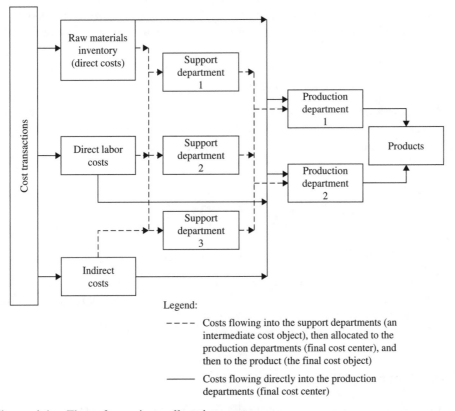

Legend:

---- Costs flowing into the support departments (an intermediate cost object), then allocated to the production departments (final cost center), and then to the product (the final cost object)

—— Costs flowing directly into the production departments (final cost center)

Figure 4-1 Flow of costs in an allocation system.

Cost transactions flow into direct raw materials, direct labor, and indirect costs. Two different cost flows result from these accounts:

1. The dotted lines depict costs flowing from these three categories directly into the support departments. Thus, the support departments are intermediate cost objects and the materials and labor cost flowing into them are direct costs. Costs that cannot be directly traced to the support departments are allocated elsewhere. From the support departments, all of these costs are allocated to the production departments and combined with other indirect costs directly allocated earlier (depicted by the solid line from indirect costs). For example, building depreciation costs would be initially allocated to both the support *and* the production departments, since they usually occupy the same building.

2. The solid lines depict raw material and direct labor costs flowing directly from the three cost categories to the production departments. From the production departments, the direct costs are traced directly to a product. The indirect costs would be charged to the product using a predetermined (budgeted) overhead rate. The base for allocating the indirect costs to the product would likely be different from the base used to allocate indirect costs from the support departments.

As we will see in Chapter 6, departments can be further broken down into activities in order to obtain more accurate costing. This concept is called *activity based costing* and can be extended to activity based budgeting.

Methods of Allocating Support Department Costs

The methods discussed below are an extension of the overhead allocation procedures discussed in Chapter 3 (specifically step 4). It would be worthwhile for you to review those procedures at this time. The two main methods that are discussed in detail below are the **direct method** and the **step method**. We begin with the direct method.

Direct Method

The direct method is used to allocate the support department's costs directly to the production departments without considering services rendered to other support departments. This method is widely used in business because of its simplicity and low cost to implement, but it may give less accurate cost information than other methods.

Illustration

Consider the budgeted data in Exhibit 4-3A for Johnson Aluminum Container Company during 20XX. The company has one plant in which there are three support departments and three operating departments:

- *Support departments*: Buildings and grounds, stockroom, and general plant and administration
- *Operating departments*: Cutting, molding, and assembly

The company uses the following allocation bases to allocate support center costs:

- *Building and grounds*: Square feet occupied
- *Stockroom*: Number of requisitions
- *General plant and administration*: Labor hours used in departments

The company uses predetermined (budgeted) overhead rates by department and allocates production indirect costs to products based on machine hours.

Exhibit 4-3A.	Departmental Budgets for 20XX The Johnson Aluminum Container Company					
	Departments					
	Support			Production		
Item	Buildings and Grounds	General Plant & Admin.	Stockroom	Cutting	Molding	Assembly
Departmental overhead	$21,000	$30,000	$18,000	$30,000	$28,000	$42,000
Number of square feet occupied by departments		2,000	1,000	3,000	2,000	2,000
Labor hours by department			5,000	5,000	4,000	6,000
Number of requisitions				2,500	1,500	2,000
Machine hours in production departments				5,000	3,000	2,000

Required

1. Allocate the support center costs to the production department using the direct method.

2. Compute the overhead rate for each production department.

Solution

The solution is shown in Exhibit 4-3B.

	Departments					
	Support			**Production**		
Item	**Buildings and Grounds**	**General Plant & Admin.**	**Stockroom**	**Cutting**	**Molding**	**Assembly**
Exhibit 4-3B. Allocation of Support Department Costs Using the Direct Method The Johnson Aluminum Container Company						
Total overhead costs	$21,000	$30,000	$18,000	$30,000	$28,000	$42,000
Allocation of Buildings & Grounds ($21,000 ÷ 7,000 sq ft = $3.00 sq ft)	(21,000)			9,000	6,000	6,000
Allocation of General Plant Administration ($30,000 ÷ 15,000 DL hours = $2.00 per DL hour)		(30,000)		10,000	8,000	12,000
Allocation of Stockroom ($18,000 ÷ 6,000 requisitions = $3.00 per requisition)			(18,000)	7,500	4,500	6,000
Totals				56,500	46,500	66,000
Divided total machine hours				5,000	3,000	2,000
Overhead rate per machine hour				11.30	15.50	33.00

Step-Down Method

The **step-down method** (sometimes called the step-down allocation method) gives partial consideration to reciprocal services between departments when allocating support department costs. It requires that support departments be sequenced or ranked in a predetermined order before the allocation process can begin. The most common approach to determining this ranking is to use the highest percentage of services provided to other supported departments. That is, the support department that provides the highest percentage is ranked first and the remaining support department's costs are allocated in descending order. Under this method, once a support department's costs are allocated, none of these costs can be reallocated back to this department. Thus this method gives some recognition to reciprocal services between support departments.

Illustration

1. Use the step method to allocate the Johnson Aluminum Company support department costs to the production departments (see Exhibit 4-3A).

2. Compute the budgeted overhead rate to allocate indirect costs to the products.

3. Compare these rates to those computed using the direct method. Comment on this comparison.

Solution

The solution is shown in Exhibit 4-3C.

In comparing these rates to those computed by the direct method, we find that there is no significant difference between the two. This means that in this example the direct method probably provides a fairly accurate allocation of service department costs. Thus, because the direct method is less complicated and less costly than the step method, the company should select the direct method. However, the company should also periodically test the two methods to ensure that conditions don't change.

Exhibit 4-3C:	Allocation of Support Department Costs Using the Step Method The Johnson Aluminum Container Company					
	Departments					
	Support			**Production**		
Item	**Buildings and Grounds**	**General Plant & Admin.**	**Stockroom**	**Cutting**	**Molding**	**Assembly**
Total overhead costs	$21,000	$30,000	$18,000	$30,000	$28,000	$42,000
Allocation of Buildings & Grounds Maintenance ($21,000 ÷ 10,000 sq ft = $2.10 sq ft)	(21,000)	4,200	2,100	6,300	4,200	4,200
Allocation of General Plant Administration ($34,200 ÷ 20,000 DL hours = $1.71 per DL hour)		34,200				
Allocation of Stockroom ($28,650 ÷ 6,000 requisitions = $4.775 per requisition)		(34,200)	8,550	8,550	6,840	10,260
			28,650)			
Totals			(28,650)	11,938	7,162	9,550
Divided total machine hours						
Overhead rate per machine hour				56,788	46,202	66,010
				5,000	3,000	2,000
				$11.3576	$15.40	$33.005

Other Methods for Allocating Support Department Overhead

While most companies use one of the two methods discussed above, neither method completely considers reciprocal services provided among support departments, which means the results from applying them are usually inaccurate.

To provide for the inclusion of costs that considers all reciprocal services provided among support departments, some larger companies may use what is called the **reciprocal method**. This method develops a set of linear equations to compute the reciprocated costs of each support department. Those familiar with using linear equations will see that when you have many support departments the computations can become very detailed and cumbersome, if one attempted the necessary calculations manually. Companies that use this approach will use computer programs that can easily compute the reciprocated costs for any number of support departments. The reciprocal method is not covered in this book but can be found in any advanced textbook on management or cost accounting.

Summary

Cost allocation is a process for assigning overhead or indirect costs to two or more cost objects. Its purposes are to provide information (1) for tax reporting and financial statement preparation, (2) for contract reimbursement, (3) for certain decision making, and (4) to motivate managers to make decisions consistent with those of the company.

Cost allocation works best when there is a cause-and-effect relationship between the costs and the base used to allocate them. The next best criterion is that of benefits received by the cost object.

In designing an allocation system several issues must be addressed:

1. Should an actual or predetermined rate be used?

2. What time period should be used in determining a rate?

3. How many cost pools should be used?

4. Should plant-wide or departmental rates be used?

5. Should a dual rate be used (variable and fixed)?

6. What base (cost driver) should be used in the system?

There are three methods for allocating indirect costs:

1. The direct method, which does not consider reciprocal support by the support departments

2. The step-down method, which partially considers reciprocal support

3. The reciprocal method, which considers all reciprocal support

The last was not covered in this text.

Practice Problems

4-1 XYZ Electronics Company sells three categories of electronics nationwide through advertising and direct telephone solicitation. To motivate sales managers, the three categories of products are organized into divisions. Salary raises and bonuses are awarded to divisional managers based on the control of telephone expenses, which is the main expense in each division, besides labor.

Each division has several telephone lines that are operated by an average of 25 people. The contract for all telephone lines is based on a fixed amount plus a charge for every minute used by the telephone solicitor. In the past, all telephone expenses were allocated based on a single budgeted rate multiplied by the actual number of direct labor hours used during the period. Division C's manager has complained that his bonus was unfairly computed for last year, saying that he was charged too much telephone expense, thus lowering his bonus.

The CEO is considering using a dual rate for allocating these expenses. The fixed portion's rate would be computed using budgeted telephone expense divided by direct hours available (assuming 2,000 per year per employee) and allocated using actual direct labor hours used. The variable portion would be based on the variable rate charged by the telephone company times the actual minutes used by each salesperson in the division. To help him make a decision the CEO wants to test the two methods using last year's actual data.

The following budgeted data were used in computing a single allocation rate for last year:

Total estimated billing charges to XYZ	$600,000
Total actual direct labor hours budgeted for all divisions	150,000
(2,000 hours per year × 25 × 3)	

The management accountant analyzed the actual usage data for last year and determined the following:

Total fixed telephone costs billed per contract	$360,000
Total actual variable costs	240,000
Charge per minute per the contract	$0.03
Minutes used per billing data (rounded)	8,000,000

Actual usage by division is shown below:

Division	DL Hours Used	Telephone Minutes Used
A	49,000	2,750,000
B	47,000	2,400,000
C	49,000	2,850,000

Required

1. Compute the allocation rate using the single rate method.
2. Compute the allocation rate using the dual method.
3. Compute the total telephone expenses charged to each division under each method.
4. Compare the results. (a) Does the manager of division C have a legitimate complaint? (b) Is the dual rate better than the single rate? (c) Is there a better method for evaluating the divisional manager's performance?
5. Why are the "total costs allocated" less than the $600,000 under both methods?

The following information pertains to questions 4-2 through 4-4.
   Timms Super Autostore sells two brands of automobiles: Ford and GMC. Each brand is organized as a division, and the managers are held responsible for achieving a sales target and for controlling costs. The overall dealership has a buildings maintenance department and a human resources department that provide services to both divisions. The maintenance department's costs of $100,000 were allocated on the basis of service hours used. The human resources department's costs of $30,000 were allocated based on the number of employees. The actual direct costs of the Ford Division are $160,000 and the costs of the GMC Division are $180,000.

The management accountant has provided the following data on service hours and number of employees in the various departments and divisions.

Item	Maintenance Department	Human Resources Department	Ford Division	GMC Division
Service hours used	2,000	2,000	2,400	1,600
Number of employees	10	20	40	120

4-2 What is the cost of the maintenance department allocated to the GMC Division using the direct method?

A. $24,000

B. $40,000

C. $39,000

D. $48,000

4-3 What is the cost of the human resources department reassigned to GMC using the direct method?

A. $75,000

B. $40,000

C. $12,000

D. $22,500

4-4 What is the cost of the maintenance department allocated to the GMC division using the step method, if the service with the highest percentage of interdepartmental service is allocated first?

A. $16,000

B. $26,667

C. $28,667

D. $33,333

The following information pertains to questions 4-5 and 4-6.

XYZ Company manufactures two finished products. Listed below are budgeted items for next year. Two operating departments of the company, the molding department and the assembly department, utilize one plant location.

Repair and maintenance department costs—fixed	$900,000
Available capacity for operating departments	2,500 hours
Budgeted long-term usage of capacity:	
Molding department	2,000 hours
Assembly department	700 hours
Budgeted variable cost per hour, which is within the relevant range	$600 per hour

4-5 If the molding department used 1,750 hours, what is its allocated cost, assuming budgeted usage is the base for fixed costs and actual usage is the base for variable costs?

  A. $1,525,000

  B. $893,620

  C. $1,716,667

  D. $1,000,063

4-6 If the assembly department used 200 hours, what is its allocated cost, assuming budgeted usage is the base for fixed costs and actual usage is the base for variable costs?

  A. $60,000

  B. $102,128

  C. $353,333

  D. $147,056

4-7 Peters Furniture Company manufactures computer desks of various sizes. It has a sawing and cutting department, an assembly department, and a finishing department. The following data were collected during January 20XX:

Direct materials requisitioned by sawing & cutting	$300,000
Direct materials requisitioned by finishing	50,000
(There were no raw materials issued to assembly)	
Actual indirect cost of all departments	220,000
Indirect costs allocated:	
Sawing and Cutting	$75,000
Assembly	125,000
Finishing	50,000

If 40,000 machine hours were budgeted in all departments for January, what was the plant-wide, budgeted cost allocation rate per machine hours used for the month?

A. $4.20 per hour

B. $5.50 per hour

C. $6.25 per hour

D. $8.75 per hour

Use the following information for questions 4-8 through 4-10:

Providing audit and tax services to clients, Pattillio and Sons is a medium-sized CPA firm with four departments: administration, computer services, audits, and tax. To more accurately determine the costs of services provided to clients, Pattillo allocates the costs of the administration and computer services to the audits and tax departments. The administration department costs of $40,000 are allocated on the basis of direct labor hours. The computer services department costs of $10,000 are allocated based on the number of computer hours used by the audits and tax departments. Costs of departments of audits and tax are $20,000 and $30,000, respectively.

Data on service hours for the month of May 20XX are as shown below:

Standard Service	Administration	Computer Services	Audits	Tax
Direct labor hours	100	100	1,200	800
Computer hours used	500	1,000	200	600

4-8 What is the cost of the administration department allocated to the audits department using the direct method?

A. $12,000

B. $16,000

C. $19,500

D. $24,000

4-9 What is the cost of the computer services department reassigned to the tax department using the direct method?

A. $2,500

B. $4,000

C. $6,000

D. $7,500

4-10 What is the cost of the administration department allocated to the tax department if the service department—using the step method with the highest percentage of interdepartmental service—is allocated first?

A. $8,000

B. $17,538 rounded

C. $14,333 rounded

D. $16,000

Solutions to Practice Problems

4-1

1. The single rate is computed as follows:

    $600,000 \div 150,000$ hours $= \$4$ per DL hour

2. The dual rates are computed as follows:

    Fixed rate: $360,000 \div 150,000 = \$2.40$ per direct labor hours available

    Variable rate: $0.03 per minute per the contract

3. The single rate is computed as follows

    Division A: Total costs allocated: $4 \times 49,000$ hours $= \$196,000$

    Division B: Total costs allocated: $4 \times 47,000$ hours $= \$188,000$

    Division C: Total costs allocated: $4 \times 49,000$ hours $= \$196,000$

    And the dual rate is computed as follows:

Division A:

Fixed rate:	$2.40 \times 49,000$ hours =	$117,600
Variable rate:	$0.03 \times 2,750,000$ minutes =	$82,500
Total costs allocated:		$200,100

Division B:

Fixed rate:	$2.4 \times 47,000$ hours =	$112,800
Variable Rate:	$0.03 \times 2,400,000$ minutes =	$72,000
Total costs allocated:		$184,800

Division C:

Fixed rate:	$ 2.40 × 49,000 hours =	$117,600
Variable rate:	$0.03 × 2,850,000 minutes =	$85,500
Total costs allocated:		$203,100

4. The allocated costs for all divisions using for both methods are shown below:

(1) Division	(2) Single Rate (SR)	(3) Dual Rate (DR)	(4) Difference (3) – (2)
A	$196,000	$200,100	$4,100
B	188,000	184,800	–3,200
C	196,000	203,100	7,100
Total	$580,000	$588,000	$8,000

(a) In terms of costs, the manager of Division C used more minutes than the other two divisions, resulting in higher total costs allocated. Thus, using this allocation system, he does not have a legitimate complaint because he would not improve his bonus under the dual method.

(b) The dual method would be better since it more accurately allocates the true costs charged to the company based on a fixed rate and a set rate per minutes used.

(c) The missing factor here is the amount of sales generated by the extra minutes used by Division C. If those extra minutes result in higher marginal income, then the manager of Division C would have used his allotted capacity more effectively. Therefore, a better measure of performance would be the use of operating income (sales – telephone expenses allocated to that division).

5. The total costs allocated are lower than actual under both methods because the actual direct labor hours were less than the budgeted direct labor hours, thus underallocating the fixed costs.

4-2 B.

$$[1,600 ÷ (1,600 + 2,400)] × \$100,000 = \$40,000$$

4-3 D.

$$[120 ÷ (40 + 120)] × \$30,000 = \$22,500$$

4-4 B.

Which support department should be allocated first:

Maintenance to human resources: $2,000 \div (2,000 + 2,400 + 1,600) = 33.3\%$

Human resources to maintenance: $10 \div (10 + 40 + 120) = 5.9\%$

Hence, the maintenance department is allocated first.

$1,600 / (2,000 + 2,400 + 1,600) \times \$100,000 = \$26,667$

4-5 C.

$$\$900,000 \times (2,000 \div 2,700) + (1,750 \times \$600) = \$1,716,667$$

4-6 C.

$$\$900,000 \times (700 \div 2,700) + (200 \times \$600) = \$353,333$$

4-7 C.

$$\$75,000 + 125,000 + 50,000 \div 40,000 \text{ hours} = \$6.25$$

4-8 D.

$$[1,200 \div (800 + 1,200) \times \$40,000 = \$24,000$$

4-9 D.

$$[600 \div (200 + 600)] \times \$10,000 = \$7,500$$

4-10 B.

Admin. to computer services: $100 \div (100 + 1,200 + 800) = 4.76\%$

Computer services to admin.: $500 \div (500 + 200 + 600) = 38.5\%$

Therefore, the computer services department is allocated first:

Computer services to administration dept.: $[500 \div (500 + 200 + 600)] \times$
$\$10,000 = \$3,846$ rounded

Administration to the tax department: $[800 \div (1,200 + 800)] \times$
$(\$40,000 + \$3,846) = \$17,538$ rounded

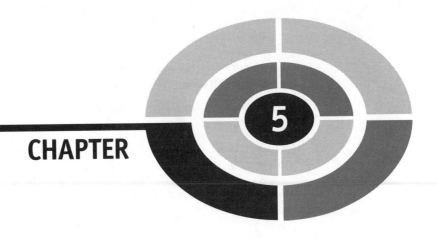

Process Cost Systems

This chapter describes process cost systems used to determine production costs in a manufacturing company. It explains the major steps in designing a process cost system, the concept of equivalent units, and the weighted average and first in–first out methods for determining the costs of production.

Process Costing and Job Order Costing Compared

In Chapter 3 we explained the meaning of and steps in designing a **job order cost system**. We described the job order system as having the following characteristics:

- The company produces several different (heterogeneous) products or services—usually simultaneously—each period.

- The cost object is usually a small quantity of a distinct product or service that is produced as one unit, a batch or a lot.

- The products are often custom-made for a customer, whether they are furniture, a printing job, or a cruise ship.

The **process cost system**, on the other hand, is quite different. It has the following characteristics:

- It creates a single product in a continuous process or over a long period of time. An example is syrup produced by Pepsi Cola or paper produced by Georgia Pacific. In a service company, a bank would use a process-like system in handling checks.

- The cost object is usually a mass production of the same unit, for which the unit costs are accumulated by a department or activity process.

A Description of Process Costing

First, Figure 5-1 presents an overview of cost flows through the accounting system under the process cost system.

From a review of Figure 5-1, it can be seen that products are started in Department A, the first process, moved to Department B, and completed in Department C. In the general ledger, each department has a work in process account representing

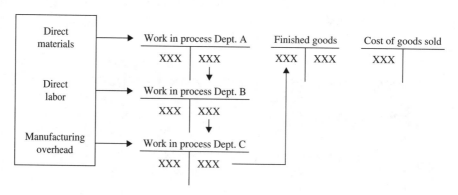

Figure 5-1 Flow of costs in a process cost system.

each process, and the costs are moved from one work in process account to the next until the process is finished in Department C, where the product cost is moved to the finished goods ledger.

Also, from Figure 5-1 it should be noted that raw materials are usually input to Department A but could be issued to any department if further material were required. The journal entry for issuing raw material is a debit to Department A and a credit to Raw Materials Control.

Also, labor and overhead could be input into all three departments. For labor, the appropriate department's Work in Process account is debited for labor used while the general Wages Payable account is credited. For overhead each department is allocated the appropriate amount based on the predetermined overhead rate used (see Chapter 4). The appropriate department is debited the amount allocated and the Overhead Control account is credited for the offsetting entry.

Now compare Figure 5-1 to Figure 3-4 in Chapter 3, which depicted the flow of costs through the accounts using a job order cost system. The major difference is in the work in process accounts. In a job order cost system there is one Work in Process Control account, with subsidiary accounts for each job order. In a process cost system, the work in process consists of one or more accounts representing the various departments or activities in the product process.

While there are differences between the two systems, there are some similarities:

- Both systems' objective is to arrive at a unit cost to enable accountants to value the various inventories.

- Both systems use the same basic general ledger control accounts: raw materials, manufacturing overhead, work in process, and finished goods.

- Both systems have basically the same cost flow through the major accounts.

Are There Other Cost Systems?

While job order costing and process costing are by far the most common systems used in the United States, there are other systems that are used. These are called *hybrid cost systems*, which have some job order cost characteristics and some process cost characteristics. The operation cost system used by clothing manufacturers is an example of a hybrid system. In this system batches of similar items of clothing are processed through different operations to completion.

Concept of Equivalent Units

In a job order cost system, it is rather easy to determine the unit cost of the products produced. As the batches are finished, the total costs are divided by the finished units produced. The result is the unit cost of the products completed. In the process cost system, however, the computations are more complex to arrive at a unit cost. The reason is that in the various processes or departments there can be units in various stages of completion before and after the accounting period ends. More specifically, a manufacturing company may have to deal with one or more of the following situations.

- Units could be started and fully completed during the period (no beginning or ending work in process inventories).

- Units could be started during the current period but not completed until the next period (there is an ending work in process inventory).

- Units could have been started during the previous period and completed this period (there is a beginning work in process inventory).

Since the objective is to arrive at a unit cost, it is necessary to determine the total costs of production (the numerator) and the equivalent units of production (the denominator). The equivalent units of production (EUP) are an approximation of the number of *whole* units of output during a given period. Obviously, if all units started in production are completed before the end of the period, there is no need for computing equivalent units. This makes the determination of unit cost simple: divide the total costs of production by the total number of finished units. This, however, is a rare occurrence and usually the EUP must be computed.

I'm Still Confused—What is the Difference Between "Whole" Units and "Equivalent" Units?

Equivalent units of production are computed for each category of inputs into the production process because the work in process could have a different percentage of completion for material, labor, and overhead. However, most process cost systems combine labor and overhead together to arrive at the **conversion cost**, which is material plus direct labor. To ascertain the percentages of completion, at the end of the period the management accountant receives a report from production personnel on the estimated completion of inventory in process as to both materials and conversion costs. For example, at Georgia Pacific inventory teams are sent out each period to inventory and estimate the degree of completion of various paper products. This is a very important estimation, because the correct valuation of inventory hinges on it.

In process cost systems there are two methods used to compute equivalent units and unit cost: the weighted average method and the first in–first out (FIFO) method. The method selected depends on the way in which the management accountant assumes the cost flows will occur in the production process. The **weighted average method** assumes an average use of resources and computes an *average* cost per unit of beginning inventory and the current period's production. The FIFO method assumes that the beginning inventory will be completed first during the period; hence, it separates the beginning inventory from the current period's production and computes a unit cost for the current period costs only.

An Overview of the Major Steps in a Process Cost System

Before the details are covered, Table 5-1 presents an overview of the major steps in a process cost system. As you review these steps remember that the ultimate objective is to determine a unit cost of production to be used for computing the total cost of production that is transferred to the next department, and to compute the ending work in process for the period.

A Visual Look at Computing Unit Costs Under the Weighted Average Method and the FIFO Method

From the three situations described under the Concept of Equivalent Units section and the steps described in Table 5-1, we can infer that there are four layers of costs in each department's production. These are depicted in Table 5-2.

Weighted Average Method

As the term implies, the weighted average method is an average unit cost of all production done to the date at the time of the computation (usually at the end of a given period). Thus, the weighted average unit cost of production is computed as follows:

(Cost layers $1 + 2 + 3 + 4$) ÷ (EUP in layers $1 + 2 + 3 + 4$)

Major Steps	Method Used: FIFO or Weighted Average	Comments
1. Compute the number of whole units to be accounted for.	Same under both methods	This equals the number of units a department worked on during the period (beginning inventory + units started during the period).
2. Compute the whole units accounted for. The results of steps 1 and 2 should balance.	Same under both methods	This equals the number of whole units completed and transferred out during the period + number of whole units in work in process (WIP) at the end of the period.
3. Compute the equivalent units of production (EUP) for use in computing the unit costs in step 5.	Weighted average	Determine the number of EUP completed and transferred plus ending work in process separated by raw materials and conversion.
	FIFO	Determine the number of EUP on work done in the current period only separated by raw materials and conversion (see below).
4. Aggregate the total costs to account for.	Weighted average	This includes the cost of beginning (WIP) and costs added during current period.
	FIFO	This includes the costs of work done in the current period only (see below).
5. Compute the cost per equivalent unit for raw materials and conversion.	Weighted average	Divide beginning WIP + costs added by the EUP of work done to date.
	FIFO	Divide costs added during current period only by EUP done in current period.
6. Use EUP and unit costs to assign total production costs.	FIFO or weighted average	Compute for completed and transferred costs and ending work in process costs.
7. Compute total costs accounted for. The results of steps 4 and 7 should balance.	FIFO or weighted average	This equals the total costs of EUP completed and transferred + ending WIP separated by raw materials and conversion.

Table 5-1 An Overview of the Steps In a Process Cost System Using the Weighted Average and First In–First Out (FIFO) Methods

Layer	Costs	Related Equivalent Units of Production (EUP)
1	Beginning work in process (costs added last period)	EUP of materials and conversion costs completed last period
2	Costs added this period to complete the beginning work in process	EUP necessary to complete the beginning work in process (100% – EUP in beginning work in process)
3	Costs for units *started and completed* this period	Whole units started and completed this period
4	Costs added for units started this period but not completed at the end of the period	EUP of materials and conversion costs in work in process at the end of the period

Table 5-2   Layers of Costs and Related Equivalent Units of Production Under the Process Cost System

Since the unit cost computed under the weighted average method is an average of all costs to date, it is used to value the total costs of production transferred to the next department and the ending work in process of the transferring department.

FIFO Method

As previously defined the FIFO method assumes that the inventory in layer 1 in Table 5-2 is completed and computes a unit cost of production of costs added for all production in this period only (layers 2 + 3 + 4). Thus, the FIFO unit cost of current production is computed as follows:

(Cost of layers 2 + 3 + 4) ÷ (EUP in layers 2 + 3 + 4)

Assigning Costs Using the Weighted Average Method

The format of a production report will be used to show the computation of unit costs and cost assignment. This report is used to summarize all of the activity in a production process during the current period. To illustrate the steps described in Table 5-1, the following data will be used:

The Coverall Company manufactures aluminum cans for sale to beverage companies. It has a cutting department and a molding and assembly department. Assume that aluminum materials are added at the beginning of the process. Conversion costs are added evenly during the process. The accountant has aggregated the production data in Exhibit 5-1 for the Coverall Company for June 20XX.

Exhibit 5-1. Production Data for the Cutting Department			
	Equivalent Units		
	Whole Units	**Aluminum Materials**	**Conversion**
Work in Process, June 1 (materials 100% complete; conversion 40% complete)	$60,000	$60,000	$24,000
Started during June	280,000		
Completed and transferred during June	300,000	300,000	300,000
Work in process, June 30 (materials 100% complete; conversion 25% complete)	40,000	40,000	10,000
Total costs for June 20XX	**Total Costs**	**Aluminum Materials**	**Conversion**
Work in process June 1	$71,500	$56,600	$14,900
Costs added during June (costs added to complete the beginning WIP + costs added for units started and completed this period + costs added for units in ending WIP)	599,500	385,000	214,500
Total costs to account for	$671,000		

Required

Assume that the company uses the weighted average method. Prepare a production report that shows:

1. The equivalent units of production
2. The unit cost per equivalent unit
3. The total costs transferred to the molding and assembly department

After completion of the report, prepare the proper journal entry to transfer costs to the molding and assembly department.

Solution

The solution to requirements 1, 2, and 3 is presented in Exhibits 5-2A and 5-2B (see Table 5-1 for a description of each step).

Exhibit 5-2A. Solution Using the Weighted Average Method of Process Costing (Steps 1–3)

| | | Step 3: Equivalent Units | |
Production	Whole Units	Aluminum Materials	Conversion
Step 1			
Units in work in process, beginning	60,000		
Units started during current period	280,000		
Units to account for	340,000		
Step 2 & 3:			
Whole units completed and transferred this period	300,000	300,000	300,000
Units in work in process at June 30 (40,000 × 100%); (40,000 × 25%)	40,000	40,000	10,000
Units accounted for	340,000		
Equivalent units on work done to date		340,000	310,000

Exhibit 5-2B. Solution Using the Weighted Average Method of Process Costing (Steps 4–7)

Production	Total Production Costs	Aluminum Materials	Conversion
Step 4			
Costs in work in process, June 1	$71,500	$56,600	$14,900
Costs added during June	599,500	385,000	214,500
Total costs to be accounted for	$671,000	$441,600	$229,400
Step 5			
Divide by equivalent units of work done to date		340,000	310,000
Cost per equivalent unit of production done to date		1.2988	0.74

Exhibit 5-2B. *(Continued)*			
Step 6			
Assignment of total production costs:			
Completed and transferred out (300,000 units)	<u>611,640</u>	(300,000 × 1.2988)	(300,000 × 0.74)
Work in process, at June 30 (40,000 whole units)			
Materials added	51,952	(40,000 × 1.2988)	
Conversion costs	<u>7,400</u>		(10,000 × 0.74)
Total cost of work in process at June 30	<u>59,352</u>		
Step 7			
Total cost accounted for (rounded)	$671,000		

The journal entry for transfer of the production costs would be:

     Work in process (molding & assembly dept.) $611,640

     Work in process (cutting dept.)   611,640

     $(300,000 \times (1.2988 + 0.74)) = 300,000 \times 2.0388 = \$611,640$

Assigning Costs Using the FIFO Method

Next we will illustrate the steps in Exhibit 5-3 using the FIFO method. Under this method, the management accountant will assume that the first layer of work in process inventory in a given department will be the first to be completed.

Required

Using the data in Exhibit 5-1 and assuming the company uses the FIFO method, prepare a production report that shows:

1. The equivalent units of production

2. The unit cost per equivalent unit

3. The total costs transferred to the molding and assembly department

After completing the report, prepare the proper journal entries to transfer costs to the molding and assembly department.

Solution

The solution to requirements 1, 2, and 3 is presented in Exhibits 5-3A and 5-3B (see Table 5-1 for a description of each step).

Exhibit 5-3A. Solution Using the FIFO Method of Process Costing (Steps 1–3)				
			Step 3: Equivalent Units	
Production	**Whole Units**	**Aluminum Materials**	**Conversion**	
Step 1				
Units in work in process, beginning	60,000	(work done before current period)		
Units started during current period	280,000			
Units to account for	340,000			
Step 2 & 3:				
Whole units completed and transferred this period:				
To complete beginning work in process (60,000 × 100%); (60,000 × 60%)	60,000	0	36,000	
Units started and completed this period (300,000 completed and transferred – 60,000 whole units in beginning work in process)	240,000	240,000	240,000	
Units in work in process at June 30 (40,000 × 100%); (40,000 × 25%)	40,000	40,000	10,000	
Whole units accounted for	340,000			
Equivalent units on work done in current period only		280,000	286,000	

Exhibit 5-3B.   Solution Using the FIFO Method of Process Costing (Steps 4–7)

Production	Total Production Costs	Aluminum Materials	Conversion
Step 4			
Costs in work in process, June 1	$71,500	(costs of work done before the current period)	
All costs added during June	599,500	385,000	214,500
Total costs to be accounted for	671,000		
Step 5			
Divide by equivalent units of work done in June (Exhibit 5-3A)		280,000	÷286,000
Cost per equivalent unit of production done in June		1.375	0.75
Step 6			
Assignment of total production costs:			
Completed and transferred out (300,000 units):			
To complete beginning work in process (60,000)	71,500		
Aluminum material added during current period	0	0 × 1.375	
Conversion costs added during current period	27,000		(36,000 × 0.75)
Total from beginning inventory	98,500		
Started and completed during current period (240,000)	510,000	(240,000 × 1.375	240,000 × (0.75)
Total costs of units completed and transferred out	608,500		
Work in process, at June 30 (40,000 whole units)			
Materials	55,000	(40,000 × 1.375)	
Conversion costs	7,500		(10,000 × 0.75)
Total cost of work in process at June 30	62,500		
Step 7			
Total cost accounted for (rounded)	671,000		

The journal entry for transfer of the production costs would be:

Work in process (molding & assembly dept.)	608,500	
Work in process (cutting dept.)		608,500

The unit cost of current production is not the same as the unit cost of production transferred to the next department since the costs in the beginning inventory are not included. It is necessary to compute the unit cost of a whole unit by adding the costs in the beginning work in process inventory to all costs added during the current period, and divide by the number of whole units transferred to the next department. From Exhibit 5-3B the unit cost of units transferred to the Molding and Assembly Department is ($608,500/300,000 units = $2.0283).

Costs Transferred in from Other Departments

Thus far, this chapter has explained how costs are computed and transferred to another department using the weighted average and FIFO methods. Now, the actual procedures for transferring costs to another department will be discussed, along with how costs are accounted for once they are in the next department.

The same basic approaches described above are used to compute production costs in the next department for a given period. The only difference is that transferred-in costs are tracked as a separate category and treated as 100% complete in terms of prior department costs.

Transferred-In Costs Using the Weighted Average Method

Continuing with the Coverall Company, the computation of production costs for the molding and assembly department for June 20XX using the weighted average method will be discussed. In the Molding and Assembly Department, additional material is added at the beginning of the process. Conversion costs are added evenly throughout the process.

Required

The production data for the Molding and Assembly Department are presented in Exhibit 5-4. Note that for purposes of this illustration, the costs transferred in are not the same as those transferred out in Exhibits 5-2B and 5-3B. Using the data given, prepare a production report that shows:

1. The equivalent units of production
2. The unit cost per equivalent unit
3. The total costs transferred to finished goods

After completing the report, prepare the proper journal entry to transfer costs to finished goods.

Exhibit 5-4. Production Data for the Molding and Assembly Department				
			Equivalent Units	
	Whole Units	**Transferred In**	**Materials Added**	**Conversion**
Work in process, June 1 (materials 100% complete; conversion 30% complete)	50,000	50,000	50,000	15,000
Transferred in during June	300,000			
Completed and transferred during June	290,000	290,000	290,000	290,000
Work in process, June 30 (materials 100% complete; conversion 40% complete)	60,000	60,000	60,000	24,000
Total costs for June 20XX	**Total Costs**		**Materials Added**	**Conversion**
Work in process June 1	$184,000	$100,000	$60,000	$24,000
Costs added during June (costs added to complete the beginning WIP + costs added for units transferred and completed this period + costs added for units in ending WIP)	1,440,000	580,000	440,000	420,000
Total costs to account for	$1,624,000			

Solution

The solution to requirements 1, 2, and 3 is presented in Exhibits 5-5A and 5-5B.

Exhibit 5-5-4A. Solution Using the Weighted Average Method of Process Costing (Steps 1–3)				
			Step 3: Equivalent Units	
Production	**Whole Units**	**Transferred In**	**Materials**	**Conversion**
Step 1				
Units in work in process, June 1	50,000			
Units transferred in during current period	300,000			
Units to account for	350,000			
Step 2 & 3:				
Whole units completed and transferred this period	290,000	290,000	290,000	290,000
Units in work in process at June 30				
(60,000 × 100%); (60,000 × 100%); (60,000 × 40%)	60,000	60,000	60,000	24,000
Units accounted for	350,000			
Equivalent units on work done to date		350,000	350,000	314,000

Exhibit 5-5-4B. Solution Using the Weighted Average Method of Process Costing (Steps 4–7)				
Production	**Total Production Costs**	**Transferred In**	**Materials Added**	**Conversion**
Step 4				
Costs in work in process, June 1	$184,000	$100,000	$60,000	$24,000
Costs added during June	1,440,000	580,000	440,000	420,000
Total costs to be accounted for	1,624,000	680,000	500,000	444,000

Exhibit 5-5-4B. *(Continued)*

Step 5				
Divide by equivalent units of work done to date		350,000	350,000	314,000
Cost per equivalent unit of production done to date		1.9429	1.42857	1.414
Step 6				
Assignment of total production costs:				
Completed and transferred out (290,000 units)	$1,387,786	290,000 × $1.9429	(290,000 × $1.42857)	(290,000 × $1.414)
Work in process, at June 30 (60,000 whole units)				
Transferred in	116,574	(60,000 × 1.9429)		
Materials added	85,714		(60,000 × 1.42857)	
Conversion costs	33,936			(24,000 × 1.414)
Total cost of work in process at June 30	236,224			
Step 7				
Total cost accounted for (rounded)	$1,624,000			

The journal entry to transfer the costs of units completed is:

Finished goods inventory control	1,387,786	
Work in process (molding & assembly dept.)		1,387,786

Transferred-In Costs Using the FIFO Method

Continuing with the data in Exhibit 5-4, the computation of production costs for the molding and assembly department will be discussed for June 20XX using the FIFO method. As stated above, additional material is added at the beginning of the process in the molding and assembly department. Conversion costs are added evenly throughout the process.

Required

Prepare a production report that shows:

1. The equivalent units of production
2. The unit cost per equivalent unit
3. The total costs transferred to the finished goods

After completion of the report, prepare the proper journal entries to transfer costs to finished goods. The solution to requirements 1, 2, and 3 is presented in Exhibits 5-5A and 5-5B.

Exhibit 5-5A. Solution Using the FIFO Method of Process Costing (Steps 1–3)				
			Step 3: Equivalent Units	
Production	**Whole Units**	**Transferred In**	**Materials**	**Conversion**
Step 1				
Units in work in process, June 1	50,000			
Units transferred in during current period	300,000			
Units to account for	350,000			
Steps 2 & 3:				
Whole units completed and transferred this period:				
To complete beginning work in process	50,000	0	0	35,000
(50,000 × 0%); (50,000 × 0%); (50,000 × 70%)				
Units started and completed this period	240,000	240,000	240,000	240,000
(290,000 completed and transferred – 50,000 whole units in beginning work in process)				
Units in work in process at June 30	60,000	60,000	60,000	24,000
(60,000 × 100%); (60,000 × 100%); (60,000 × 40%)				
Units accounted for	350,000			
Equivalent units on work done in current period only		300,000	300,000	299,000

Exhibit 5-5B. Solution Using the FIFO Method of Process Costing (Steps 4–7)

Production	Total Production Costs	Transferred In	Materials Added	Conversion
Step 4				
Costs for work in process, June 1				
	$184,000	(costs of work done before the current period)		
All costs added during June	1,440,000	580,000	440,000	420,000
Total costs to be accounted for	1,624,000			
Step 5				
Divide by equivalent units of work done in June only (Exhibit 5-6A)		300,000	300,000	299,000
Cost per equivalent unit of production done during June		1.93333	1.46667	1.4047
Step 6				
Assignment of total production costs:				
Completed and transferred out (290,000 units):				
Beginning work in process	$184,000			
To complete beginning WIP (50,000 units)				
Transferred in	0	0	0	
Material added during June	0	0	0	
Conversion costs added during June	49,165			(35,000 × $1.4047)
Total from beginning inventory	233,165			

Exhibit 5-5B.   *(Continued)*

Started and completed during June (240,000)	1,153,128	240,000 × 1.93333)	(240,000 × 1.46667)	(240,000 × 1.4047)
Completed and transferred out (290,000 units):	1,386,293			
Work in process, June 30 (60,000 whole units)				
Transferred in	116,000	(60,000 × 1.93333)		
Materials	88,000		(60,000 × 1.46667	
Conversion	33,713			(24,000 × 1.4047)
Total costs, work in process, June 30	237,713			
Step 7				
Total cost accounted for (rounded)	$1,624,000			

The journal entry to transfer the costs of units completed is:

Finished goods inventory control	1,386,293
Work in process (molding & assembly dept.)	1,386,293

Summary

The process cost system is used in a manufacturing operation that creates a single product in a continuous process and/or over a long period of time. The cost object is usually a mass production of the same unit, the cost of which is based on costs accumulated by process (usually a department). This unit cost is used to compute the cost of products transferred and the value of the ending work in process.

A critical part of the process costing system is to compute the equivalent units of production. The equivalent units of production are an approximation of the number of *whole* units of output during a given period. The equivalent units of production are usually computed for materials and conversion costs.

The seven-step approach to determining the costs of production output is:

1. Compute the number of whole units to be accounted for.

2. Compute the cost of the whole units accounted for and compare to the results of step 1.

3. Compute the equivalent units of production.

4. Aggregate the total costs to account for.

5. Compute the cost per equivalent unit for raw materials and conversion.

6. Use the equivalent units of production to assign total production costs.

7. Compute the total costs accounted for and compare to the total costs to account for.

The two methods used in process cost systems are the weighted average method and the first in–first out (FIFO) method.

The journal entries used are similar to those in job order costing, but in process costing there are two or more work in process accounts representing the processes or departments. In the job order system the work in process account has several subsidiary ledgers that are not found in process costing.

Practice Problems

The following information is to be used in problems 5-1 through 5-5.

Easy Talk produces and assembles high-end cell phones from parts purchased from outside vendors. These cell phones are Internet capable and will send, receive, and display photos and e-mail. They also include word processing and spreadsheet capabilities. Easy Talk uses a process cost system that includes two cost categories: raw materials and conversion. Each phone is assembled in the Assembly Department and transferred to the Testing Department, where extensive tests are completed. The products are then moved to a warehouse for storage until they are shipped. Raw materials are requisitioned from the stock room and added at the beginning of the process. Conversion costs are added evenly throughout the process. Easy Talk uses the weighted average costing method in its process costing system.

The management accountant has aggregated the data for the Assembly Department for December 20XX in the table below.

Production Data for the Assembly Department	
Work in process, December 1, 20XX	2,500 units
Raw materials (100% complete)	
Conversion costs (50% complete)	
Units started in December 20XX	8,000 units
Work in process at December 31	1,500 units
Raw materials (100% complete)	
Conversion costs (75% complete)	
Costs for December 20XX	
Work in process, December 1	
Direct materials	$1,800,000
Conversion costs	$2,700,000
Raw materials added during December 20XX	$10,000,000
Conversion costs added during December 20XX	$10,000,000

5-1 The equivalent units for raw materials and conversion costs, respectively, for work done to date are:

A. 10,500; 10,500

B. 10,500; 10,125

C. 12005; 11,606.4

D. 10,250; 10,250

5-2 The total amount debited to the work in process control account for the Assembly Department during the month of December is:

A. $24,500,000

B. $20,000,000

C. $4,500,000

D. $22,700,000

5-3 The raw material's cost per equivalent unit (rounded) during December is:

A. $1,579.00

B. $1,980.00

C. $1,729.00

D. $1,124.00

5-4 The conversion cost per equivalent unit (rounded) during December is:

A. $1,254.00

B. $1,980.00

C. $1,579.00

D. $1,370.00

5-5 The amount of conversion costs assigned to the Assembly Department's ending work in process for December 20XX is:

A. $1,888,148

B. $1,019,567

C. $1,410,750

D. $1,264,505

The following information pertains to problems 5-6 and 5-9.

The Altoona Oar Company uses a process costing system that includes the FIFO method of costing production. The Sawing Department started the month with 20,000 units in its beginning work in process inventory that were 50% complete with respect to conversion costs. There were 18,000 units in the ending work in process inventory of the Sawing Department that were 20% complete with respect to conversion costs. The conversion cost in the beginning work in process inventory was $65,000. An additional 50,000 units were started into production during the month. A total of $300,000 in conversion costs was incurred in the department during the month. When units are completed in the Sawing Department they are transferred to the Staining Department.

5-6 What would be the whole units started and completed during the month?

A. 30,000

B. 32,000

C. 50,000

D. 38,000

5-7 What would be the cost per equivalent unit for conversion costs for the month on the department's production report? (Round off to three decimal places.)

A. $6.579

B. $6.881

C. $5.800

D. $5.167

5-8 What would be the amount of conversion costs transferred to the Staining Department during the month?

A. $328,160

B. $407,108

C. $341,318

D. $342,500

5-9 In the Staining Department there is a beginning inventory of 10,000 units, 40% complete as to material and 70% complete as to conversion costs. What would be the completion percentage for units transferred in using the weighted average method?

A. 100% complete

B. 70% complete

C. 40% complete

D. Not enough information is provided to determine

5-10 XYZ Manufacturing has three production departments, #1, #2, and #3. Production moves sequentially from Department #1 to Department #2, and finally to Department #3. Department #2 started the month with 30,000 units in its work in process inventory. An additional 350,000 units were transferred in from Department #1 during the month to begin processing in Department #2. There were 20,000 units in the ending work in process inventory of Department #2. How many units were transferred to Department #3 during the month?

A. 333,000

B. 362,000

C. 360,000

D. 314,000

Solutions to Practice Problems

5-1 B.

First, compute the number of whole units completed and transferred:

$$(2,500 + 8,000 - 1,500) = 9,000$$

Next, compute the equivalent units of production as shown in the table below:

	Raw Materials	Conversion
Units completed and transferred	9,000	9,000
Work in Process, December 31	1,500	$(1,500 \times 0.75) = 1,125$
Total Equivalent Units	10,500	10,125

5-2 B.

Total costs debited equals total raw materials and conversion costs added:

$10,000,000 + $10,000,000 = $20,000,000

5-3 D.

(Costs in beginning inventory + costs added) ÷ equivalent units of raw materials = cost per equivalent unit

($1,800,000 + $10,000,000) ÷ 10,500 = $1,124 per unit (rounded)

5-4 A.

(Costs in beginning inventory + costs added) ÷ equivalent units of raw materials = cost per equivalent unit

($2,700,000 + $10,000,000) ÷ 10,125 = $1,254 per equivalent unit (rounded)

5-5 C.

(Number of equivalent units × % complete) × cost per equivalent unit

$(1,500 \times 0.75) \times \$1,254.00 = \$1,410,750$

5-6 B.

Whole units started and completed = whole new units put into production less whole units in ending work in process

$(50,000 - 18,000 = 32,000)$

5-7 A.

(Total costs incurred during the current period) ÷ (EUP to complete beginning WIP + units started and completed this period + EUP in ending WIP)

$(\$300,000) \div [(20,000 \times 0.5) + (50,000 - 18,000) + (18,000 \times 0.2)] = \$6.579$

5-8 C.

(Total costs in beginning WIP) + (costs to complete beginning WIP) + (costs started and completed during the current period)

($65,000) + (20,000 × 0.5 × $6.579) + (32,000 × $6.579) = $341,318

5-9 A.

Transferred in units are always 100% complete in the receiving department.

5-10 C.

(Units in beginning WIP + units transferred from department # 2) – (units in ending WIP) = (units transferred to department #3)

$(30,000 + 350,000) – 20,000 = 360,000

CHAPTER 6

Activity-Based Management Systems

This chapter presents the concept of activity-based management (ABM) systems, including activity-based costing (ABC), the uses and applications of ABM, the differences between ABC and traditional cost allocation, and the steps in designing an ABM system.

Activity-based costing systems have evolved since the late 1980s as a methodology for identifying activities in all links of the business value chain within an organization (research and development, design, production, marketing, distribution, quality control, and customer service), and for tracing costs of resources consumed by these activities. Over the years ABC has evolved into what is now called an **activity-based management system**, in that it not only encompasses the determination of activity

Traditional	ABC
• Focuses on information for determining costs for external reporting	• Focuses on information for management decision making and control
• Assumes that costs can be managed	• Assumes that what is being done (the activity) can be managed in a way that brings change in costs
• Identifies a very limited number of allocation bases	• Identifies many activity measures that drive costs
• Assumes the cost object consumes resources	• Assumes the cost object consumes activities
• Uses volume-related bases for allocation	• Uses drivers at various levels of allocation
• Is structure oriented, i.e., emphasizes organizational segments, such as departments	• Is process oriented and cuts across organizational units

Table 6-1   Traditional Cost Allocation Systems vs. Activity-Based Costing System

costs but also identifies systematic ways to use these costs in management decision making.

Table 6-1 summarizes the advantages of ABC systems compared with traditional allocation systems.

Activity-Based Management Systems

ABC as a Management System

ABM is a system that provides improved information to management for use in planning, decision making, and control responsibilities. Over the years the ABC concept has expanded to encompass applications in profitability analysis, pricing decisions, cost reduction, control, and even budgeting and internal audit. Chapter 4 has already shown how taking manufacturing cost allocation to the departmental level provides more accurate cost information than a plant-wide rate for valuing inventory based on generally accepted accounting principles. An ABM system goes beyond product costing and traces both manufacturing and appropriate nonmanufacturing costs to an intermediate cost object (activities) and then to final cost objects. The final cost object may be a product, a customer, a market channel, a line of service, or whatever object for which management needs improved cost information for decision making purposes. The heart of an ABM system is the identification of activities. An **activity** is any distinct task or unit of work undertaken by an organization to create and sell a product or service. As will be seen shortly, identification of activities and tracing or allocating costs to each activity is a significant improvement in cost systems.

Since a manufacturing ABM system usually traces or allocates both manufacturing and nonmanufacturing costs to each activity, the company will usually have to track two sets of costs: those used for product costing and those used for management purposes, since the cost output for the two could differ. Why? Because generally accepted accounting principles and tax regulations specify how and what types of costs must be accumulated and require that only costs incurred in creating products be included. As we saw in Chapter 2, selling and administrative expenses are period expenses: they cannot be included in production, but they may be included in an ABC system.

ABM systems were originally developed in the manufacturing sector but now are used in many types of organizations, including service companies, nonprofit groups, and governmental organizations. In reality, ABM could be used in virtually any organization as long as activities can be identified, reasonable cost drivers can be associated with these activities, there is a reasonable system for allocating indirect costs, and the resulting activity costs are used by management in its decision making.

In concluding this section, it should be pointed out that ABM systems are rather expensive to design, implement, and operate, which can be a significant disadvantage. Companies that are considering the use of this system should perform an extensive cost-benefit analysis in deciding whether to design and implement an ABM system. Further, in implementing such a system it is wise to limit the number of activities during the initial phase. This is important because of the massive amount of detail involved in ABM and the need for personnel to be trained in its day-to-day operation. Because of the cost of designing and implementing ABM systems, some companies limit their use to parts of the company or limit the number of activities to which it is applied. Thus, there is considerable variation of ABM in practice.

ABC in Product Costing

ABC is used by some companies to improve the cost accuracy of products for inventory and external financial reporting purposes. In this situation, only costs to produce the product would be included in costs of the activity. This would require the traditional system depicted in Figure 4-3 in Chapter 4 to be adjusted to include activities. With improved computer technology and sophisticated software, ABC can improve departmental rates in the traditional cost system by going a step further and allocating costs, first to activities and then to the products, based on the product's use of resources. For example, in an assembly department that is principally machine intensive, the number of machine hours is often used as its allocation base (cost driver). However, there may be activities within the department with cost consumption that don't correlate well with machine hours, for example, quality control, various moving activities, setup of machinery, machine power costs, and occupancy costs. This is particularly true when there are several different products moving through these activities, each making varying demands on the activities' resources. In these situations, using the single departmental rate based on machine hours may result in overcosting of some products and undercosting of other products. ABC usually will result in improved cost allocation and, thus, improved accuracy of product costs.

Finally, when used in product costing, ABC is not another costing system but supplements an existing job order or process costing system. For example, as the job order moves through the various manufacturing processes in a job order system, there may be two or more activities involved each process. Each activity has its own allocation rate, which is used to allocate costs to the product as it moves through these activities.

An Overview of the Flow of Costs in an ABM System

The graph in Figure 6-1 shows the general flow of costs through an ABM system. This graph shows that resources are acquired in the form of cost transactions and entered into the general ledger. The overhead costs are usually entered into department overhead accounts. Likewise, direct costs are usually entered into individual accounts, for example, raw materials, advertising, etc.

In an ABM system, costs that can be directly traced to a cost object should be assigned so (see the box labeled "1"). For example, if a custom order of furniture was the cost object, typical direct costs charged directly to the batch of products may include raw materials, direct labor, and costs of any special equipment required for the order.

Note that both manufacturing and nonmanufacturing overhead costs are considered for allocation to activities. The allocation of overhead costs to activities is sometimes referred to as **first level** or **first stage allocations** and is done using **resource drivers**. A resource driver is a measure of the actual resources used by an activity, i.e., it drives the consumption of resources. An example of a resource driver

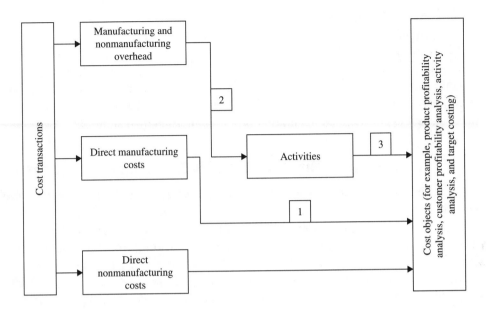

Figure 6-1   Flow of costs in an ABC system.

is the percentage of time a production supervisor spends on one activity among the several activities that he or she supervises. The box labeled "2" depicts the allocation of overhead costs using resource drivers.

After costs flow into activities, the costs of activities are allocated to the cost object for use in various decision analyses (for example, ABC budgeting (see Chapter 10), activity analysis, customer profitability analysis, product profitability analysis, and target costing) using **activity drivers**. An activity driver is a measure of the frequency and intensity with which a cost object influences activity levels. An example of an activity driver is the number of setups in a furniture production department. (Activity drivers are further discussed under step 3 later in this chapter.) The allocation of overhead costs to the final cost object is sometimes referred to as **second level** or **second stage allocations** and is represented by the box labeled "3" in Figure 6-1.

The following is a summary of the steps employed in designing and implementing an ABM system.

1. Identify the activities that consume resources.
2. Identify and trace all direct costs to cost objects.
3. Identify the resource drivers for allocating overhead pools to each activity.
4. Identify the activity drivers to assign activity costs to cost objects.
5. Identify and allocate all overhead costs to each activity.

6. Compute the activity driver rates.

7. Compute the total activity costs allocated to the cost object.

8. Use activity costs in decision making.

Having presented an overview of the steps in designing an ABM system, we will now present each step in more detail. We will provide examples as we move through these steps and an extended illustration problem after the final step.

Step 1: Identify the Activities That Consume Resources

This may be the most important step in the whole process, because the selected activities will serve as an underpinning for the entire system. The objective is to identify the key activities performed to produce and deliver products or services. The methods used in this step are survey instruments, interviews, and flow charting. Some companies may even use time and motion studies to estimate the amount of time consumed in the activities. This step is very time consuming and requires a cross-functional team to collect all of the necessary information from overhead and operating departments and perform analysis to identify the activities and time spent on the various activities by the support departments. For example, in studying activities in a manufacturing operation the team could include members from product design, manufacturing operations, and accounting. Instead of using teams staffed by its own personnel, some companies hire outside consultants to design its ABM system.

Designers of ABM systems have generally identified four different levels of activity costs pools in an attempt to determine cause-and-effect relationships between the costs and activity drivers. Determining cause and effect becomes more difficult as a company increases in size. Generally, as the company becomes more automated and complex the number of activities and activity drivers increase. Thus, it is helpful to categorize the different levels of activity costs. This categorization by level is called **cost hierarchy**.[1] The levels are:

- **Unit-level costs** are incurred each time a unit of output is completed. That is, the quantity of usage relates to the volume of output of production. This output may be a product or a service. In manufacturing a product, specified amounts of raw material and labor are consumed for *each* product along with overhead costs.

- **Batch-level costs** are incurred when each batch of products is processed through the activity. That is, the group of products involved are all processed together, regardless of the number of items in the batch. The best

---

[1]Some companies separate resources consumed for customer specific activities, such as activities required for a specific job or contract. In the four hierarchies used here, these costs would be included at the unit or batch level.

example of this level of costs is setup costs. In the production of chairs a batch of a dozen chairs of a specific style would arrive at a stitching activity for processing, and a machine set up with a specified stitching pattern would be required to complete the entire batch.

- **Product-level costs** are incurred by activities that provide services for an entire product line regardless of how many items are eventually produced. For example, original product design and design modifications are product-sustaining activities.

- **Facility-level costs** are incurred when running a production facility, an organization, or a business as a whole, regardless of the product or service mix, how many objects are produced, or how much of the products or services are sold. Some examples of facility-level costs are administration, occupancy costs (depreciation, utilities, etc.), and computer systems.

Step 2: Identify and Trace All Direct Costs to Cost Objects

As discussed above, ABC systems require that direct manufacturing and nonmanufacturing costs be traced to the cost object.

Step 3: Identify the Resource Drivers for Allocating Overhead (indirect cost) Pools to Each Activity

Resource drivers are used to allocate overhead pools to each activity on the basis of actual consumption of these resources. The major overhead resources are usually occupancy costs, indirect labor, and computer systems. The cross-functional team must spend considerable time interviewing personnel in each activity to determine the percentage of the overhead resources that is consumed by each activity. Some overhead cost percentages are easier to determine because they can be based on more precise measurements. For example, occupancy costs are usually based on the percentage of square footage an activity occupies in a building. The major resource drivers are shown in Exhibit 6-1.

Exhibit 6-1. Overhead Pools and Associated Resource Drivers	
Overhead Pool	**Resource Driver**
1. Occupancy costs	Percent of square feet used by the activity
2. Indirect labor costs	Percent of time spent on each activity
3. Computer systems	Computer usage by activities

Step 4: Identify and Allocate All Overhead Costs to Each Activity (first level allocation)

The flow of costs to activities was summarized in Figure 6-1. All overhead costs indirectly associated with a group of activities should be allocated among those activities based on their actual consumption of the overhead. This is done through an allocation process that is a refinement of the system discussed in Chapter 4. The major difference is that overhead resources will be allocated to activities instead of departments and both nonmanufacturing and manufacturing overhead will be allocated. Some overhead costs may not be left in overhead accounts after the allocation process has been completed. These costs are usually labeled **excess capacity**. Companies are increasingly using ABC systems to identify and manage excess capacity for productive purposes.

The allocation of costs is normally computed by multiplying the resource driver rate times the overhead cost pool. This rate is usually a percentage of the overhead costs consumed by the activity as described in step 3 above. These percentages are determined by cross-functional team interviews or surveys of support personnel. During the interviews the team estimates the amount of time spent by the support function in the various activities.

Step 5: Identify the Activity Drivers to Allocate Activity Costs to Cost Objects

The identification of the four levels of activity cost pools was discussed in step 1. This section will discuss the selection of activity drivers to assign the activity costs.

The actual selection of the activity drivers is the responsibility of the cross-functional team and must be periodically reviewed for relevancy. One important factor in choosing an activity driver is the availability of data for the driver selected. Data for output-level cost drivers are much easier to aggregate because the volume of an activity is usually readily available or can be easily added to the data system. However, because of complexity the measure of batch-level and product-level activities are more difficult to identify. For example, a cost driver for measuring the cost of designing a product relates to the complexity of the size and shape of the product's surface. Often the size of the product and/or the number of parts in the product is used as the cost driver.

What are the criteria for selecting an activity driver? As we discussed above, the best criterion is a causal relationship. Such a relationship exists when a change in the activity driver "drives" or causes a similar change in the related costs. In the absence of a causal relationship, designers may use the benefits-received criterion, which may be difficult to establish.

Some examples of activity drivers in a production facility are listed in Exhibit 6-2.

Activity or Cost Pool	Function/Process	Activity Cost Level	Activity Driver(s)
Exhibit 6-2. Activities and Activity Drivers in a Production Facility			
1. Designing a new product by a team from design, engineering, and production	Design department	Product level	Number of parts to produce; size of product surface; time spent designing product
2. Designing improvements to several products	Design department	Product level	Number of modifications made; time spent on redesign of each product
3. Moving materials from stockroom to production	Stockroom	Batch level	Number of batches of materials moved; time spent moving materials
4. Installing tires on an automobile on the assembly line	Production operations	Unit level	Labor hours; labor cost
5. Boring shape of product	Production operations	Unit level	Machine hours
6. Testing of products upon completion	Production operations	Unit level	Direct labor hours
7. Setting up machine for batch of products	Production operations	Batch level	Number of batches process; time spent setting up
8. Moving finished goods to shipping area	Shipping and receiving	Batch level	Number of batches of products moved; time spent moving batches.
9. Incurring electricity for the production facility	Production operations	Facility level	Square feet; actual usage from meters
10. Paying the salary of the plant superintendent	Production operations	Facility level	Number of production employees; production employee hours

Some examples of activity drivers in a service company are shown in Exhibit 6-3. A bank illustration has been selected because banks have made extensive use of ABM in the pricing of services and assessing customer profitability. The activities in this illustration are very detailed. To limit the number of activities, some may be combined.

Exhibit 6-3. Activities and Activity Drivers in a Bank Commercial Lending Department	
Activity	**Activity Driver(s)**
1. Call to a potential customer	Number of calls made; minutes spent per call
2. Direct-mail solicitations	Number of mailings; minutes spent per mailing
3. Credit analysis	Number of loan applications; hours or minutes per application
4. Discussion of loan with manager	Minutes spent with manager per loan
5. Creation of loan documents	Number of documents; hours (minutes) spent per loan decision package
6. Review of loan package	Minutes spent per package
7. Preparation of approval or disapproval letters	Minutes spent per letter
8. Loans booked	Minutes spent per booking

Step 6: Compute the Activity Driver Rates

Once overhead costs have been allocated to each activity the total costs of each activity will be divided by the total quantity of each activity's driver during the same period of time. Thus, the formula for this computation is: Activity rate = (overhead costs allocated to each activity) ÷ (total units of the activity driver).

Step 7: Allocate the Total Activity Costs to the Cost Objects (second stage allocation)

For example, as a product cost object moves through each activity the activity driver rate is multiplied by the quantity of activity driver related to the cost object to determine the amount of overhead costs assigned to that object. Some direct costs (materials and labor) may have been assigned to the cost object; if so, these costs are added to the allocated activity costs to obtain the full cost of the product object.

Step 8: Use Activity Costs in Decision Making

Activity costs are computed for a major reason, which is to assist management in making decisions about the company. There are several management situations where these costs are very helpful: strategic analysis (Chapter 14), product costing (Chapters 4 and 5), profitability analysis (see below), ABM budgeting (Chapter 10), value-added analysis (Chapter 9), and target costing (Chapter 9).

Illustration

The Executive Chair Company manufactures several different designs of executive chairs in leather or fabric. Chairs normally move through the various activities in batches and require machine setup in the cutting department. No special setups are required in the other activities. In the past, the company sold to individuals or small furniture stores that place special orders.

The chairs are sold on a special order basis; therefore, the company uses a job order cost system. In addition to this system, the company partially implemented an ABC system that helps in pricing and in measuring the profitability of customers. Since Executive is a small company it uses only six different activity pools in the ABC system.

Concurrent with implementing the ABC system, Executive Chair is testing a new strategy that seeks to market its chairs to large office supply companies that would result in much larger size orders. These efforts have resulted in five orders being received during the past month from five different office supply companies, for a total of 100 executive chairs. The actual material costs per chair are $200 and the actual labor costs per chair are $100 under both the old and new strategies. The 100 chairs are sold for $800 each, $100 less than the $900 sales price to individual customers. Exhibit 6-4 reports overhead costs for the past year—including costs for the 100 chairs—for each cost pool and the related resource drivers used to allocate to activities.

Before testing the use of the ABC system, the company used labor hours to allocate overhead cost pools. The controller, in consultation with the production and sales managers, estimates that each chair requires approximately 5 hours each. During the year the company produced and sold 1,500 chairs, including the 100 chairs under the new strategy. Thus, it would have required an estimated 7,500 hours to produce the total number of chairs.

Exhibit 6-4. Overhead Cost Pools		
Overhead Pool	**Cost**	**Resource Driver**
Manufacturing Overhead		
Occupancy costs (depreciation, utilities, taxes, etc.)	$300,000	Percent of square feet occupied by each activity
Factory supervision	100,000	Estimated percent of time spent on each activity
Building maintenance	50,000	Estimated percent of time spent in maintaining each activity
Selling and Administrative Overhead		
Selling	$100,000	Estimated percentage of support to each activity
Administrative support	$100,000	Estimated percentage of support in each activity
Total overhead costs	$650,000	

Exhibit 6-5 shows the resource driver rates for distribution of overhead to each activity on an annual basis. The estimated percentage of time spent on each activity was determined from interviews by a cross-functional team in the supporting departments.

Exhibit 6-5. Resource Allocation Rates

Overhead Cost Pools	Activity Cost Pools							
	Cutting	Stitching	Assembly	Processing Orders	Customer Support	Shipping & Receiving	Other	Total
Occupancy costs	20%	20%	20%	10%	10%	15%	5%	100%
Factory supervision	20%	20%	30%	5%	5%	10%	10%	100%
Building maintenance	30%	30%	20%	5%	5%	5%	5%	100%
Selling	0	0	5%	30%	20%	30%	15%	100%
Admin. support	10%	10%	20%	20%	10%	15%	15%	100%

Exhibit 6-6 presents the activity cost pools and their related activity drivers identified for allocating the activity costs to the final cost object.

Exhibit 6-6.   Activity Cost Pools and Activity Drivers

Activity Cost Pool	Activity Driver
Production Activities	
Cutting	Number of batches
Stitching	Number of units
Assembly	Number of units
Sales and Administrative Activities	
Processing orders	Number or orders
Customer support	Number of customers
Shipping and receiving	Number of orders

Exhibit 6-7 presents the volume data on the activity drivers used to allocate the activity costs.

Exhibit 6-7. Activity Driver Volume	
Activity	**Activity Driver Volume**
Production Activities	
Cutting	300 batches
Stitching	1,500 units
Assembly	1,500 units
Sales and Administrative Activities	
Processing orders	300 orders
Customer support	200 customers
Shipping and receiving	300 orders

Required

The activities, direct costs, and overhead costs have already been identified in this problem. The controller wants to test the new strategy using both the old method of allocating overhead cost pools using direct labor hours and using the new ABC method.

1. Using the data in the preceding tables allocate activity costs using the old, traditional method of allocation used by the company.

2. Allocate overhead costs to activities using ABC.

3. Compute the activity driver rates for each activity.

4. Compute the overhead costs allocated from the activities for the five batches of chairs (the final cost objects).

5. Compute the profitability of the five batches of 100 chairs using:

   a. The old method of allocation, including assigning any direct costs to cost objects.

   b. The ABC method, including assigning any direct costs to cost objects.

   c. Which method is better? Why?

   d. What if the company had compared the new strategy to the old strategy using the company's previous method of allocation? Would the decision have been different? Assume that the past year's sales were 1,400 units (excluding the 100 chairs made to the large office suppliers under the new strategy) and were sold at an average of $900.

Solution

See Exhibits 6-8 through 6-12.

1. The allocation of the costs using the traditional method is:
   a. Total overhead rate = $650,000 ÷ 7,500 labor hours = $86.67/ labor hour.
   b. Total overhead cost per chair = 5 × $86.67 = $433.35.
2. Using the ABC system, the allocation of overhead costs to activities using the rates in Exhibit 6-5 is shown in Exhibit 6-8:

Exhibit 6-8.   Allocation of Overhead Costs to Activities

Overhead Cost Pools	Activity Cost Pools							
	Cutting	Stitching	Assembly	Processing Orders	Customer Support	Shipping & Receiving	Other	Total
Occupancy costs	$60,000	$60,000	$60,000	$30,000	$30,000	$45,000	$15,000	$300,000
Factory supervision	20,000	20,000	30,000	5,000	5,000	10,000	10,000	100,000
Building maintenance	15,000	15,000	10,000	2,500	2,500	2,500	2,500	50,000
Selling	0	0	5,000	30,000	20,000	30,000	15,000	100,000
Admin. support	10,000	10,000	20,000	20,000	10,000	15,000	15,000	100,000
Total costs	$105,000	$105,000	$125,000	$87,500	$67,500	$102,500	$57,500	$650,000

3. The activity driver rates for each activity overhead pool are shown in Exhibit 6-9.

Exhibit 6-9.   Activity Driver Rates

Activity Cost Pool	Total Cost	Total Activity	Activity Rate (1) ÷ (2)
Cutting	$105,000	300 batches	$350.00 per batch
Stitching	105,000	1,500 units	$70.00 per unit
Assembly	125,000	1,500 units	$83.33 per unit
Processing orders	87,500	300 orders	$291.67 per order
Customer support	67,500	200 customers	$337.50 per customer
Shipping and receiving	102,500	300 orders	341.67 per order
Other (excess capacity)	57,500	Not applicable	

4. The overhead costs allocated from the activities for the five batches of chairs are shown in Exhibit 6-10.

Exhibit 6-10.   Activity Overhead Costs Allocated to Five Batches of Chairs (Rounded)

Activity Cost Pool	Activity Rate (1)	Activity (2)	ABC Cost (1) × (2)
Cutting	$350.00 per batch	5 batches	$1,750
Stitching	$70.00 per unit	100 units	$7,000
Assembly	$83.33 per unit	100 units	$8,333
Processing orders	$291.67 per order	5 orders	$1,458
Customer support	$337.50 per customer	5 customers	$1,688
Shipping and receiving	$341.67 per order	5 orders	$1,708

5. The profitability of the five batches of 100 chairs, including assigning the direct costs, is:

   a. Profitability using the traditional method is shown in Exhibit 6-11:

Exhibit 6-11.   Profitability of New Strategy Using the Traditional Method

Sales ($800 × 100)		$80,000
Cost:		
Direct materials ($200 × 100 units)	$20,000	
Direct labor ($100 × 100 units)	10,000	
Overhead costs (100 × $433.35)	43,335	73,335
Strategy margin		$6,665
Average margin per chair: $6,665 ÷ 100 = $66.65		

   b. Profitability using the ABC method is shown in Exhibit 6-12:

Exhibit 6-12.   Profitability Analysis of New Strategy Using ABC

Product Margin		
Sales ($800 × 100)		$80,000
Cost:		
Direct materials ($200 × 100 units)	$20,000	
Direct labor ($100 × 100 units)	10,000	
Batch production (Exhibit 6-10)	1,750	
Volume production (Exhibit 6-10) ($7,000 + 8,333)	15,833	
Order related overhead (Exhibit 6-10) ($1,458 + $1,708)	3,166	50,749
Product margin		$29,251
		(Continued)

Exhibit 6-12. *(Continued)*

Strategy Profitability Analysis

Profit margin (above)	$29,251
Less: Customer support overhead (Exhibit 6-10)	1,688
Strategy margin	$27,563

Average margin per chair: $27,563 ÷ 100 = $275.63

---

c. The difference between the two methods is in the way that overhead costs are allocated. The existing labor hour method distorts the costs for the new strategy, because there is little correlation between labor hours and overhead. Different activities, consumer resources at different rates, and a broad measure of activity—such as labor hours—do not measure these differences. Activity-based costing is more accurate, because it allocates the overhead resources to activities and then to the chairs based upon their consumption of overhead components. Thus, ABC provides a more accurate estimate of a product's full costs (manufacturing, sales, and order processing). In this situation, the result will be a more accurate evaluation of the new strategy vs. the old strategy (see item # 6). Further, the company can use the data from ABC to evaluate activities and reduce costs of more expensive overhead operations. Further, the ABC method identified $57,500 worth of excess capacity that should be useful for management in better managing its capacity, i.e., efforts should be made to seek new sales to fill this capacity.

6. The profitability of the old strategy under the traditional method is shown in Exhibit 6-13. The profitability of the new strategy using the traditional method is shown in Exhibit 6-11.

Exhibit 6-13. **Profitability Analysis of Old Strategy Using the Traditional Method**

Product Margin:

Sales ($900 × 1,400)		$1,260,000
Cost:		
Direct materials ($200 × 1,400 units)	$280,000	
Direct labor ($100 × 1,400 units)	140,000	
Total overhead costs (1,400 × $433.35)	606,690	1,026,690
Product margin		$233,310

Average profit per chair: $233,310 ÷ 1,400 chairs = $166.65

The profitability of the new strategy using the traditional method is $66.65 per chair (Exhibit 6-11). The profitability of the old strategy using the traditional method is $166.65 (Exhibit 6-13). Thus, using the old method allocation instead of ABC would have resulted in the company erroreously deciding that the new strategy was not as profitable as the old one and probably discontinuing it.

Summary

This chapter has explored the concept of activity-based costing (ABC) and activity-based management (ABM). ABC was compared with traditional cost allocation and was shown to be a superior method for product costing and for decision making purposes. The chapter presented an overview of the flow of costs through an ABM system. The steps in designing an ABM system were presented:

1. Identify the activities that consume resources.
2. Identify and trace all direct (input-level) costs to cost objects.
3. Identify the resource drivers for allocating the overhead (indirect cost) pools to each activity.
4. Identify and allocate all overhead costs to each activity.
5. Identify the activity drivers to assign activity costs to cost objects.
6. Compute the activity driver rates.
7. Compute the total activity costs allocated to the cost objects.
8. Use activity costs in decision making.

Practice Problems

6-1 ABC in a service company. Brand One Banking Company is a medium-sized bank that has 10 branches within its market area. Currently the bank is practicing the traditional method of tracing direct costs and allocating overhead costs down to the branch level, and evaluating costs at that level.

A recent corporate retreat led by the CEO resulted in a decision to initiate ABC systems in the bank. It was decided to implement ABC in the commercial lending departments of each of the branches on a test basis. The test will be used to evaluate the cost efficiency of the activities within

the branches. If the test is successful, the company will expand the ABC system to include customer profitability analysis.

The branch manager has commercial lending responsibilities and each branch has an average of two commercial loan officers. The following cost data pertaining to the Jackson branch were assembled by the corporate accounting department for the past year:

Salary of the branch manager	$90,000
Salaries of two commercial loan officers	120,000
Administrative assistant to loan officers	30,000
Clerical staff salaries	40,000
Telephone and mailing costs	4,000
Computer systems usage	6,000
Total costs	$290,000

All other overhead costs are facility-level costs and cannot reasonably be allocated to commercial loan activities.

The chief accountant led a cross-functional team that evaluated the commercial loan departments in each branch, which included interviews, surveys, and document analysis. The results of their analysis identified the activities and resource driver percentages as shown below for Jackson branch.

Distribution of Resource Percentage Consumption in the Jackson Branch's Commercial Lending Department

Costs	Customer Solicitation	Credit Analysis	Creation of Loan Documents	Review of Loan Package	Creation of Loan Letters	Total
Branch manager's salary	20%	10%	0%	15%	0%	45%
Commercial loan officers' salary	25%	40%	20%	10%	5%	100%
Admin. assistant's salary	20%	10%	40%	15%	15%	100%
Clerical salaries	30%	5%	50%	5%	10%	100%
Telephone & mailing	70%	5%	10%	5%	10%	100%
Computer usage	10%	30%	30%	10%	20%	100%

Note: Commercial lending consumed only 45% of the branch manager's time.

Required

Allocate the overhead resources consumed by the activities in commercial lending based on the resource driver percentages in the preceding table and using a worksheet similar to Exhibit 6-8.

6-2 Computing activity rates in a service company (Continuation of problem 6-1) The cross-functional team identified the activity drivers listed in table below for the Jackson branch. In addition, the activity data for the past year are included in the right-hand column.

Activity Drivers and Related Activity in the Jackson Branch		
Activity	**Activity Driver**	**Activity**
Customer solicitation	Number of calls	2,000
Credit analysis	Number of loans	300
Creation of loan documents	Number of documents	1,000
Review of loan package	Number of loans	300
Creating loan letters (acceptance and rejection)	Number of letters	800

Required

Compute the activity driver rates for each activity.

6-3 Using activity rates to evaluate efficiency in a service company (Continuation of problem 6-1) All branches reported their activity results to the home office, which shared them with all branches. The manager of the Jackson branch computed an average activity driver rate for each activity across all branches. The following table lists these average rates.

Average Activity Driver Rates in Brand Bank One Branches	
Activity	**Average Activity Driver Rates**
Customer solicitation	$26.00
Credit analysis	190.00
Creation of loan documents	54.00
Review of loan package	101.00
Creating loan letters (acceptance and rejection)	19.25

Required

Compare the average results of all branches to the results in the Jackson branch.

6-4 Product development and design changes for a product are an example of:

A. Unit-level activity

B. Batch-level activity

C. Product-level activity

D. Facility-level activity

6-5 XYZ Manufacturing Company produces two products: S1 and S2. XYZ uses an ABC system. The estimated total cost and expected activity for each of the company's three activity cost pools during the coming year are shown in the table below:

Activity Cost Pool	Estimated Cost	Expected Activity		
		Product S1	**Product S2**	**Total**
Assembly	$36,000	600	400	1,000
Order processing	$32,000	1,000	200	1,200
Customer support	$45,000	900	600	1,500

The activity driver rate under the activity-based costing system for customer support is closest to:

A. $30.00

B. $50.00

C. $75.00

D. $67.78

6-6 Easy Find Research is a market research firm located in Atlanta. Easy Find uses an ABC system for its main service lines of research. The firm has two activity cost pools: general service and research service. These costs are then allocated to specific jobs that are provided to clients. Information for three jobs to be completed next year related to this activity-based costing system is shown in the two following tables:

Activity Cost Pool	Activity Measure	Estimated Overhead Cost
General service	% of time devoted to jobs	$1,400,000
Research service	Computer time	$280,000

Estimated data for three large jobs for next year are shown in the following table:

	% of Time Expended on Jobs	Computer Time
Job 1	30%	400,000 minutes
Job 2	60%	300,000 minutes
Job 3	10%	100,000 minutes

How much of the headquarters' cost allocation should be allocated to Job #2 next year?

A. $560,000

B. $519,500

C. $945,000

D. $1,008,000

The following data apply to questions 6-7 and 6-8.

Boco Wholesale Company is a small wholesale distributor that serves mainly mom-and-pop stores in a large county. Last year Boco implemented an ABC system for all of its overhead costs. The accountant has aggregated the information in the following three tables for the year 20XX.

Distribution of Resource Consumption				
	Activity Cost Pools			
Overhead Pools	Filling Orders	Customer Support	Other	Total
Wages and salaries	40%	50%	10%	100%
Other expenses	50%	30%	20%	100%

Overhead Cost Pools	Costs
Wages and salaries	$800,000
Other expenses	300,000
Total	$1,100,000

The "Other" activity cost pool consists of the costs of idle capacity and facility-level costs. The amount of activity for the year is as follows:

Activity Cost Pool	Activity Drivers
Filling Orders	10,000 orders
Customer support	500 customers

6-7 What would be the overall activity driver rate for the *filling orders* activity cost pool? (Round numbers to the nearest whole cent.)

A. $32.00

B. $183.00

C. $53.75

D. $47.00

6-8 What would be the overall activity driver rate for the *customer support* activity cost pool? (Round to the nearest cent.)

A. $980.00

B. $800.00

C. $780.00

D. $650.00

6-9 Human resource administration is an example of:

A. Unit-level activity

B. Batch-level activity

C. Product-level activity

D. Facility-level activity

6-10 Pine Door Company manufactures custom-made doors for sale to large home improvement retail stores. The company is considering an ABC system but is having difficulty developing activities. Presently there are a cleaning and painting department and an assembly department. A partially completed door is received into the cleaning and painting department unfinished with vacant panels in the door. After completion by the cleaning and painting department the doors are transferred to the assembly department for completion, including the installation of various styles of glass in the vacant panel spaces. Suggest some activity cost pools that could be used instead of a single departmental cost pool.

Solutions to Practice Problems

6-1 The allocation computations are found in the table in the next page.

6-2 The activity driver rates computations are shown in the following table.

Activity Driver Rates			
Activity Cost Pool	**Total Cost**	**Total Activity**	**Activity Rate (1) ÷ (2)**
Customer solicitation	$69,400	2,000	$34.70 per call or mailing
Credit analysis	64,000	300	$213.33 per loan
Creating loan documents	58,200	1,000	58.20 per document
Review of loan package	32,800	300	109.33 per loan
Creating loan letters (acceptance and rejection)	16,100	800	20.13 per letter

6-3 The cost per activity at the Jackson branch is higher than the average compared to all of the activities at other branches. It is significantly higher in the customer solicitation activity and credit analysis activity. The creation of loan letters activity is only slightly below the average, which suggests that the administrative staff is performing near normal. The two remaining activities are marginally below the average. The results suggest that the branch manager should evaluate the efforts of the loan officers—and even his own contribution—in the more technical aspects of solicitation, credit analysis, and review.

6-4 C

6-5 A

$45,000 ÷ (900 units + 600 units) = $30.00

6-6 C

($1,400,000 × 0.6) + [(280,000 ÷ (400,000 + 300,000 + 100,000)] × 300,000 = $945,000

6-7 D

($800,000 × 0.4) + ($300,000 × 0.5) = $470,000

$470,000 ÷ 10,000 orders = $47.00

6-8 A

($800,000 × 0.5) + ($300,000 × 0.3) = $490,000

$490,000 ÷ 500 orders = $980.00

Allocation of Overhead Costs to Activities in Jackson Branch's Commercial Lending Department						
Costs	Customer Solicitation	Credit Analysis	Creation of Loan Documents	Review of Loan Package	Creation of Loan Letter	Total
Branch manager salary	$18,000	$9,000	$0	$13,500	$0	$40,500
Commercial loan officers' salary	30,000	48,000	24,000	12,000	6,000	120,000
Admin. assistant's salary	6,000	3,000	12,000	4,500	4,500	30,000
Clerical salaries	12,000	2,000	20,000	2,000	4,000	40,000
Telephone and mailing	2,800	200	400	200	400	4,000
Computer usage	600	1,800	1,800	600	1,200	6,000
Total costs	$69,400	$64,000	$58,200	$32,800	$16,100	$240,500

6-9 D

6-10 Answers will vary but the following is a list of activities that Pine Door Company could use instead of a single departmental cost pool:

- Sand and clean door
- Paint door
- Inspect door
- Transport door to the assembly activity

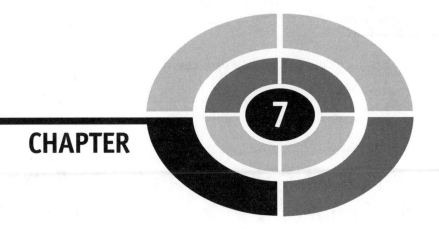

CHAPTER

Costs for Decision Making: Cost Estimation and Cost-Volume-Profit Analysis

In this chapter we will discuss the basic cost behavior concepts, the steps in estimating costs from various activity levels, the basic cost-volume-profit (CVP) model, how to perform (CVP) analysis, and using CVP to evaluate potential strategic decisions that influence profit.

Why Cost Behavior and Cost Estimation Is So Important

Cost estimation underlies many management decisions in business. Managers often ask such questions as, "If I add a new product to my business, how many units do I need to sell in order to break even?," "If I want a profit increase of 10% for the coming year, how many units do I need to sell?," and "How will the purchase of a new computer system affect profit?" Cost estimation and CVP analysis can aid management in answering these and other similar questions.

What is the Difference Between Cost Estimation and Cost Prediction?

Cost estimation has to do with estimating costs from past relationships. Cost prediction has to do with estimating *future* costs from predicted relationships. The same basic model is used in both.

Review of Cost Behavioral Terms

Cost behavior was covered in Chapter 2 but, for review purposes, the concepts that we will use in this chapter are summarized below.

- **Total Variable Costs**   Costs that vary in direct proportion to changes in the level of some measure of activity are defined as *total* variable costs. As we saw in Chapter 6, this measure of activity is also called a *cost driver* in that it is assumed to cause the change in total variable costs. The measure of activity could be the production volume, machine hour volume, sales volume of the finished product, or some other measure of volume or activity.

- **Total Fixed Costs**   Those costs that do not vary with changes in some level of activity are total fixed costs. Fixed costs relate to the capacity to produce or to sell the product or services of the business.

- **Mixed Variable Costs**   Many costs are not true variable or true fixed costs and are referred to as mixed or semivariable costs. In fact, it can be said that most costs are not either true variable or true fixed costs.

- **Stepped Fixed Costs**   Stepped costs are not true variable or true fixed costs. They act similar to a fixed cost during a range of production but eventually there is a significant increase in fixed costs in production. For example, at an assembly line in a factory all supervisors' salaries would be fixed within the capacity of a given range. When the company decides to add another assembly line because of an increase in sales, another supervisor would have to be added.

Illustration

Listed below are various types of costs in a manufacturing or service company. Identify each as a variable (V), fixed (F), mixed (M), or stepped (S) cost.

1. Raw materials that are issued to production based on a set amount per finished unit.

2. The annual depreciation of equipment computed on the straight-line method of depreciation.

3. The fee paid to a temp agency for a handyman in the maintenance department, where the fee is based on an hourly rate.

4. The city power bill for the production facility that is based on a flat charge, plus a variable rate after a specified number of kilowatt hours are used.

5. The production-line supervisor's salary aligns to a certain level of production, when another production line is added, which requires an additional production supervisor.

6. Maintenance expenses that require some fixed investment but vary with production volume thereafter.

Solution: 1. V; 2. F; 3. V; 4. M; 5. S; 6. M.

To answer the question "Why is cost behavior so important?" we will illustrate the use of cost behavior in setting prices.

Illustration

Let's assume a laboratory facility performs tests for doctors and hospitals at a set fee per procedure. The accountant for the facility has used total costs to aid in the setting of contract bids to hospitals. Based on past costs she forecasts that total costs will be $200,000 and that the number of total tests performed will be 10,000. Thus, the average cost is projected to be $20 per procedure. However, without the contract the total costs are projected to be $150,000 for 7,500 procedures. Further, $75,000 of the $150,000 total costs, or $10 per procedure, are variable costs. This means that the incremental costs for these tests in the short run are $75,000 in total, or $10 per procedure ($20 less $10 for fixed costs), since the other half of the costs is fixed. If the accountant uses the $20 average as the basis for the bid, the hospital may lose the contract. The price could realistically be set somewhere between the $10 incremental (variable) cost and $20, the total cost. Why? Because fixed costs are irrelevant in the short run (see Chapter 8), since they have already been incurred and won't be changed by the decision.

From this illustration we can see that cost behavior is very important in estimating costs for decision making. This requires the decision maker to separate total costs into their variable and fixed components. In order do this, the decision maker must have a good understanding of the cost function.

The Basic Linear Cost Function

As described above, there are four types of costs relating to behavior: variable, fixed, mixed, and stepped. The basic **linear cost function** used to estimate or predict variable and fixed costs is shown in the following equation:

$$TC = TFC + X(UVC)$$

where

TC = Total costs

TFC = Total fixed costs

X = Total number of some measure of activity

UVC = Unit variable costs

This cost function is depicted graphically in Figure 7-1.

Assumptions Underlying the Linear Cost Model

- Within the estimated or predicted **relevant range** of activity, all costs are totally fixed or totally variable in relation to some measure of volume.
- The dependent variable (total costs) can be predicted by one independent variable (the cost driver).
- A-cause-and-effect relationship exists between the dependent and independent variables.

Again, What Is the Relevant Range?

The relevant range is the range of volume in which the company normally operates, based on capacity and sales constraints. Often, it is the expected volume for the coming year.

Very few costs are either pure variable or pure fixed. Most costs contain some elements of both and are labeled mixed or semivariable costs. The problem that we

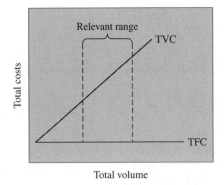

Figure 7-1 Basic cost function.

encounter in using cost estimation or prediction as well as CVP analysis is that the total *mixed* costs must be separated into their fixed and variable components. In the next section we discuss some basic methods for distinguishing these costs.

Methods for Estimating Variable and Fixed Costs

The methods used to separate variable and fixed costs range from subjective appraisals to sophisticated analysis. Four methods will be discussed: account analysis, industrial-engineering estimates, the scatter diagram, and the high-low method. Regression analysis, a more sophisticated statistical method, will be discussed briefly.

The Account Analysis Method

The account analysis method is based on a review and analysis of the cost accounts in the general ledger and on relating each to some measure of activity, usually a cost driver similar to that used in an ABC system described in Chapter 6. The analysis may be performed by an individual or a conference of individuals experienced in evaluating costs in the process involved. For example, in a manufacturing facility, the conference group could be personnel from production, process engineering, purchasing, and accounting. This estimate should not be made solely by accounting personnel, as their knowledge of the technical aspects of the process may be inadequate for this purpose.

Illustration

Assume the accountant has assembled the cost accounts for XYZ Manufacturing Company as shown in total cost column in Exhibit 7-1. The company accountant calls a meeting of production, engineering, and purchasing personnel to estimate how much of each total cost is variable and how much is fixed. The group estimates the costs based on an average of 10,000 units of production during a yearly period. The result of their analysis is shown in the last two columns of Exhibit 7-1.

Exhibit 7-1.   Estimating Variable and Fixed Costs Using the Account Analysis Method (10,000 units of output)

Account	Costs at the 10,000 Units of Output (Relevant Range)		
	Total	Variable	Fixed
Raw materials	$30,000	$30,000	$0
Direct labor	40,000	40,000	0
Indirect materials	5,000	3,000	2,000
Indirect labor	20,000	0	20,000
Building depreciation	30,000	0	30,000
Electricity	5,000	3,000	2,000
Heating	5,000	3,000	2,000
Equipment repair and maintenance	20,000	8,000	12,000
Quality testing	20,000	5,000	15,000
Total	$175,000	$92,000	$83,000

From Exhibit 7-2, we can compute the unit variable cost (UVC) of the costs from above as

UVC = $92,000/10,000 units = $9.20

The variable cost is directly related to the 10,000 units of output; therefore, we can insert UVC and the total fixed costs into the cost model for this level of activity and obtain an estimation model for total costs at any level of production within the relevant range:

TC = TFC + UVC (X)

TC = $83,000 + $9.20 (X)

For example, in order to estimate the total costs at the 11,000 unit level, the computation is TC = $83,000 + $9.20 × 11,000 = $184,200.

The advantage of this method is that it is relatively inexpensive to implement and does give some degree of accuracy when there are experts available to analyze the accounts. The weakness of this method is that it is largely subjective and can result in significant errors, even when used by experts. However, it is used frequently in smaller companies because of the higher cost of more sophisticated methods.

Industrial Engineering Method

This method breaks down processes into repetitive operations and operations into repetitive steps. Thus, it is a "bottom up" approach to estimating variable costs, as well as the most detailed of all cost estimating methods and the most expensive to implement. The costs of performing each step in a process or operation are estimated, including the time required to perform the steps and the quantities of direct materials. The labor time is normally determined by an industrial engineer using time and motion studies. The material requirements are derived from engineering drawings and/or specifications. Fixed costs are estimated in total and, together with the UVC of each completed unit derived from the engineering method, are inserted into the cost formula used above to derive total costs.

The advantage of this method is that it provides relatively accurate estimates of variable costs as long as the engineering estimates remain current. The main disadvantage is that it is very expensive to develop and implement. Sometimes it is used in combination with a standard cost system (discussed in Chapter 12), which facilitates its use and makes it less expensive.

Scatter Diagram Method

This method uses a spreadsheet to plot past costs on a graph, usually called a scatter diagram. Past data—at least 2 to 3 years' worth—relating to the volume of the cost driver and total costs are entered into the spreadsheet and plotted as points by the spreadsheet program. Using "eyeball judgment," a line is drawn through the points to intersect with the y-axis (total costs). The analyst attempts to draw the line through the points where there is the least amount of variance between the line and all of the points on the graph. The point of intersection on the y-axis is identified as the total fixed costs. Next a representative point on the line is selected and its related point on the y-axis is the total costs. With these two pieces of information the fixed costs are deducted from the total costs to arrive at total variable costs. This figure is divided by the volume at the level at which the total costs were determined to arrive at the UVC. This procedure provides enough information to construct a cost model.

Illustration

Assume the following data from the analysis of past costs at various levels of activity, as shown in Exhibit 7-2A.

Exhibit 7-2A.   Total Costs and Related Levels of Activity

Volume of Units	Total Costs
1,000	$50,000
2,000	60,000
3,000	70,000
4,000	75,000
5,000	91,000
6,000	97,000
7,000	115,000
8,000	119,000
9,000	132,000
10,000	145,000
11,000	148,000
12,000	166,000

Figure 7-2 depicts a scatter diagram using the data in Exhibit 7-2A. From this scatter diagram we can "eyeball" and draw a line that intercepts the total cost line (y-axis) at about $40,000, which would be the total fixed cost. The total variable cost would be computed by selecting a point on the cost line that "looks" representative of the other points. In this case we selected the point that represents approximately $139,000 in total costs and the related volume or cost driver is 8,500 (see the dashed line). The total variable cost is $139,000 less the fixed cost of $40,000, which equals $99,000. The UVC is computed as $99,000/8,500 = $11.647. Thus, the cost model for prediction of costs at any level within the relevant range is TC = $40,000 + $11.647(X), where X = the

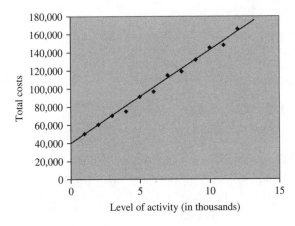

Figure 7-2   Scatter diagram.

number of units selected or predicted. Using this equation the total costs at the 6,000 unit level is $40,000 + $11.647(6,000) = $109,882.

The scatter diagram method is marginally accurate only if the activity of operations has followed a consistent pattern and the points used to construct the line do not vary significantly from the cost line itself, which is rarely the case. Even in the above diagram with points that vary little from the cost line, there could be a significant level of error in drawing the line to the *y*-intercept point. However, the method does have its uses; for example, it can be used to "eyeball" the relationship of costs at various levels of activity. This diagram is often used with more sophisticated methods, such as regression analysis, to aid in constructing a good model for estimation or prediction.

The advantage of the scatter diagram method is that it is very inexpensive to use but the major disadvantage is that it has a potential for a significant error level. Thus, it should only be used to obtain a "picture" of the cost relationships for use with statistical methods.

The High-Low Method

The simplest statistical method for estimating cost relationships is the high-low method. This method is useful when the cost patterns between costs and volumes can be described with a straight-line function and there is a small amount of variance between the points on the line and the line itself. We select the highest and lowest points within a given range of production, usually the relevant range, and assume that these two points are representative of the other points within the range of activity used for estimation. Using the cost formula from above, we find the slope of the line, which is the UVC, then use it to compute total fixed costs. From this information we can then construct the cost function to estimate or predict costs.

Illustration

Using the data in Exhibit 7-2A, we will assume that the relevant range of production is from 4,000 units to 9,000 units; therefore, we compute the UVC as follows:

$$\text{UVC} = \left(\frac{\$132,000 - 75,000}{9,000 - 4,000} \right) = \$11.40$$

To find the TFC, we select either the total cost at the highest level of activity or the total cost at the lowest level activity and then, using the above UVC, subtract the total variable cost from the total cost at the level selected. For this problem, we select $132,000:

$$\text{TFC} = \$132,000 - (\$11.40 \times 9,000 \text{ units}) = \$132,000 - 102,600 = \$29,400$$

Hence, the cost function for estimating or predicting costs along the relevant range is:

TC = $29,400 + $11.40(X), where X = the number of units selected or estimated.

Therefore, if 6,000 units were selected, the predicted total costs would be:

TC = $29,400 + ($11.40 × 6,000) = $97,800

Comparing this to the $109,882 computed using the scatter diagram, we find a difference of $12,082, which is a significant difference. Assuming that the two points selected are relatively representative of other points on the line, then the high-low method provides a more accurate measurement or prediction.

The advantage of this method is that it is relatively easy to compute, the data can be relatively easily obtained, and if there is not a significant amount of variance, it is relatively accurate. The biggest disadvantage is that there may be significant variance between the points along the line and the line itself. How do you determine the degree of variance? The scatter diagram discussed previously is the best method for "eyeballing" the variance, using the high-low method in order to get some idea of its accuracy.

Regression Analysis

A more sophisticated method of estimating or predicting total costs is regression analysis. The mathematical description of how the regression equation is derived and tested is beyond the scope of this book and can be reviewed in any statistics or intermediate managerial accounting textbook. However, since we can use the regression equation simply by entering the required data into the more sophisticated hand-held calculators or through the use of relatively inexpensive software, a brief overview of this approach is given below. These programs use the formula:

Y = a + b(X)

where

Y = TC

a = TFC

b = UVC

X = Volume

The regression equation (sometimes called the least-squares regression equation) is similar to the cost formula used in the high-low method but goes much further by considering along the equation line *all* points that are listed in Exhibit 7-2A. The formula computes the "best fit" line based on the data used within the relevant range. In regression analysis the objective is to find TFC and UVC, or a and b, and construct the TC formula the way we did with the methods described above.

The software will require you to input the observed values of Y and X and the number of data points labeled *n*. Y is called the dependent variable and X is called the independent variable. For example, in Exhibit 7-2A the observed values of Y are all of the total cost data points within the relevant range; the observed values of X are all of the volume data points and *n* would equal 9. After inputting these values into the computer or the hand-held calculator, the software would compute the TFC and the UVC or a and b. With these results we would be able to construct the TC function as we did with the high-low method. For example, if the computed values are a = $30,000 and b = $11.75 the total cost formula is:

TC = $30,000 + $11.75X

The major advantages of using regression analysis is that it considers *all* points on the cost line and it computes a measure of the goodness of fit, which tells how well the predicted values (TC or Y) based on the cost driver volume (X) match the actual cost observations. This measure of goodness of fit is called the **coefficient of determination**, or r^2. The coefficient of determination is a measure of the percentage of variation in Y (TC) explained by X (volume). This measure is between 0 and 100%. Generally, the higher the measure the better, but a rule of thumb is that it should exceed 50% for the estimation or prediction model to be reasonably accurate. The biggest disadvantage is that the user may have difficulty making the computations and not fully understand the results. However, the accountant should be able to aid in its computation and interpretation.

Finally, there are other tests of the regression equation and even more sophisticated versions of regression analysis but these are beyond the scope of this book.

Putting It All Together—The Steps in Developing a Cost Estimation or Prediction Formula

This section summarizes the previous discussion by listing the steps used in deriving the cost function based on actual data. These steps can be used for prediction purposes by projecting the data based on assumptions made by the decision maker.

Step 1: Choose the Cost Object for Which the Costs Are to be Estimated

Which cost object is chosen is based on why the costs are to be estimated or predicted. If we want cost-volume-profit analysis, the analysis normally would be at the company level and all related costs (manufacturing and nonmanufacturing) and volume should be included. If we want product costing (i.e., to separate variable and fixed costs for more accurate costing), then all manufacturing costs and relating volume for a specific product should be included.

Step 2: Choose the Cost Driver or Measure of Volume

This measure can be a volume of output or input. For example, output could be the finished product. A measure of input could be machine hours or labor hours. The criterion for selecting of one of these variables is how well it aids in estimating or predicting the total costs; that is, how well the volume measure selected relates the total costs.

Step 3: Collect the Data on the Cost Object and Related Volume

For cost estimation, the data are normally collected from the general ledger accounts or cost reports. For cost prediction, the general ledger could be used as the starting point to develop past trends and then be supplemented by interviews with knowledgeable personnel (sales and production) or by use of forecasting methods, which are discussed in Chapter 10.

Step 4: Plot the Data on a Scatter Diagram

As discussed above, this helps us "eyeball" the data in order to discern patterns and variability as an aid in selecting the estimating or predicting model.

Step 5: Select the Cost Estimation or Prediction Model

This is one of methods discussed in the previous section that will be used to separate the total costs into their fixed and variable components. Relevant methods include:

- Account analysis
- Industrial engineering

- Scatter diagram
- High-low
- Regression analysis

Step 6: Evaluate the Model Selected

This would include the following points:

- Does the relationship between the cost driver and the total cost that it is predicting make sense? That is, is there a good cause-and-effect relationship?

- If prediction is the purpose of the computation, draw a scatter diagram for a representative range from past actual data and then draw a scatter diagram for the predicted range of data. The "eyeballed" variability should be similar in both.

- For regression analysis, compute the coefficient of determination. The percentage computed should be greater than 50% to have a reasonable accuracy. More sophisticated methods of assessing the cost prediction model are found in more advanced statistics texts or advanced management accounting texts.

Cost-Volume-Profit Analysis (CVP) and Its Uses

Now that we have presented how to compute variable and fixed costs, we are ready to present CVP analysis as a powerful tool for management decision making. **Cost-volume-profit** analysis is method for studying the interrelationship between total revenues, total costs, operating income, and total volume. Specifically, it analyzes the impact on profit of changes in the sales price, unit variable costs, total fixed costs, or total volume or a combination of any two or more of these. CVP is sometimes loosely called "breakeven point analysis" but we will go further than computing the breakeven point—although a manager may find it useful to know that in certain situations. Managers may find it more useful to find how many units are required to be sold to break even *and* attain a specified profit objective. Computing the breakeven point is just a first step in the multiple uses of CVP, which can be used for several decision making purposes, including:

- Deciding on whether to add a new product
- Filling a "budget" gap in financial planning
- Performing "what if" analysis involving several financial variables such as:
  - Impact of changing the sales price on profit
  - Impact of decreasing the unit variable cost of an input factor like direct labor or raw materials
  - Increasing of the amount of advertising (a fixed cost) on profit, based on impact on the sales quantity
  - Impact of purchasing a fixed cost item (e.g., computer system, piece of machinery) on profit

The CVP Model

The CVP model is depicted graphically in Figure 7-3. Note that this graph is an extension of the basic cost function depicted in Figure 7-1 by changing the y-axis to total dollars and including a total sales dollar line. With this new information one can construct a loss area, a breakeven point, and a profit area. The relationships in this chart are very important and we will use them extensively in CVP analysis.

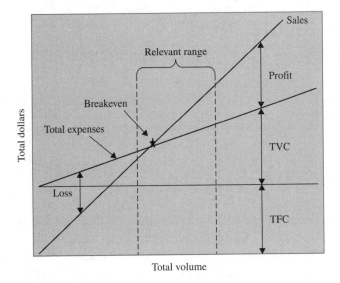

Figure 7-3   CVP graph.

The CVP model can also be depicted in equation form. The basic equation is:

$$OI = TR - (TVC + TVC) + TI$$

where

OI = Operating income

TR = Total revenue

TVC = Total variable costs

TFC = Total fixed costs

TI = Target income

These components can be broken down further:

$$OI = (SP \times Q) - [(UVC \times Q) + TFC] + TI$$

where

SP = Sales price

Q = Units produced and sold

The same assumptions that were made for the basic cost function in Figure 7-1 also apply to the CVP graph, with three additional assumptions:

- Cost, revenue, and output and sales quantities can be determined with certainty.
- A single-product or multiple-product sales mix remains constant as the total units sold changes.
- The same quantity that is produced is sold.

Obviously, these assumptions won't hold over the entire sales and production range, but they are close enough within the relevant range to use CVP for decision making purposes.

Total Costs vs. Unit Costs

As has already been discussed, total variable costs (TVC) vary in direct proportion to the changes in volume, within the relevant range. The unit variable cost (UVC), however, remains constant throughout the relevant range because it is the slope of the TVC line and is always a constant. On the other hand, total fixed costs (TFC) remain constant over the relevant range of production but the unit fixed cost (UFC) decreases when production increases. This can easily be seen by dividing TFC by the number of units at one level and then dividing the same fixed costs at a higher level. This is an important concept, because management always wants to increase sales and production up to capacity in order to spread the fixed costs over more units. Stated another way, management always wants to fill excess capacity and this is an important step in the planning process.

It should also be pointed out that the unit sales price (SP) is the slope of the total sales line (see Figure 7-3). The SP times each level of sales volume equals the total sales at the point selected. Obviously, as you increase volume, the total sales will also increase.

Next, two approaches used in CVP analysis will be discussed: the contribution margin approach and the formula approach.

Contribution Margin Approach in CVP Analysis

At this point we introduce the concept of contribution margin (CM). Contribution margin can be described in two ways: **total contribution margin (TCM)** = TR – TVC, and **unit contribution margin (UCM)** = SP – UVC. Both TCM and UCM have the same percentage relationship. In the CM format all variable costs and expenses must be included. In a manufacturing company, this means that both manufacturing costs and nonmanufacturing expenses must be included.

The concept of contribution margin is very important, as it tells the decision maker how much net revenue is left over after covering total variable costs that contribute to covering TFC and achieving a target profit. Obviously, in the long run all costs and expenses must be covered and a reasonable profit attained for the business to remain viable. However, as will be seen in Chapters 8 and 9, in the short run, the decision maker may assume that TFC are not necessarily relevant in certain decision situations. For example, the decision maker may receive a special order that is priced below the going market price. In a situation where the company has excess capacity the decision making will be motivated to accept such an offer because it will contribute more to profit than by not accepting it (assuming that the special sales dollars exceeds the total variable costs). Why? Because regardless of whether the offer is accepted or not the fixed costs will not change in the short run but profit will increase.

The contribution margin concept is used in many decision questions: Should a product or service line be added or dropped? What price should be charged for a product or service? What happens if the sales price decreases or increases? The CM can be used in these and many more situations. Exhibit 7-3 illustrates how a CM income statement is constructed.

Exhibit 7-3.   Contribution Margin Income Statement for XYZ Manufacturing Company

	Total	Per Unit	Percent of Sales
Sales (10,000 units)	$500,000	$50	100%
Less: Total variable expenses	350,000	35	70%
Contribution margin	$150,000	$15	30%
Less: Total fixed expenses	125,000		
Net operating income	$5,000		

With these data the contribution approach is used below to address several decisions scenarios.

- **Should I add a new product or service?** Contribution margin analysis can aid in this decision. The question really is how many units or sales dollars are required to break even. In this case a target income (TI) of zero is included in the equation, because we are interested only in the breakeven point. There are two CM equations that can help answer this question:

  1. For the breakeven (BE) point in number of units, divide the TFC by the unit contribution margin (UCM):

  $$BE = \left(\frac{TFC}{UCM}\right) = \left(\frac{TFC}{SP - UVC}\right)$$

  Using the data from Exhibit 7-3, the number to break even is:

  $$BE = \left(\frac{\$125,000}{\$50 - 35}\right) = 8,333 \text{ units}$$

  2. For BE in dollars, divide the TFC by the CM ratio:

  To compute the CM ratio $= \left(\frac{UCM}{SP}\right) = \left(\frac{\$50 - 35}{\$50}\right) = 30\%.$

  The contribution margin ratio simply means that for every sale dollar, $0.30 of it goes to cover fixed costs and contribute to profit.

Using the data in Exhibit 7-3 the BE dollars is:

$$BE = \left(\frac{TFC}{CMRatio}\right) = \left(\frac{\$125,000}{.30}\right) = \$416,667$$

In some cases the SP or the UVC is not available to compute the BE but the total sales and total variable costs will be available (on contribution margin income statements). In such a case the computation is:

$$CM \text{ ratio} = \left(\frac{500K - 350K}{500K}\right) = 30\%$$

$$BE = \left(\frac{\$125,000}{.30}\right) = \$416,667$$

Notice that the result is the same whether one uses a total or unit basis, because as we stated above, the relationship between sales and variables cost is exactly the same in both cases.

The decision to add a product or not cannot be completely determined from the BE computations. Why? Long-term decisions are part of an overall strategic planning process and must take into account factors like the size of the market, potential competitors, competing products and services, and an analysis of discounted cash flows. The BE computation simply tells the decision maker how many units must be sold to BE, and whether the company can reach that level is based on careful strategic analysis. Long-range decisions will be further discussed in Chapter 8.

- **How do I close a budget gap?** When a budgeted income statement is prepared and the project operating income doesn't meet the company's profit objective, CVP analysis can be used to consider different alternatives to achieve it. What are these alternatives? We can identify the possible alternatives by looking at the CVP equation shown above:

$$OI = (SP \; Q) - (UVC \; x \; Q) - TFC$$

What Is a Budget Gap?

It is the difference between the company's profit objective in dollars and the operating income derived from the preparation of a projected income statement (pro forma income statement).

From this equation several alternatives that will affect profit can be identified:

- Change the sales price (SP)
- Change the variable costs (UVC)
- Change the fixed costs (TFC)
- Change two or more of the above components

Any alternative will require strategic or tactical considerations, because the CM analysis only provides a tool to compute the results of various scenarios. Some strategic considerations include increasing TFC (advertising) in hopes of increasing Q (units sold), lowering the SP (sales prices) in hopes of increasing Q, or considering more productive operations to lower UVC or more effective purchasing practices to lower the UVC (unit cost of material). CVP analysis using the contribution margin approach is used only as a tool to show the manager the impact of various strategic considerations.

Illustration

Assume that XYZ Manufacturing (Exhibit 7-3) desires to increase net operating income by $10,000 (100%) next year or a projected OI of $15,000. Management decides to undertake a marketing campaign that will cost $5,000 and estimates that it will increase sales volume by 10%. Is this a viable strategy? Again, only a good market strategy analysis will answer this question but the CM approach can be used as a part of this analysis.

If TFC is increased by $5,000, the new TFC would equal $130,000. If sales volume is increased by 10% then both TR and TVC will be affected:

TR = (10,000 units 1.10 $50) = $550,000

TVC = (10,000 units 1.10 $35) = $385,000

The OI from this strategy would be $550,000 – $385,000 – $130,000 = $35,000.

Comparing the projected OI of $35,000 from this strategy to the desired $15,000 OI, we see that it is certainly a viable strategy. Of course, the projections may be too optimistic and cannot be achieved. A way of evaluating these projections is to compute the **margin of safety**, which is:

Margin of safety = Expected sales – Breakeven point sales

From the above information the margin of safety for the proposed strategy is:

Margin of safety = (11,000 × $50) – (8,333 units × $50) = 133,350

$$\text{Margin of safety percentage} = \left(\frac{\$133,350}{\$550,000}\right) = 24.2\%$$

This is the percentage that sales can drop before the strategy becomes a breakeven proposition. The objective is to have a high margin of safety in case the target objective is not met and, worse, the sales drop below the breakeven point. What is a high margin of safety? This is subjective and based on management's risk tolerance.

- **Which product or product mix should be pushed?** Another use of contribution margin analysis is when one has to decide which of two or more competing products or services to push for sale. This question involves product mix. Generally, the answer is that the product or service with the greater total contribution margin should be pushed. However, this question really revolves around capacity constraints, so the product with the higher CM may not be the final answer. This question is further evaluated in Chapter 8.

From these illustrations, we can see that CVP analysis, using the contribution margin approach, is a very useful tool in evaluating various decision scenarios. It is particularly helpful in assessing the impact of various scenarios relating to cost, volume, and profit.

The Formula Approach in CVP Analysis

As has already been discussed, the formula for the CVP model is:

$$OI = (SP \times Q) - (UVC \times Q) + TI$$

Some management accountants and decision makers prefer to use the formula approach instead of the contribution margin approach in CVP analysis. The formula approach is easier to work with, if you know the SP and UVC. As pointed out above, if you only have TR and TVC it is necessary to work with the CM approach. The use of the formula approach can be illustrated with the following problem data. In this problem we will consider the **impact of income taxes on operating income**. In order to do this the CVP model is modified by changing the TI element:

$$OI = TR - TVC - TFC + \left(\frac{NetTI}{1 - TaxRate} \right)$$

Illustration

Easy Storage Company manufactures golf racks to store golf clubs, shoes, and golf balls. The company's growth has stagnated and management is evaluating various strategies to increase sales. One strategy is to undertake an aggressive advertising campaign during the coming year. Exhibit 7-4 lists the costs and other data for the previous year.

Exhibit 7-4. Easy Storage Company	
Variable costs (per rack)	
Direct materials	$ 9.75
Direct manufacturing labor	24.00
Variable overhead (manufacturing, sales, and administrative)	7.50
Total variable costs	$41.25
Fixed costs	
Manufacturing	$75,000
Selling and administrative	330,000
Total fixed costs	$405,000
Selling price	$75.00
Expected sales, 60,000 units	$4,500,000
Federal income tax rate	40%

1. What is breakeven point in units for the past year?

2. Management proposes to spend an additional $33,750 on a marketing campaign it expects will boost sales by 10%. What is the breakeven point in dollars for this new level of sales if the $33,750 is spent?

3. (a) Compute the past year's net income after taxes using the data in Exhibit 7-4. (b) Compute the net income after taxes using the new strategy. Compare the result with 4.

4. Assume that the company proposed another alternative to increase income that will involve the purchase of a highly automated machine to assemble the golf racks. Management, in consultation with engineers from the company selling the machine, estimates that the machine will lower direct labor costs by 12%. The machine will cost $500,000. Ignoring the strategy proposal in # 2, compare the net income after taxes from this proposal with the net income from last year.

Solution

1. Using the CVP formula approach:

$$\$75Q - \$41.25Q - \$405,000 = 0$$

$33.75Q - \$405,000 = 0$

$\$405,000 \div \$33.75 = 12,000$ units

2. $\$75Q - \$41.25Q - (\$405,000 + \$33,750) = 0$

 $Q = \$33.75Q - \$438,750 = 0$

 $Q = \$438,750 \div \$33.75 = 13,000$ units

 $13,000 \times \$75,000 = \$975,000$

3. (a) The net income after taxes for the past year is computed as follows:

$$[(\$75\ 60,000) - (\$33.75 \times 60,000)] - (\$405,000) = \left(\frac{NI}{1-.40}\right)$$

$$\$4,500,000 - 2,025,000 - \$405,000 = \left(\frac{NI}{.60}\right)$$

NI = $1,242,000

4. (b) The target net income (TNI) after taxes, if the $33,750 were spent, is computed as follows:

$$[\$75\ (60,000 \times 110\%)] - [\$33.75 \times (60,000 \times 110\%)] - (\$405,000 +$$

$$\$33,750) = \left(\frac{TNI}{1-.40}\right)$$

$$\left(\frac{TNI}{.60}\right) = \$4,950,000 - 2,227,500 - 438,750$$

$$\left(\frac{TNI}{.60}\right) = \$2,283,750$$

TNI = $1,370,250

Comparing the projected TNI using the proposed strategy with last year's NI will result in an increase of NI of $128,250, or 10.3%. This appears to be a good strategy.

4. The NI from purchasing the machine would depend on the number of years that it depreciated. Assume that it will depreciate over 10 years. Thus, the depreciation charge each year is $50,000. The 12% decrease in UVC would result in a new UVC of ($33.75 × (1– 0.12)) = $29.70. The computations for the NI under this proposal are:

$$\left(\frac{TNI}{1-.40}\right) = \$75\ (60,000) - \$29.70 \times (60,000) - (\$405,000 + \$50,000)$$

$$\left(\frac{TNI}{.60}\right) = \$4,500,000 - \$1,782,000 - \$455,000$$

$$TNI = 0.60 \times \$1,787,000$$
$$TNI = \$1,357,800$$

The NI of $1,357,800 shows an increase in NI of $115,800 compared with the NI of the past year of $1,242,000. If we assume that the savings would continue into the future, the $500,000 would be recouped in 4.32 years ($500,000/$115,800), if the time value of money is not taken into account. Since the machine is estimated to last for 10 years, this appears to be a worthwhile purchase.

Shortcut Approaches to CVP Analysis

While the analyst should use one of the approaches discussed above in CVP analysis, there are some shortcut computations that are useful when discussing CVP relationships and their impact on profit. These approaches are pretax and listed below.

- If the proposed change is in SP, UVC, or UCM, the impact on TI can be computed as follows:

  (Dollar change in the unit variable) × (volume) = Change in TI (assuming that volume remains the same)

  For example, assume that UCM can be increased by $2.00 and the current volume is 10,000 units. TI would increase by $2.00 × 10,000 units or $20,000.

- If the proposed change is in TFC, the change has a dollar-for-dollar impact on TI. For example, assume that a company eliminated a training program that was a fixed cost valued at $10,000. The TI would increase by $10,000.

- If the proposed change is in volume only and everything else remains the same, the impact on TI can be computed as follows:

  (Change in volume) × (UCM) = Change in TI

  For example, if a company forecasts a decrease in sales volume of 1,000 units and the UCM is $13.00, the impact on TI is:

  1,000 units × $13.00 = $13,000 decrease in TI

- If there is a change in two or more variables in the CVP model, the shortcut approaches cannot be used. The analysis will need to use the contribution margin approach or the equation approach.

CVP Analysis and the Multiproduct Firm

Up to now it has been assumed that a business sells only one product or service. Most companies sell more than one product and the sales mix has a large impact on the breakeven point and change in target profit. Computing the breakeven point with two or more products becomes much more complex. In large companies where several products are involved, these computations are made with the help of a computer software. For our purposes, only the two-product situation will be discussed. When computing the breakeven point in this situation, it is assumed that the product mix remains constant. If it changes, the breakeven point will change, which requires a new computation.

The computation of the breakeven point is done in three steps:

Step 1: Obtain the sales volume ratio of one product to the other.

Step 2: Set two equations for the products involved.

Step 2: Solve the equations for both products to find BE in units for one product. Then substitute the quantity obtained into the other equation and find its quantity.

To illustrate these steps: Assume that ZYZ Manufacturing Company manufactures two products: A and B. The projected income statement is shown in Exhibit 7-5.

Exhibit 7-5. Budget Data for XYZ Company for Year 20XX			
	Product A	**Product B**	**Total**
Total units sold	90,000	30,000	120,000
Total sales ($30 and $40 each)	$2,700,000	$1,200,000	$3,900,000
Total variable costs ($21 and $27 each)	1,890,000	810,000	2,700,000
Total contribution margin	$810,000	$390,000	$1,200,000
Total fixed costs			900,000
Operating income			$300,000

Required

Compute the breakeven point, assuming that the sales mix remains.

Solution

Step 1: Determine the sales ratio of one product to another.

Let Q = the number of units of Product B to break even

Let $3Q$ = the number of units of Product A to break even (sales A is three times those of B)

Step 2: Set the equations.

$$[\$30(3Q) + \$40Q] - [\$21(3Q) + \$27Q] - \$900{,}000 = 0$$

Step 3: Solve the equations.

$$(\$90Q + \$40Q) - (\$63Q + \$27Q) = \$900{,}000$$

$$\$130Q - \$90Q = \$900{,}000$$

Q = 22,500 units of Product B to break even

$3Q = 3 \times 22{,}500 = 67{,}500$ units of Product A to break even

Breakeven point computations in a multi-product firm can be made for different product mixes experimentally to determine how each mix might affect the target profit. This is useful in deciding which products have the biggest impact on the bottom line. In the next chapter we will see that we should also look at the constraining factor of capacity.

Summary

In this chapter the cost behavior concepts of variable costs, fixed costs, mixed costs, and contribution margin were discussed. These concepts are described using a graph of the basic cost function. Methods for separating mixed costs into their variable and fixed components were discussed. These methods are:

- The account analysis method
- The industrial engineering method
- The scatter diagram method
- The high-low method
- The regression analysis method

The basic cost-volume-profit (CVP) model and two approaches to determine the breakeven point and to reach a target profit were presented. These were the contribution margin and the formula approaches. These were applied to several situations to illustrate that CVP analysis is a powerful tool in helping the manager evaluate different strategic decisions that influence profit. Finally, breakeven analysis in a multi-product firm was briefly discussed.

Practice Problems

7-1 Review the nine numbered items in Figure 7-4 and identify each.

7-2 XYZ Manufacturing sells golf shoes for $50 per pair. The unit variable costs are $40. During the past year the sales volume was 30,000 pairs per year. Assume that the company is operating at the breakeven point. What are the total fixed costs?

   A. $2,700,000

   B. $300,000

   C. $250,000

   D. $1,500,000

7-3 JB Manufacturing Company produces steel molding in units that are sold to fabricators. In projecting next year's budget, it was assumed that at the 6,000-unit level the total costs would be $80,000 and at the 8,000-unit level

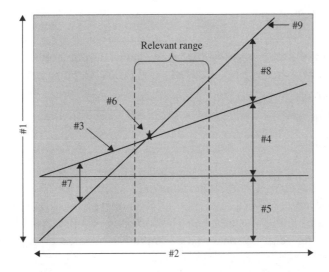

Figure 7-4   CVP graph.

the costs would be $100,000. The management accountant has determined that the costs have some variable and some fixed characteristics. Using the high-low method, what are the predicted costs at the 7,500-unit level?

A. $90,000

B. $95,000

C. $87,500

D. $92,500

7-4 CVP analysis assumes that:

A. The unit sales price and the unit variable cost are constant.

B. Total revenue is constant.

C. Unit fixed cost is constant.

D. Total variable costs are constant.

7-5 Suppose an architectural firm has an objective to attain a profit of $1,000,000 in the coming year. Further, assume that the unit variable cost is $200, total fixed costs are $400,000, and the average fee charged per client hour is $300. How many charged client hours is required to achieve the profit objective?

A. 14,000 hours

B. 12,000 hours

C. 6,000 hours

D. 2,800 hours

7-6 Margin of Safety Assume the same data as in problem 7-5 but also assume that the expected total fees are $1,900,000. What is the margin of safety?

A. 5.263%

B. 4.500%

C. 6.200%

D. 36.8%

The following information pertains to 7-7 through 7-10.

The Fairway Golf Cart Company manufactures golf carts for sale to golf shops in the tri-state area. The company is considering strategies for the coming year. The data in the Exhibit 7-6 have been projected for the coming year.

Exhibit 7-6 Fairway Golf Cart Company Financial Projections for the Year 20XX	
Variable costs per golf cart	
Direct materials	$1,000
Direct labor	800
Variable manufacturing overhead	600
Sales commissions	500
Total variable costs	$2,900
Total fixed costs	
Fixed manufacturing overhead	$1,100,000
Salaries (fixed)	$400,000
Total fixed costs	$1,500,000
Selling price per unit	$6,000
Projected sales	1,200 carts
Income tax rate	40%

7-7 Based on the above data, compute the contribution margin and the contribution margin ratio.

A. $3,600; 47.54%

B. $3,100; 51.667%

C. $3,100; 47.54%

D.   None of the above

7-8 What is the break even in number of units and dollars, before taxes?

A.   625 carts; $2,903,207

B.   250 carts; $2,812,518

C.   484 carts; $2,903,207

D.   None of the above

7-9 Suppose that management has set a profit goal of $1,500,000 after tax for next year. Will the projections in the above table achieve this goal after tax?

A.   No, the target income will only be $1,332,000.

B.   Yes, the target income will be $2,220,000.

C.   No, the target income will only be $1,115,000.

D.   None of the above

7-10 If the projected sales will not reach the profit goal, what are some alternatives for the company to consider?

Solutions to Practice Problems

7-1

1. Total dollars
2. Total volume
3. Total cost line
4. Total variable costs
5. Total fixed costs
6. Breakeven point
7. Loss area
8. Profit area
9. Total sales line

7-2 B

Using the CVP equation:

$SP(Q) - UNC(Q) - TFC = 0$

$\$50\,(30{,}000) - \$40\,(30{,}000) - TFC = 0$

$TFC = \$300{,}000$

7-3 B

Using the high-low method:

$$UVC = \left(\frac{\$100{,}000 - 80{,}000}{8{,}000 - 6{,}000}\right) = \left(\frac{\$20{,}000}{2000}\right) = \$10$$

Using the 8,000 unit level: $TFC = \$80{,}000 - (6{,}000 \times \$10) = \$20{,}000$

At the 7,500 level: $TC = 20{,}000 + 7{,}500(\$10) = \$95{,}000$

7-4 A

The SP is the slope of the total revenue (sales) line and is a constant. The UVC is the slope of the total variable cost line and is a constant.

7-5 A

$SP(Q) - UVC(Q) - TFC = TI$

$300Q - 200Q - \$400,000 = \$1,000,000$

$100Q = \$1,400,000$

$Q = 14,000$ hours

7-6 D

First, calculate the breakeven point. It is $\left(\dfrac{\$400,000}{\$300 - \$200}\right) = 4,000$ hours.

In dollars, the breakeven point is $4,000 \times \$300 = \$1,200,000$. Alternatively, the BE point could be calculated as $\$400,000 \div 33.333\%$.

The margin of safety is $\$1,900,000$ minus $\$1,200,000 = \$700,000$.

$\$700,000 \div \$1,900,000 = 36.8\%$

The margin of safety $= \$1,900,000 - 1,800,000 = \$100,000$

The margin of safety percentage $= \left(\dfrac{\$100,000}{\$1,900,000}\right) = 5.263\ \%$, which is a very low margin of safety.

7-7 B

The CM $= \$6,000 - 2,900 = \$3,100$; the CM ratio $= \left(\dfrac{6,000 - 2,900}{\$6,000}\right) = 0.51667$

7-8 C

The breakeven point in carts sold $= \left(\dfrac{\$1,500,000}{\$3,100}\right) = 484$ carts

The breakeven point in dollars $= \left(\dfrac{\$1,500,000}{.51667}\right) = \$2,903,207$

7-9 A

The equation to compute the after-tax net income is:

$SP(Q) - UVC(Q) - TFC = \left(\dfrac{TI}{1 - .40}\right)$

$(\$6,000 \times 1,200) - (\$2,900 \times 1,200) - \$1,500,000 = \left(\dfrac{TI}{.60}\right)$

$\$7,200,000 - 3,480,000 - \$1,500,000 = \left(\dfrac{TI}{.60}\right)$

$TI = \$2,220,000 \times 0.60 = \$1,332,000$

Since the projected sales will result in only $1,332,000 income, the business will not achieve its profit goal.

7-10 The projected net income after taxes is $168,000 ($1,500,000 – $1,332,000) short of the profit goal. The company has a budget gap and has to cut costs or increase revenue. Since the proposal must be something that will be put into effect in the very near future, time is short and the company's options are limited.

- The easiest course would be to look for discretionary fixed costs that could be cut. These are costs that could be made by management decisions such as training or advertising. However, both actions may cause more problems in the long run.

- Management could look for ways to cut labor costs, perhaps by laying off some personnel. However, this course needs to be thoroughly evaluated because it could result in a decrease in quality and efficiency and have negative long-range consequences.

- Management could increase advertising with the goal of increasing sales. However, management would need a good knowledge of its market to make a reasonable estimate of the impact of this option.

- What really should happen is for management to perform strategic analysis to determine what course of action would be viable in the long run. For example, are there additional markets that could be tapped? Could management purchase a more efficient piece of manufacturing equipment that would improve productivity? Could it improve its purchasing practices to lower the cost of raw materials?

- CVP analysis could be a very useful tool in evaluating each of the above alternatives.

CHAPTER

8

Costs for Decision Making: Relevant Costing and Capital Expenditure Analysis

In this chapter we cover costing for managerial decision making. The following topics will be discussed: the managerial decision making model, the cost concepts relating to decision making, application of the model to various short-run decisions faced by management, pitfalls in using relevant costing in decision making, and costs for long-run decision making including capital expenditure analysis.

Managers in every company make important decisions every day. A manager at Bank of America may be considering whether to close a branch office or keep it open. A Home Depot executive may wonder whether the company should buy facilities to make lawn mowers or purchase them already finished from an established vendor. A Coca-Cola technology manager could be faced with a problem of whether to recommend the replacement of the company's existing information system. Smaller companies may ask such questions as: "Should I replace a piece of equipment?" or "Should I accept a special offer to sell my product below my established selling price?" These and a host of other problems present themselves to managers in large and small companies every day. In making decisions managers are always guided by the company's overall mission, strategic goals, and objectives. However, they need a carefully constructed decision paradigm and process to ensure a successful outcome.

This chapter will discuss the decision process and how the management accountant can aid managers by gathering information, arranging the data for evaluation, and assisting in its interpretation.

Decision Making Model

The alternative-choice decision model that managers often use in problem solving situations is shown in Figure 8-1. The decision model works as follows.

1. *Clearly Define the Problem.* This may be easier said than done, because the problem usually requires refining. For example, defining the overall problem as unsatisfactory earnings growth is much too broad. Is the problem caused by poor marketing strategy, poor cost control, outdated equipment, or something else? Management may hold a strategy meeting or a company retreat of key executives to identify specifics and to develop viable solutions. For example, the executives in a small bank may decide that the problem is poor profit performance, decide that the problem is cost control, and, using analysis described in this chapter, consider closing underperforming branches.

2. *Identify the Alternatives.* This really involves projecting all possible solutions for consideration. This provides an opportunity for all relevant

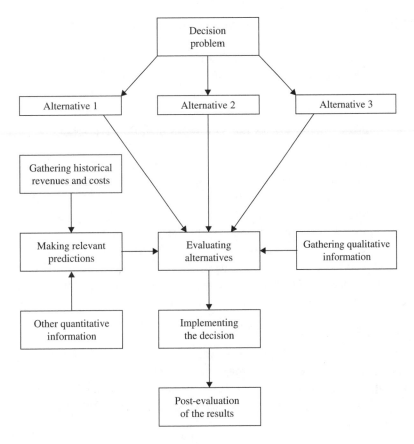

Figure 8-1 Alternative-choice decision model.

managers to suggest ways to solve the problem. In our bank example above, management may consider closing Branch A and Branch D or it may focus on one branch, which means the alternatives are close the branch or not close the branch. In projecting alternatives, management is often faced with too many alternatives to evaluate. So part of the process is to whittle the number down.

3. *Gather Relevant Information.* This stage involves gathering two broad types of information: quantitative and qualitative. Gathering *quantitative information* usually starts with historical revenues and costs. We will see shortly that historical revenues and costs, per se, cannot be used in formulating the final decision model. However, they may serve as the starting point for projecting the revenues and costs into the future.

Management will also need other quantitative data for analysis. In our banking example, management needs to know data on projected population growth, competition threats, and other economic trends relevant to the location where a branch may potentially close.

The management accountant is particularly helpful in this step because most of the data needed to quantify each alternative reside in the accounting department. The management accountant can also help present the information in a logical, understandable format.

Gathering *qualitative information* is also very important, for it may contribute something different from what quantitative analysis can. Qualitative information may be important in ensuring the selected alternative is in agreement with company goals. In the banking example above, management may have a goal to serve low-income areas. A branch in the bank's market area may be underperforming all other branches and appear to be a good candidate to close. However, this conflicts with management's goal of serving all of the communities in its market area. Closing the branch would not be in agreement with the company's goal and, in fact, may generate negative media attention that could harm the company's image.

Another example of qualitative information relates to the environment. A company may be considering several locations in which to place its headquarters. One location may provide strong economic incentives for the company, but be in an area with severe air pollution, a factor that would conflicts with a company objective of providing a healthy environment for its employees and maintaining their high morale.

4. *Evaluate the Information.* To do this effectively, the data need to be in a format that facilitates the evaluation. One approach used by companies is called a **decision tree**, which is a graphic representation of various decision alternatives and their outcomes and related probabilities (risks) that are visually available to the decision maker. This technique is particularly useful when there are more than two alternatives to be considered. It helps ensure that all relevant information is included and errors minimized. Each "limb" of the tree represents an alternative and normally contains both revenues (or benefits) and costs pertaining to that alternative. The outcome of each alternative would be stated in both quantitative and qualitative format.

5. *Select the Best Alternative and Implement the Decision.* Generally, the alternative with the higher return or the alternative that has the greater relevant revenues over related costs will be selected, considering qualitative

factors. Implementation of the decision may require training personnel, reorganizing operations, integrating a merger, or any other action dependent on what the decision involves.

6. *Evaluate the Decision.* Sometimes decision applications do not succeed, and management needs to know what went wrong, in order to "learn from your mistakes," as the old adage goes. Thus, some companies perform a postaudit of the implementation results to provide the necessary feedback for this important stage of future decision processes.

Important Accounting Concepts for Decision Making

Relevant revenues and costs are critical to the decision making process. For revenues and costs to be relevant, they must meet two tests. First, they must be *future* revenues and costs. Costs that occurred in the past are not relevant. These are usually labeled **sunk costs** because they have already happened and thus cannot be affected by any future decision. Second, the revenues and costs must *be different* for each alternative. If there is no difference, they are irrelevant and can be left out of the analysis. For example, a company may be considering the replacement of a machine in the production process. The *book value* of the old machine is historical— it is a sunk cost. The relevant cost in this case is the cost of a new machine. Of course, if the old machine were to be sold, then the cash flow from the sale would become relevant, because it would become a future cash flow.

Accountants and managers may also call relevant revenues and costs **differential revenues and costs** or **incremental revenues and costs**. The economists may also use the term **marginal costs**. The terms all mean essentially the same thing.

Opportunity costs were introduced in Chapter 2. Briefly, an opportunity cost is the potential benefit (cost savings or profit) that is foregone by selecting one alternative over another. For example, a company may have excess capacity and has an offer to produce an object similar to the one it normally produces, but the selling price the special offer is lower than the market price of its normal product. If the company has no other opportunity to use its excess facilities, it will have no opportunity costs to consider in the short run. However, if it had had a competing offer, then the amount of contribution margin foregone by not accepting the alternative offer would be an opportunity cost. Thus, even though identified opportunity costs are not be included in accounting records, the concept remains very important to decision analysis.

Hazards in Using Relevant Costing

When performing decision analysis using costs and revenues there are some important hazards to consider:

- **Allocated Fixed Costs.** Generally, these costs are irrelevant because they are sunk costs and don't have a bearing on the decision.

- **Identifying All Variable Costs as Relevant and All Fixed Costs as Irrelevant.** Some variable costs may vary depending on volume but are irrelevant. An example of a variable cost that is irrelevant is a telephone charge that varies with the amount of usage but the contract with the telephone company requires a minimum level of usage. An example of a fixed cost that is relevant is a special offer that requires a special piece of equipment to produce the order. In this case the cost is fixed but relevant to the decision.

- **Using Unit Costs Instead of Total Costs.** Unit or average costs at different output levels may include unit fixed costs; these change as output increases and may result in an erroneous decision. Some managers may mistakenly assume that all unit costs remain the same at different levels of production within the relevant range.

Now that we have discussed the decision making model and defined the concepts that will be used, we can turn to specific applications of the alternative-choice decision process.

Problem: Should a Product, Service, or Business Segment Be Dropped?

Managers are often faced with a product or service line that has declining sales and profitability. There could be several reasons for the decline. Some notable examples are a competitor has developed a competing product or service of higher quality, the market area has changing population patterns resulting in a decrease in demand, and a new technology has made the product obsolete. The decision model using relevant revenues and relevant costs can be helpful in framing the analysis.

Here are some key points to remember when considering dropping a product or service or closing a business unit:

- Take the overall company perspective in deciding whether revenues and costs can be eliminated. Eliminating a product or service may affect the sales of other products or services. For example, a product may be a loss leader and bring customers into a retail store where they buy other products. This effect should be considered. Also, if costs are eliminated in a department but they are still shouldered by the company as a whole, then those costs have not been avoided. For example, if a large supermarket is considering dropping a section in its store, it will not reduce its utility bills because the section's location is part of the store's overall open space.

- The use of the idle space is a major factor in the analysis. If the space can be used for a viable alternative purpose, such as producing a new product or selling a new service, then the resulting incremental revenues and costs are relevant.

Illustration

The Dude Saddle Company is a large retailer of saddles and tack, riding apparel, and gifts and accessories. Each of the three product lines is sold in its own department but all are housed in the same building. The company is considering dropping the gifts product line because of decreasing profitability. The accountant estimated that neither the sales of other products nor the total assets of the company would be affected. At the present time, management has not found another use for the idle store space. The direct fixed expenses, such as the area supervisor's wages, could be avoided by not operating the department selling the gifts and accessories. The accountant gathered the data shown in Exhibit 8-1. Should management drop the accessories product line?

Exhibit 8-1. The Dude Saddle Company				
	Saddles and Tack	**Riding Apparel**	**Gifts and Accessories**	**Total**
Sales	$450,000	$350,000	$150,000	$950,000
Less:				
Total variable expenses	250,000	200,000	100,000	550,000
Direct fixed expenses	50,000	40,000	30,000	120,000
Joint fixed expenses	50,000	50,000	50,000	150,000
Net income (loss)	$100,000	$60,000	($30,000)	$130,000

Solution

The relevant revenues and relevant expenses are shown in Exhibit 8-2.

Exhibit 8-2. Gifts and Accessories: Revenues and Expenses			
	Keep Product Line	Drop Product Line	Incremental Revenue/Costs
Sales	$150,000	$0	$150,000
Total variable expenses	100,000	0	$100,000
Direct fixed expenses	30,000	0	$30,000
Net income (loss)	$20,000	$0	$20,000

Notice that Exhibit 8-2 does not include any revenues or expenses relating to the tack and apparel lines. Why? Because based on the information given, they are not relevant to the decision, since they would be the same under both alternatives. The Drop Product Line alternative would give no revenues or costs. However, another approach to the "two alternatives" format shown in Exhibit 8-2 would be to prepare a full income statement and include the total revenues and expenses of the tack and apparel lines along with a deduction of the total joint fixed expenses of $150,000. The resulting income would total $110,000. This format simply leaves out the relevant revenues and costs for the gifts and accessory lines. Comparing this figure with that of Exhibit 8-1, we arrive at a difference of $20,000, the same figure as the "two alternative" format. Either format could be used, as long as relevant revenues and relevant costs were used in both.

So what would be the best decision? In the short run, the gift and accessories line is contributing $20,000 to cover joint fixed costs and should not be dropped. In the long run the company should attempt to find a more profitable line and use the fixed costs that cannot be avoided.

Why is keeping the gift and accessories a valid decision? While the company would save $30,000 in direct expenses relevant to the gift and accessories line, it would be losing $50,000 in contribution to joint expenses and profit. Thus, it is $20,000 better off.

Problem: How to Make Capital Investment Decisions

Capital investment decisions are part of the overall strategic planning process used by most companies. Strategic planning involves making decisions that affect the type of business the company will be in and the course it will undertake in pursuing that business in the long run. The decisions often involve whether to add a product or service, whether the company should move into a new market, where facilities should be located, and whether to replace a major system or piece of equipment. These and a host of other long-term decisions require a carefully designed decision process, since they involve the future of the company.

In making capital investment decisions, companies incorporate the **payback** or **discounted cash flow methods** into the model we have discussed. In addition, a company will consider tax implications, since this is an important component in the analysis. Also, since the consequences of these decisions stretch far into the future, perhaps 10 or more years, the company must consider the time value of money. The chapter appendix covers the basics of the concept of present value and how to compute it.

Illustration

The XYZ Manufacturing Company is considering replacing its partially automated assembly line with robotics. The machinery on the assembly line has a book value of $650,000 and an estimated disposal value of $200,000. The tax basis for the old equipment is $350,000. The robotics assembly line could be installed at a cost of $840,000. It is estimated to have $200,000 in differential savings on labor and other costs per year, compared with the old machinery, for at least 5 years. The present machine will not have a salvage value at the end of its useful life. The company uses straight-line depreciation on the new equipment over the 5-year period, less any disposable value at the end of project life, which for the robotics equipment is assumed to be $50,000. Assume there is a 40% income tax rate for both deductions and gains and losses. The company expects a 12% return on its investments. Based solely on this information, should the company invest in the new assembly line or keep the present one?

The Payback Method of Evaluating Capital Investment Projects

The payback method asks the question, "How long does it take for me to recoup my initial investment?" Management may want an investment to pay for itself rather quickly in order to reduce the risk of investing in the project, that is, the quicker the payoff, the lesser the risk. This method is often used to screen potential investment projects. The data for each investment opportunity are arrayed and, all else being equal, the projects with the quickest payoff would be considered first. Income taxes are not normally considered under this approach. The payback is computed as follows:

Payback period = Initial investment ÷ Net annual cash inflow

According to the data given above for XYZ Manufacturing, the initial investment is computed as $840,000 – $200,000 = $640,000. The $200,000 is offset against the $840,000 purchase price because the old machine can be sold for this amount and is therefore a cash inflow. The $650,000 book value is a sunk cost and not relevant to this decision.

$$\text{Payback period} = \left(\frac{\$640,000}{\$200,000}\right) = 3.2 \text{ years}$$

Management would have to evaluate the payback period to determine whether 3.2 years is a reasonable guess, based on the fact that the machinery has an estimated life of 5 years. Also, since this is pretax, the actual payback will be longer. Thus, on the surface this appears to be a risky project and should not be undertaken. The discounted flow method, discussed in the next section, will provide a better analysis.

The advantage of the payback method is that it is simple and it is particularly a good screening mechanism. The obvious disadvantage is that it does not consider the time value of money. This could make a significant difference in the outcome of the analysis, because it means the payback method does not show the true net benefits of the investment. Also, the payback period often is shorter than the useful life of the asset. Thus, it does not take into consideration the use of the asset after the payback period cutoff.

The Discounted Cash Flow (DCF) Method of Evaluating Capital Investment Projects

There are several important variables to consider in the discounted cash flow method:

- **Discount rate.** Management must select a rate to use in discounting the cash flows to be received in the future. As stated above, this is based on the projected inflation rate and the amount of estimated risk.

- **Estimate of future cash flows.** The project analyst must estimate future cash flows from the project. These could be future revenues offset by future costs or cash flows resulting from savings of costs derived from purchasing a more efficient piece of equipment, for example. These estimates should be made by personnel knowledgeable of the project processes, outcomes, and environment, such as production engineers, accountants, design personnel, and even economists.

- **Tax implications.** Federal and some state tax laws are sometimes amended to allow for specific tax credits and deductions on business investments. Some of the more common credits and deductions are discussed below. To determine if either of these apply to a given investment situation, the reader should consult the current tax laws or a tax professional.

- **Depreciation tax shield.** Depreciation of the project can be deducted on the company's income tax return, thus shielding revenue from income taxes. This results in a saving of tax payments (cash outflow). For this reason depreciation is often referred to as a *source* of funds, which is technically incorrect. The depreciation, per se, does not provide any funds; it is the savings on taxes that affect funds flow. Stated another way, if there is no revenue to offset the depreciation, there is no tax benefit. In addition to deducting normal yearly depreciation, the company can deduct the loss on a sale or disposal of an asset, which can occur for either the old asset when the new is bought or the new when the project has ended. These actions also result in additional tax savings for the company.

- **Investment tax credit.** The United States Congress from time to time has passed legislation that allows an investment tax credit on the purchase of certain assets. This is usually a dollar-for-dollar deduction on the tax return. The company should determine whether such a credit is applicable during the time of a potential project.

- **Other deductions.** The rules for asset depreciation deduction and investment tax credit are complex. There could be deductions other than the two most popular ones described above. For example, there could be tax deductions for installation expenses.

Exhibit 8-2 displays cash flows and current value computations based on the data presented for the XYZ Manufacturing Company. This type of chart could easily be translated to a spreadsheet and "what if" analysis could be performed by projecting the relevant values for the key variables.

In addition to the information on XYZ Manufacturing, the following additional assumptions are made:

- A 7% investment tax credit is assumed for investment in this type of equipment.

- All cash flows are assumed to occur at the end of the period, except for year 0, which refers to the beginning of the year and has no time value or money effect.

- The tax credit and deductions are assumptions and simplifications for illustration purposes only and do not necessarily reflect federal and state tax laws.

The analysis in Exhibit 8-3 shows that the project does earn the company's required rate of return of 12% and has a $28,330 of negative cash flow. Based on the quantitative analysis, the project should be rejected.

Exhibit 8-3.   Schedule of Cash Flows for XYZ Manufacturing Company

		Cash Flows from Investment in Project	Cash Flows at End of Each Year				
		0	**1**	**2**	**3**	**4**	**5**
1.	Cost of equipment and installation	($840,000)	0	0	0	0	0
2.	Investment tax credit savings	58,800	0	0	0	0	0
3.	Proceeds from sale of old asset	200,000	0	0	0	0	0
4.	Tax savings from sale of old asset	60,000	0	0	0	0	0
5.	Annual cash savings before taxes	0	200,000	200,000	200,000	200,000	200,000
6.	Taxes on annual cash flows	0	(68,000)	(68,000)	(68,000)	(68,000)	(68,000)
7.	Proceeds on sale of asset	0	0	0	0	0	50,000
8.	Tax from gain on asset sold	0	0	0	0	0	(20,000)
9.	Net cash flows for each period	(521,200)	132,000	132,000	132,000	132,000	162,000
10.	Present value factor at 12%	1.00	0.893	0.797	0.712	0.636	0.567
11.	Present value of cash flows	($521,200)	$117,876	$105,204	$93,984	$83,952	$91,854
12.	Net present value of the project	($28,330)					

Notes:

2.   840,000 × 0.07 = $58,800

4. $350,000 tax basis – $200,000 sale of old asset = $150,000 loss × 0.40 = $60,000

5. $200,000 annual savings before taxes

6. $200,000 annual savings – $\left(\dfrac{\$200,000 - 50,000}{5} \right)$ depreciation × 0.40 = $68,000

8. $50,000 sales value of robotics machinery (fully depreciated) × 0.40 = $20,000

10.   Present value factors are taken from Exhibit 8A-1. (See chapter appendix.)

11.   Row 9 × Row 10

12.   The cash outflows at the time of the investment less the sum of cash savings from years 1–5

Problem: Should a Product or Service Be Produced Internally or Outsourced?

Outsourcing has become a controversial topic in the media, particularly outsourcing to overseas vendors. However, it remains a viable strategy for management. Outsourcing means that the overall company or a segment of it purchases goods and services from outside the company rather than producing the same goods or services itself. Many companies choose to produce from within so that they can control quality and delivery dependability. Others have decided to outsource activities that are not part of their core functions. Outsourcing can involve questions such as whether to make a part for a product or purchase it from outside the company, outsource food services rather than produce them in the company, or outsource service center functions or retain them in the company. These and a host of other functions have been outsourced to contractors. For purposes of our discussion, these will be called *make or buy decisions*.

The relevant costing decision model can be applied to make or buy decisions. Suppose that Generation A makes an electronic device that requires several parts in assembly. The company is vertically integrated and makes all of its parts. Generation A has received an offer from a producer of transistors to supply one of its key parts for $50 per unit. The transistor company has no use for the idle facilities. The accountant for Generation A has prepared the estimated cost for making the product internally, which is displayed in Exhibit 8-4.

Exhibit 8-4. Direct Costs for Production of 5,000 Transistors		
	Total	**Per Unit**
Direct materials	$100,000	$20.00
Direct labor	50,000	$10.00
Variable manufacturing overhead	25,000	5.00
Allocated fixed overhead	80,000	
Total costs	$255,000	

The decision data can be structured as shown in Exhibit 8-5.

Exhibit 8-5. Make or Buy Analysis

	Make Transistor	Outsource Transistor	Differential Costs
Direct materials	$100,000	(a)$250,000	($150,000)
Direct labor	50,000		50,000
Variable manufacturing overhead	25,000		25,000
Total costs	$175,000	$250,000	($75,000)

(a) 5,000 × $50 = $250,000

Note: The fixed costs are irrelevant because the company has no use for the idle facilities. However, for information purposes they could have been included in the analysis as long as the same amounts are shown under both alternatives.

Based on the data given, the company should continue to make the transistors because it would pay $75,000 more in differential costs to the outside source. However, let's assume that the company has developed a new electronics item that it is planning to manufacture and that the facilities made free by outsourcing the above transistor could be converted to making a small transistor for this new product. Further, the production of the smaller transistor could be purchased outside at a cost of $30 for 3,000 units. Would this new information change the decision? The $90,000 ($30 × 3,000) would become an *opportunity cost* for the make alternative, because buying the smaller transistor would represent the cost of an opportunity foregone. The analysis is shown in Exhibit 8-6:

Exhibit 8-6. Make or Buy Analysis with Opportunity Costs

	Costs to Make Transistor	Costs to Outsource Transistor	Differential Costs
Direct materials	$100,000	$250,000	($150,000)
Direct labor	50,000		50,000
Variable manufacturing overhead	25,000		25,000
Total costs before opportunity costs	$175,000	$250,000	($75,000)
Opportunity costs of using facilities to make the smaller transistors and save purchasing outside	90,000		
Total costs, including opportunity costs	$265,000	$250,000	$15,000

The decision now would be to outsource the manufacture of the existing transistors and use the idle facilities to manufacture the smaller transistor for the new product. In outsourcing decisions, one of the key questions is what will be done with existing facilities or, in the case of personnel, what will be done with the existing personnel. If the existing facilities cannot be used, then the opportunity costs would be zero. If the personnel providing services that could be outsourced can be laid off or used elsewhere in the company, then that cost becomes an opportunity cost to keeping the function internally.

Problem: Which Product Mix Provides the Greater Profitability?

In Chapter 8 we stated that, in general, the product with the greater contribution should be sold over products with a lower contribution margin. This is true if there are no capacity constraints—either in production or selling. If there is a limited capacity to make multiple products or if there is a limited capacity to sell products, as in a retail operation, then the focus turns to the contribution per the limiting factor, as in machine hour or shelf space, for example.

Illustration

Assume that Jiffy Supermarkets has a dairy products section. It sells four types of milk: regular, 2% butterfat, 1% butterfat, and nonfat. The store manager wants to offer all four types of milk in 1-gallon containers and he argues that the milk that has the greater contribution margin per gallon should have greatest amount of shelf space. The total amount of shelf space is limited to 16 feet. He wants to offer at least 2 feet of shelf space and a maximum of 8 feet of shelf space for each type of milk. Exhibit 8-7 provides the relevant revenues and costs for the four types of milk.

Exhibit 8-7. Contribution per the Limiting Factor for Jiffy Supermarkets				
	Regular Milk	**2% Butterfat**	**1% Butterfat**	**Nonfat**
Sale price per gallon	$4.00	$4.25	$4.50	$4.75
Less: Variable cost per gallon	2.50	2.60	2.70	2.80
Gallons sold per foot of shelf space per day	50	40	36	30

Required

1. If the store manager has his way, what will be the contribution margin per gallon of each type of milk?

2. Sam, who works part time at the supermarket, has just completed a course in management accounting. He advises the store manager that there is a limited amount of space and therefore, the milk product that has the most contribution (sales minus cost) per foot of shelf space should be used to determine which type of milk needs to be pushed. How would this change the computations?

3. Make a recommendation on what mix of milk should be sold.

Solution

1. The contribution per type of milk is shown in Exhibit 8-8.

2. The contribution margin per foot of shelf space in shown in Exhibit 8-9.

Exhibit 8-8. Contribution Margin per Type of Milk				
	Regular Milk	**2% Butterfat**	**1% Butterfat**	**Nonfat**
Sale price per gallon	$4.00	$4.25	$4.50	$4.75
Less: Variable cost per gallon	2.50	2.60	2.70	2.80
Contribution margin per gallon	$1.50	1.65	$1.80	$1.95

Exhibit 8-9. Contribution Margin per Shelf Space				
	Regular Milk	**2% Butterfat**	**1% Butterfat**	**Nonfat**
Contribution margin per gallon	$1.50	1.65	$1.80	$1.95
Milk sales in gallons per foot of shelf space per day	×50	×40	×36	×30
Contribution margin per foot of shelf space per day	$75.00	$66.00	$64.80	$58.50

3. The contributions in Exhibit 8-9 show that using the contribution margin per foot of shelf space (the constraining factor) provides a better measure of contribution margin, compared to using the contribution of each product shown in Exhibit 8-8. Therefore, it should be used to allocate shelf space. The use of the maximum and minimum of shelf space devoted to each type of milk set by the store manager would result in shelf space being allocated as shown in Exhibit 8-10.

Exhibit 8-10. Shelf Space Allocation for Each Type of Milk			
	Daily Contribution of Shelf Space	Feet of Shelf Space Allocated	Total Contribution per Day
Regular milk	$75.00	8	$600.00
2% Butterfat	66.00	4	264.00
1% Butterfat	64.80	2	129.60
Nonfat	58.50	2	117.00

Summary

This chapter defined the concepts of relevant revenues, relevant costing, and opportunity costs. It presented an alternative-choice decision model that often incorporates these concepts.

The steps used in making decisions were described in six steps:

1. Clearly define the problem.
2. Identify the alternatives for solving the decision problem.
3. Gather relevant information for predicting.
4. Evaluate the information, identifying relevant revenues and/or relevant costs.
5. Make and implement the decision.
6. Evaluate the decision.

Some hazards that may be encountered when using the decision model were introduced:

- Allocated fixed costs
- Identifying all variable costs as relevant and all fixed costs as irrelevant
- Using unit costs instead of total costs

After presentation of the decision model and the process for using it, several applications of the model were presented:

- In deciding whether to drop a product, service, or business segment
- In deciding how to make capital investments
- In deciding whether to produce a product or service internally or outsource it
- In determining product or service mix

Appendix: Computing Present Value of a Lump Sum of Money

The purpose of this chapter is to cover the basics of the present value of money and explain how it is computed.

The Present Value of Money

We all know that the value of an amount of money expected in the future is different from which it would be if we received it today. To take the time value of money into consideration, we must adjust the amount expected in the future based on its timing and a **discount rate**. The discount rate is similar to an interest rate except that it reflects the rate of return that the company desires to earn on a particular investment project, including the effects of inflation and risk. The future cash flows associated with an investment opportunity are adjusted to their present value using the discount rate. Note that we use cash flows, not revenues and expenses, as the latter are based on accrual accounting and may result in an incorrect decision.

By way of clarification, the future value of money has a reciprocal value today. Instead of asking the present value of a lump sum expected at a specific point in the future, as in 10 years, for example, future value relates to how much a present investment will be worth at that specified point in the future, or the 10 years we used as an example above. A difference between present and future value also exists for annuities. For our purposes, we will only use the present value of a lump sum, although in large investment projects the present value of an annuity may be used.

Computing the Present Value of Money

The mathematical formula for computing the present value of a lump sum is

$$PV = \frac{FV_n}{(1 + i^n)}$$

where

PV = present value

FV = future value

i = discount rate

n = period(s)

Let us assume that a young woman is to inherit $20,000 in 10 years, when she is 25. What is the present value of that amount, if the going rate of interest is 5%? We can insert these data into the equation, but the computations would become cumbersome. Instead, Exhibit 8A-1 is a present value table that will provide us a present value factor that we can insert into the equation. The equation would change to become

$$PV = FV^n \times (PVF), \text{ where:}$$

PVF = Present value factor

To obtain the present value factor we look in Exhibit 8A-1 under 5% and at 10 years, where we find the PVF to be 0.614. Inserting this into our equation we have:

$$PV = \$20,000(0.614) = \$12,280$$

There are also present value tables of an annuity. In this case we would multiply the amount to be received at the end of each period by the PVF of an annuity found in the PV annuity table. Present value and future value tables can be found in any intermediate management accounting text or on the Internet.

Exhibit 8A-1. Present Value of $1 (Lump Sum)											
Yrs	1%	2%	3%	4%	5%	6%	7%	8%	9%	10%	12%	14%
1	0.990	0.980	0.971	0.962	0.952	0.943	0.935	0.926	0.917	0.909	0.893	0.877
2	0.980	0.961	0.943	0.925	0.907	0.890	0.873	0.857	0.842	0.826	0.797	0.769
3	0.971	0.942	0.915	0.889	0.864	0.840	0.816	0.794	0.772	0.751	0.712	0.675
4	0.961	0.924	0.888	0.855	0.823	0.792	0.763	0.735	0.708	0.683	0.636	0.592
5	0.951	0.906	0.863	0.822	0.784	0.747	0.713	0.681	0.650	0.621	0.567	0.519
6	0.942	0.888	0.837	0.790	0.746	0.705	0.666	0.630	0.596	0.564	0.507	0.456
7	0.933	0.871	0.813	0.760	0.711	0.665	0.623	0.583	0.547	0.513	0.452	0.400
8	0.923	0.853	0.789	0.731	0.677	0.627	0.582	0.540	0.502	0.467	0.404	0.351
9	0.914	0.837	0.766	0.703	0.645	0.592	0.544	0.500	0.460	0.424	0.361	0.308
10	0.905	0.820	0.744	0.676	0.614	0.558	0.508	0.463	0.422	0.386	0.322	0.270
11	0.896	0.804	0.722	0.650	0.585	0.527	0.475	0.429	0.388	0.350	0.287	0.237
12	0.887	0.788	0.701	0.625	0.557	0.497	0.444	0.397	0.356	0.319	0.257	0.208
13	0.879	0.773	0.681	0.601	0.530	0.469	0.415	0.368	0.326	0.290	0.229	0.182
14	0.870	0.758	0.661	0.577	0.505	0.442	0.388	0.340	0.299	0.263	0.205	0.160
15	0.861	0.743	0.642	0.555	0.481	0.417	0.362	0.315	0.275	0.239	0.183	0.140
16	0.853	0.728	0.623	0.534	0.458	0.394	0.339	0.292	0.252	0.218	0.163	0.123
17	0.844	0.714	0.605	0.513	0.436	0.371	0.317	0.270	0.231	0.198	0.146	0.108
18	0.836	0.700	0.587	0.494	0.416	0.350	0.296	0.250	0.212	0.180	0.130	0.095
19	0.828	0.686	0.570	0.475	0.396	0.331	0.277	0.232	0.194	0.164	0.116	0.083
20	0.820	0.673	0.554	0.456	0.377	0.312	0.258	0.215	0.178	0.149	0.104	0.073

Practice Problems

8-1 Opportunity costs are:

A. Recorded in the accounting records

B. Interchangeable with variable costs

C. Relevant to decision making

D. Considered historical costs

The following information pertains to questions 8-2 and 8-3.

Beck and Beck CPAs provides three types of service: tax, auditing, and consulting. The maximum amount of billable hours for next year is 10,700 (six professionals). The firm accountant has computed the information per billable hour displayed in the following table. Due to contractual obligations, the firm must provide a minimum of 4,500 hours to its audit clients and a minimum of 3,500 to its tax clients.

	Audit	Tax	Consulting
Fee charged per hour	$300	$400	$500
Variable costs per hour	100	120	140
Fixed costs per hour	150	155	160
Unit gross profit	$50	$125	$200

8-2 If the firm employs a short-run profit maximization strategy, which type of service should be emphasized?

A. Audit

B. Consulting

C. Tax

D. Either tax or consulting

8-3 What would be the amount of total contribution margin, if the firm met its minimum billable hours or responsibility and chose the best long-term pricing strategy?

A. $2,500,900

B. $1,900,000

C. $2,000,100

D. $2,852,000

The following information pertains to questions 8-4 through 8-7.

Titan Inc. purchased a new machine on July 1 for $1,000,000; it was estimated to have annual operating savings of $50,000 and a useful life of 5 years. Just 3 months later, on September 1, the purchasing director was offered a new machine that would cost $800,000, provide an annual savings of $35,000, and have a useful life of 5 years. The original machine could be sold for $600,000. Neither machine would have a salvage value at the end of its useful life. Both machines would produce output of about the same quality. The purchasing director is torn between whether he should replace the old machine with the new machine and he has asked his accountant for advice. For this problem ignore the time value of money and tax consequences. The table below displays that data collected related to this problem.

	Original Machine (July 1st)	New Machine (September 1st)
Cost	$1,000,000	$800,000
Useful life	5	5
Salvage value	0	0
Current sales value	$600,000	NA
Annual operating savings	$50,000	$35,000

8-4 What is the net outlay for the new machine?

A. $800,000

B. $150,000

C. $200,000

D. None of the above

8-5 What are the total relevant benefits (costs) of the new system over the life of the project, if it were purchased?

A. $375,000

B. ($25,000)

C. $625,000

D. ($75,000)

8-6 What are the total relevant benefits (costs) of the old machine over its useful life?

A. $250,000

B. $1,250,000

C. ($650,000)

D. ($750,000)

8-7 What should the accountant recommend?

A. Buy the new machine because it has a net benefit of $25,000.

B. Keep the old machine, the company would lose $250,000 upon its resale.

C. Buy the new machine because it would have a benefit of $375,000.

D. Keep the old machine because it has a differential benefit of $25,000.

8-8 The Yahoo Banking Company has a main office bank and two branch banks. The president wants to close the urban branch, since it is losing money. The divisions have the revenues and expenses as displayed in the table below.

	Urban Branch	Suburbia Branch
Revenues	$900,000	$1,200,000
Total variable expenses	350,000	375,000
Direct fixed expenses	450,000	525,000
Allocated common corporate expenses	120,000	125,000
Net operating income (loss)	$(20,000)	$175,000

If the urban branch were eliminated, then its direct fixed expenses could be avoided. The total common corporate expenses would be unaffected. Based on the data in the table above and if there is no qualitative information that affects the decision, what would the effect of closing have on Yahoo's net income?

A. Decrease of $100,000

B. Increase of $20,000

C. Increase of $155,000

D. None of the above

The following information pertains to questions 8-9 and 8-10.

Nobeard Company has 1,000 electric razors that have been returned because of defects. They are carried in inventory at a manufacturing cost of $20,000. If the razors are reworked for $10,000, they could be sold for $20,000. Alternatively, the razors could be sold for $9,000 for scrap.

8-9 What are the sunk costs in this situation?

   A. $1,000

   B. $30,000

   C. $20,000

   D. $50,000

8-10 Should Nobeard rework the electric razors and sell them or should they just sell them for scrap? What would be the impact on net income?

   A. $1,000 in differential income if sold for scrap

   B. $1,000 in differential income if processed further and sold

   C. $20,000 in differential income if processed further and sold

   D.   None of the above

Solutions to Practice Problems

8-1 C

8-2 B

Audit:	$300 − 100 = $200
Tax:	$400 − 120 = $280
Consulting:	$500 − 140 = $360

   The firm should emphasize consulting, since it provides the highest contribution margin per billable hour. Fixed costs would not be relevant in the short run.

8-3 D

The table below reflects the correct mix of services for the coming year. Since the number of billable hours is the capacity constraint and the firm has contractual obligations, it should allocate hours to those responsibilities first and allocate the remainder to consulting, which has the highest total contribution.

	Contribution Margin per Billable Hour	Number of Billable Hours Allocated	Total Contribution Margin
Audit	$200	4,500	$900,000
Tax	280	3,500	980,000
Consulting	360	2,700	972,000
Total			$2,852,000

8-4 C

$800,000 − $600,000 = $200,000

8-5 B

$800,000 − 600,000 − ($35,000 × 5) = $25,000 costs over benefits

8-6 A

$50,000 × 5 = $250,000 benefits

The original cost of the old machine of $1,000,000 is not relevant, since it is a sunk cost.

8-7 D

	Buy New Machine
Sell old machine and buy the new one:	
Cost of new machine	$800,000
Sale of old machine	(600,000)
Net cost of new machine	200,000
Operating savings of new machine (5 years × $35,000)	175,000
Difference in favor of keeping old machine	$(25,000)

The accountant should recommend that the old machine be retained since it will have a net benefit of $225,000. See the table above for summary of the analysis.

8-8 A

Closing the urban branch would result in its revenues being lost and all of its total variable cost and direct fixed costs being avoided. The allocated common costs would not be avoided and would have to be absorbed by the parent bank (these costs would exist under both alternatives). Thus, the impact on income would be $900,000 − ($350,000 + $450,000) = $100,000 decrease in cash inflow. Although the urban branch is losing money, it is contributing $100,000 to cover fixed costs of the parent bank. However, in the long run the bank must find a strategy for improving net income in the urban bank or find new uses of the corporate common costs.

8-9 C

The inventory cost is an historical, or past, cost and no decision can change that—it is a sunk cost.

8-10 B

If processed further: $20,000 – 10,000 = 10,000

If sold as scrap: $9,000

$10,000 – 9,000 = $1,000 in differential income in favor of processing further

Costs for Decision Making: Setting Prices

This chapter continues the coverage of costs for decision making by discussing costs used in setting prices in the short and long run. The topics covered are the economics of pricing, short-run pricing, contribution margin pricing, cost-plus pricing, and target cost pricing.

Economics of Pricing

The fundamental economic theory in pricing is that companies will sell a product or service as long as the revenue from additional units exceeds the cost of producing or providing those units. Beyond this, pricing is based on supply and demand for the

product or service in the market in which the company competes. Demand is based on what customers want and the price they are willing to pay. Supply relates to the seller's ability to provide a quality product at the lowest cost to make a satisfactory profit. At the same time, the seller must be aware of competitors in the market who may provide the product or service at a lower price, with a better quality, or sell a satisfactory substitute. Thus, pricing is a complex interaction of demand (customers), competitors, and supply (costs and ability to produce). The sensitivity of prices to demand is known in economics as **elasticity of demand**. Specifically, elasticity of demand is the responsiveness of changes in quantity to change in price, all other things being equal.

In the long run, pricing strongly relates to the degree of control the seller has in the market. If the business is a monopoly, obviously it has a significant amount of control, depending on governmental regulation. If the business is in a very competitive market where there are many customers and many competitors, then it has very little control and the prices are set by the market. Therefore, managers must give careful consideration to the market in which they compete and to the competitors they compete against.

This is a brief overview of the economics of pricing. For a more detailed analysis on pricing, consult an introductory text in economics and marketing.

Short-Term Pricing Decisions

In the long term, a business must cover all costs and make a satisfactory profit in order to remain a going concern. However, in the short term there may be situations in which the seller is willing to accept a lower price. These decisions usually relate to whether the business is operating at full capacity, that is, whether it has excess capacity. The most common short-term decision situation is that of the special order request by a customer. An illustration of a special order decision situation is provided below.

What is the Different between Short and Long Term?

The time horizon in a business usually relates to its operations. *Short term* normally means a firm's operating horizon of 1 year or less. *Long term* means the firm's operating horizon of greater than 1 year, up to 5 and even 10 years, depending on the firm's long-term planning horizon.

Illustration

Healthy Vitamin Company manufactures vitamins under its own brand and sells them to vitamin chains and large individual vitamin stores. A company that sells vitamins over the Internet makes a special offer to buy vitamins of a specified blend from Healthy, which would require the purchaser's own label to be placed on each bottle. The Internet company has proposed paying $5 per bottle of 60 vitamins and wants to purchase 5,000 bottles. Healthy sells a very similar blend for $7 per bottle through its normal distribution channels. The president of Healthy says that acceptance will result in a loss, and he is against it. Healthy can produce the special order because it has excess capacity and will not require any special equipment and personnel. Since this is a special offer, normal sales expenses will not be incurred and are not included in the costs listed in Exhibit 9-1. Healthy estimates the costs for the special offer as displayed in Exhibit 9-1.

Exhibit 9-1. Healthy Vitamin Company			
	Total	Per Unit	Percent of Sales
Sales (5,000 units)	$25,000	$5.00	100%
Less total variable expenses	15,000	$3.00	70%
Contribution margin	$10,000	$2.00	30%
Less total fixed expenses (workers in mixing and packaging + allocated costs)	$11,000		
Net income on the project	($1,000)		

Is the president correct: Should the company accept the offer?

To consider the special offer and any short-run pricing decision situation, we can use the decision model discussed in Chapter 8. Namely, the relevant revenues should exceed the relevant costs, assuming that there are no negative qualitative factors (see below). Generally, the differential revenues from the special order and the variable costs relating to the special order are relevant. As stated above, the relevancy of fixed costs in this situation depends on *whether the company has excess capacity*. If there is excess capacity, the fixed costs are normally not relevant because they cannot be avoided in the short run. However, if the company must purchase a fixed asset to complete the special order—such as a special piece of equipment—then they are relevant. Healthy Vitamin does have excess capacity and does not have any additional potential sales of its normal products on the short-term horizon. Therefore, the company would be $10,000 ($25,000 sales less $15,000

total variable costs) better off taking this special offer to fill its capacity. If the company were at full capacity it would want to sell at no less than the $7 normal price that it normally receives from its buyers. To sell at less than $7 with no excess capacity would be an opportunity cost that Healthy could not afford.

There are two pieces of qualitative information relating to any special offer. First, is the impact of selling at a lower price on existing customers. If its usual customers heard about a special sale price available only to other customers, Healthy could lose their business. This must be carefully considered in this situation. The second piece of information is whether such a sale violates the Robinson-Patman Act for price discrimination. Courts have generally ruled that a business has not engaged in predatory pricing when its prices do not fall below its average variable costs. Therefore, the short-run pricing model is acceptable.

Long-Term Pricing Decisions

In making long-term pricing decisions, management should select a target price that will cover both its variable and fixed costs *and* achieve a target profit. There are three basic methods for long-run pricing decisions: cost-plus (absorption costing), contribution margin, and target costing.

Cost-Plus Pricing

Cost-plus pricing starts with the total cost of selling a product or providing a service and adds a reasonable annual target profit. To compute the reasonable target profit, the company will normally use a target rate of return on a company's investment. Investment normally means the company's invested capital (total assets). For example, if the company's balance sheet shows $1,000,000 in assets and it desires a 12% return on its assets, the annual target profit would be $1,000,000 × 0.12 = $120,000. The company would strive to cover its variable and fixed costs plus the $120,000 target profit. In developing the price to charge, the company would forecast the amount of sales volume, then use that to convert the total costs and target profit to a unit basis.

A seller who uses the cost-plus method to negotiate a contract would start with the approach as described in the preceding paragraph, but would use the volume the contractor desires to be produced. The price would then be based on the cost plus a reasonable return on investment at the volume desired.

The cost-plus method can be expressed in formula form:

Target SP = (Unit Manufacturing Cost) + (Unit S&A Cost) + (Profit
   Markup)

Where,

SP = Unit sales price

S&A = Selling and administrative

The profit markup = A percentage markup using cost plus profit as the basis

Note that the cost-plus method's cost base is full costs, that is, manufacturing plus selling and administration. A variation of this approach is called the **absorption method** for determining prices. This method uses as its base the full manufacturing costs and computes a markup to cover selling and administrative and a reasonable profit.

The cost-plus approach to pricing is used in three situations:

1. Where there is no acceptable market for its products or services. This occurs in regulated industries, such as a utility company, and in defense contracting companies where the contract is negotiated on a cost-plus basis.

2. Where the seller has some control over pricing, such as in the automobile industry and specialized industrial products.

3. As a testing mechanism to determine whether a company's cost structure is such that it would be beneficial for it to enter a particular competitive market.

The following illustration will be used to describe the cost-plus method in more detail.

Illustration

The Solid Oak Company makes sturdy picnic tables for parks and other outdoor uses. The state recreational authority has asked for bids to build 5,000 picnic tables for use in its parks. If Solid Oak receives the contract it estimates that it will have to devote almost all of its productive capacity to the contract. Since the company is in a slump, Solid Oak has decided to make a bid and the accountant has estimated that the cost per table (including manufacturing and administrative expenses) would be $130. The contract would take at least 1 year to complete and may lead to other contracts from the state. The company has an investment base (total assets) of $1,000,000 and desires a return on investment (ROI) of 15% annually. What price should the company use to bid for the contract?

Solution

The ROI = $1,000,000 \times 0.15 = \$150,000$ = Target operating income

The target operating income per table = $\$150,000 \div 5,000 = \$30$ per table

Full cost of producing one table = $130

Selling price = $130 + 30 = $160

Markup percentage on full cost = $\left(\dfrac{\$30}{\$160}\right) = 0.1875$ or 18.75%

Contribution Margin Approach to Pricing

A variation of the cost-plus formula presented above is to break costs down into their variable and fixed components and use the **contribution margin approach to pricing** by adding a markup to the variable cost of an item. The latter is useful in considering the impact on profit of changes in the sales prices and their impact on sales demand. Using this approach, the formula becomes:

$$(\text{TSP} - \text{UVC}) \times \text{Volume} = \text{Total CM}$$

Where

TSP = Target selling price

UVC = Unit variable cost

CM = Contribution margin

To use this approach in pricing, we multiply the contribution margin per unit by each potential level of volume during an operating cycle to obtain the total contribution margin. Since *total* fixed costs would be the same at each level within the relevant range, the total fixed costs are not relevant at these levels. This method allows the decision maker to focus on the impact of prices on different levels of volume.

Illustration

Positive Action Inc. provides consulting services in a large city where the consulting business has considerable demand. The demand is based more on reputation of the firm and quality of services than on what fees are charged. However, there is some sensitivity to the amount of fees charged. Positive Action has eight professional staff, including three partners. The controller is planning next year's budget and after consulting with several partners, comes up with the project fees per professional hour and the related volume of hours displayed in Exhibit 9-2.

Exhibit 9-2.	Positive Action Decision Data		
Price per Billable Hour	Unit Variable Cost	Demand in Hours	Total Fixed Costs
$200	$110	13,500	$1,100,000
210	110	12,500	1,100,000
220	110	12,000	1,100,000
230	110	11,000	1,100,000
240	110	9,000	1,100,000

What fee should Positive Action charge?

Solution

Using the contribution margin approach, Exhibit 9-3 shows the total contribution at various levels.

Exhibit 9-3.	Positive Action Decision Analysis			
Price per Billable Hour (1)	Variable Cost per Hour (2)	Contribution Margin per Hour (3)	Demand in Hours (4)	Total Contribution (5) = (3) × (4)
$200	$110	$90	13,500	$1,215,000
210	110	100	12,500	1,250,000
220	110	110	12,000	1,320,000
230	110	120	10,500	1,260,000
240	110	130	9,000	1,170,000

Based on the information given, Positive Action should charge $220 per billable hour, since that would provide the highest amount of total contribution. This would amount to $110 per hour or a total contribution of $1,320,000 to cover the fixed costs of $1,100,000 and leave a profit of $220,000.

Target Costing

Target costing involves setting a competitive market price for a product based on market analysis, computing the maximum costs that will be allowed, and working out cost reductions made possible by the improvement of technologies and processes. This approach was first developed in Japan in the 1980s by companies such as Sony and Toyota. As a fundamentally different approach to controlling costs and setting prices, it worked by starting with the market price of a product and working back to the allowable cost. It spread to the United States and the rest of the world during the 1990s. It is now recognized worldwide as a superior method for setting long-term, market-driven prices where product life cycles are becoming shorter and shorter.

Target costing is a proactive approach to planning and managing costs early in the design and development stages of a product life cycle. It is best applied to new products during their design and development stage. It has very little effect after the product has begun production but can be used with product modifications. This approach is in sharp contrast to the cost-plus approach described above, which starts with the costs and determines a target income based on that cost and finally a price that covers both the cost and desired profit.

The Basic Concepts of Target Costing

Market-Driven Costing

Market-driven costing is more or less the same as target costing. It requires the company to have an increased knowledge of the market and the price that customers are willing to pay. In some cases the target costs of a downstream company set the target price of the upstream company. Moreover, some companies use target costing when they want to become the price leader in a particular market, which results in the lowering of the price. In this situation the lower price becomes the price that drives the target costs. In any of these three cases, once determined, the market price is used to determine the target cost by the simple formula:

Market price – Required profit margin = Target costs

Customer-Driven Product Development

Customer-driven product development requires that customer demand for low prices, product features, and high quality be taken into consideration before the design and development stages are undertaken. Market analysis is used to determine what kind of products the customer wants, what the customer's quality requirements are, how much the customer is willing to pay for design innovations, and what the customer's time requirements for delivery of the product are.

Early Cost Management

Cost management is undertaken early during the product planning, design, and development stages, because up to 80% of product costs are locked in during these stages. This requires a significantly different culture and attitude by management and workers. Trying to reduce costs after the product is in production status is usually very difficult and costly. The question is not "What does the product cost?" but "How much should it cost?"

Cross-Functional Teams

The use of cross-functional teams should involve all functions in the delivery chain. These include product design, engineering, manufacturing, purchasing, suppliers, sales, and accounting. Team sharing and interaction are critical to increase understanding of the product design and processes in order for individual members to make meaningful contributions to the target costing process. In addition, the use of cross-functional teams requires the support of top management. The team must be given the responsibility along with the authority to make the critical decisions relating to target costs.

Life Cycle Costs

Focusing on life cycle costs can help minimize costs. These include design costs, purchase price, production costs, maintenance costs, and distribution costs.

Steps in Computing the Target Cost

The key steps in developing target prices and target costs are:

1. **Determine the product price**, based on market and customer analysis.
2. **Compute the target profit per unit** by computing total annual target profit using a rate of return on investment that is based on management's profit objective. The total target profit is then divided by the annual target sales to arrive at the target profit per unit. The formula is:

$$\text{Target profit per unit} = \left(\frac{Total\ Assets \times ROI}{Total\ Annual\ Sales\ Units} \right)$$

3. **Compute the target cost per unit** by subtracting the target profit per unit from the target price per unit. The formula is:

Target cost per unit = Target price per unit – Target profit per unit

Total target cost = Target cost per unit × total target sales units

4. **Compute the cost-reduction target** by computing the probable cost using *existing* processes and subtracting the probable cost from the target cost to arrive at the cost reduction target. The formula is:

Cost reduction target = Total probable cost – total target cost

5. **Implement actions to achieve the cost reduction target**. This involves three sub-steps:

   • **Create a cross-functional team** with empowerment to devise and implement the processes to achieve the cost-reduction target.

   • **Use value engineering or value-added analysis** in the design process. Value engineering consists of breaking down the product into its design elements or functions and challenging each element to determine if it adds value to the customer at the lowest cost. Activities are divided into two categories: those that add value and those that do not add value. For those elements that don't add value the team must present alternatives that will do so. Value engineering was initially developed by General Electric to eliminate any element or function that would not reduce the utility or value to the customer. This results in providing each product, part, or service at a level of quality acceptable to the customer at the lowest cost.

What Are Value-Added Costs or Value-Added Activities?

Value-added costs and activities add value to the product or service in terms of quality or usefulness. Non-value-added costs do not add value. Both types are identified by evaluating their places in the value chain (research and development, product design, manufacturing, marketing, distribution, and customer service) and, once identified, those that do not add value are eliminated, thereby reducing costs. Activity-based costing can be used with value engineering to identify activities and cost drivers, with the focus being directed toward reducing the cost driver quantity.

   • **Use kaizen costing to pursue continuous improvement**. The concept of *kaizen* was developed in Japan and means improvement in small steps. Whereas target costing applies to the product cycle prior to entering into production, *kaizen* costing applies to the product after it is introduced into production. Together target costing and *kaizen* costing have been called *life cycle costing*. *Kaizen* costing has been compared to standard costing but it has a different focus. A standard cost system focuses on verifying that the actual costs conform to the standard estimate and identifying deviations. A *kaizen* costing system's focus is on cost reduction through continuous improvement by bettering existing production operations and reducing the costs below those that would be considered standard. The *kaizen* system also has the added objective of verifying that target costing is fully achieved.

Illustration

High Reach Ladder Company manufactures ladders of various heights and sells them to large home improvement stores. It purchases lumber and other minor materials to use in manufacturing these ladders. High Reach has several competitors whose lower prices have resulted in High Reach's losing market share. By lowering its prices by 6% the company believes that it will be more competitive, but this action may result in its failing to meet its profit objective under its current operational practices.

The accountant has developed the costs of existing activities as shown in Exhibit 9-4.

Exhibit 9-4. High Reach Ladder Company Cost Data			
Activity	**Cost Driver**	**Quantity of Cost Driver**	**Cost per Unit of Cost Driver**
Creating, placing, and paying for orders of lumber	Number of orders	300	$60
Receiving completed items from production and storing in warehouse	Loads moved	2,500	$40
Shipping ladders to customers	Number of shipments	500	$70

High Reach projects to sell 24,000 ladders next year, the same as this year. The average sales price per ladder last year was $50. If the company reduces its price by 6%, the selling price would be $47 for next year. The average manufacturing cost per ladder for the past year was $25. The company has a profit objective of $12 per ladder.

What would be the expected operating income, if no changes were made to the basic operations?

Solution

The operating income is computed in Exhibit 9-5. Based on the expected operating income, the company will not achieve the target income of $12 per ladder. The expected revenue per unit that High Reach has established, based on the competitive market price, is $47. The total cost per unit of $36.375 plus the $12.00 target income per unit is $48.375, which exceeds the selling price by $1.375 per unit. This is the gap that High Reach much close in order to remain competitive and profitable.

Exhibit 9-5. High Reach Ladder Company Analysis		
	Total for 24,000 Units (1)	Cost per Unit (1) ÷ 24,000 (2)
Revenues ($47 × 24,000)	$1,128,000	$47.00
Manufacturing cost ($30 × 24,000)	720,000	30.000
Purchasing costs ($60 × 300 orders)	18,000	0.750
Receiving and warehousing ($40 × 2,500)	100,000	4.170
Shipping ($70 × 500)	35,000	1.458
Total costs	$873,000	$36.378

Assume that High Reach has decided to use target costing and reengineer its purchasing, receiving, and warehousing functions to reduce costs but maintain its existing service to the customer. High Reach appointed a cross-functional team that has studied each of these three functions and has selected the following improvements to reduce costs.

- Negotiate longer term contracts with its major suppliers and use **just-in-time** delivery practices to move lumber directly to production to save storage costs and to cut the number of purchase orders for lumber to 200 per year and the costs per order to $50.

- Moving the receiving area to a more optimal location between the production completion area and the storage warehouses to cut down on movement time for finished ladders, and redesigning the storage areas to more efficiently store and retrieve items for shipment. These improvements are expected to reduce the number of load movements to 2,200 and the cost per load to $35. These improvements are also expected to reduce the cost of shipments to $65.

What is the target cost per unit? Compare the target cost to the currently probable cost in Exhibit 9-5. Will the company achieve its target income if the above changes are successful?

Solution

The target cost per unit is

$47 – 12 = $35

Compared with the current probable cost, the company needs cost reductions of $33,000 to achieve the operating profit objective:

$36.38 × $35.00 (24,000) = $33,120

If the reengineering succeeds, the new operational income will be as shown in Exhibit 9-6. Through reengineering the three functions as proposed, High Reach will be able to reach its target cost and target income objectives.

Exhibit 9-6. High Reach Ladder Company Analysis		
	Total for 24,000 Units (1)	Cost per Unit (1) ÷ 24,000
Revenues ($47 × 24,000)	$1,128,000	$47.000
Manufacturing cost ($30 × 24,000)	720,000	30.000
Purchasing costs ($50 × 200 orders)	10,000	0.417
Receiving and warehousing ($35 × 2,200)	77,000	3.210
Shipping ($65 × 500)	32,500	1.354
Total costs	$839,500	$34.981

Summary

This chapter discussed pricing decisions, including the economic implications and the costs that are used in the decision making process. First, pricing was discussed from the short-term perspective. In the short term, the concept of relevant costing was applied from the viewpoint of when there was excess capacity and when there was full capacity. Next, long-term decisions were considered. The cost-plus approach starts with the total cost to sell the product or provide a service, and adds a reasonable annual target profit. The contribution margin approach was described as a methodology for considering the impact on profit of changes in the sales prices and their impact on sales demand. Finally, the target costing approach was discussed as a way to plan and manage costs early in the design and development stages of a product life cycle. The detailed steps in applying target costing in a company were discussed.

Practice Problems

The following information pertains to questions 9-1 through 9-2.

The Universal Company manufactures remote control devices for sale to distributors at $60 each. The cost per remote control is shown in the table below. The fixed cost per unit is based on a normal capacity of 24,000 units per year.

Direct materials	$10
Direct labor	$15
Manufacturing overhead (75% variable and 25% fixed)	$10
Selling and administrative costs (30% variable and 70% fixed)	$15

Universal has received a special order from a large electronics manufacturer for 1,000 remote control units at $40 each. The contract would require Universal to include the electronics company's brand on each remote unit. The only selling and administrative costs that would be incurred on this order would be $2 per unit for shipping. Universal expects to sell 20,000 units through regular channels next year and the existing customers would have no knowledge of this sale, if it were accepted.

9-1 What is the amount of costs that are not relevant to this decision?

A. $50.00

B. $13.00

C. $12.00

D. $52.00

9-2 What is the minimum price that the company should accept for this offer?

A. $34.50

B. $39.00

C. $40.00

D. $52.00

9-3 In setting the price for a special order to be manufactured in the operating cycle, it is important to consider:

A. Whether the sale will be revealed to existing customers

B. Which costs are relevant in the short run

C. Whether the capacity can be used for other purposes

D. All of the above

9-4 Sure Aim Gun Company is bidding on a U.S. government contract for automatic weapons and needs to determine the best price to ask. The government will pay the cost plus a reasonable profit. The company expects to receive a 20% return on its investment. The bid calls for production of 20,000 rifles per year over a 3-year period. The following table reflects the annual costs that would be associated with the contract:

Number of units required by contract	20,000
Required investment assets	$10,000,000
Manufacturing cost per rifle	$300
Total annual administrative expenses	$1,500,000

Using the cost-plus method, what is the price the company should bid for the rifles?

A. $500

B. $450

C. $475

D. None of the above

9-5 Which of the following economic factors affect the price of a product or service in a competitive market?

A. The elasticity of demand

B. The competitors in the market

C. The desires of the buyer

D. All of the above

The following information pertains to questions 9-6 through 9-7.

ABC Manufacturing sells a product in a competitive market for $100 per unit. The product's current full cost is $83. Senior management conducted a retreat to discuss improving the profitability of the firm. The CEO believes that the company can increase its market share by about 10% by reducing the price of its product to $90 per unit and maintaining its current profitability. The product is currently earning a profit of $20 per unit. Senior management reached a consensus that the costs of the product must be reduced without decreasing the quality of the product.

9-6 What is the target price per unit?

    A. $90

    B. $70

    C. $88

    D. None of the above

9-7 What is the target cost per unit?

    A. $83

    B. $70

    C. $80

    D. None of the above

9-8 Which of the following can be used in achieving a target cost?

    A. Value engineering

    B. Activity-based costing

    C. Cross-functional teams

    D. All of the above

9-9 Easy Shovel Company is a small manufacturer of shovels that sells to distributors in a competitive market. The market-set price per shovel is $11. The company currently manufactures and sells 30,000 units per year. Its investment base is composed of current and fixed assets of $300,000. The company desires a 20% return on investment. The target cost per shovel would be:

    A. $2.00

    B. $7.00

    C. $9.00

    D. $8.00

9-10 Continuous improvement occurring after a new product has been introduced into production is normally used with which of the following:

    A. Kaizen costing

    B. Cost-plus pricing

    C. Value engineering

    D. None of the above

Solutions to Practice Problems

9-1 B

All fixed costs would not be relevant, since the company has excess capacity.

$(\$10 \times 0.25) + (\$15 \times 0.70) = \$13.00$

9-2 A

All manufacturing variable costs, including variable overhead, plus the $2 shipping costs would be relevant. All other selling and administrative costs would be avoided and not relevant.

$\$10.00 + 15.00 + (\$10.00 \times 0.75) + \$2.00 = \$34.50$

9-3 D

9-4 C

$$\$300 + \left(\frac{\$1,500,000 + (\$10,000,000 \times 0.2)}{20,000 \, \text{units}} \right) = \$300 + \left(\frac{\$3,500,000}{20,000} \right)$$

$$= \$475$$

9-5 D

9-6 A

9-7 B

$$\text{Target cost} = \text{Target price per unit} - \text{Target operating income per unit}$$
$$\text{Target cost} = \$90 - 20 = \$70$$

9-8 D

9-9 C

$$\text{Target cost} = \$11.00 - \left(\frac{\$300,000 \times .20}{30,000} \right) = \$11.00 - \$2.00 = \$9.00$$

9-10 A

CHAPTER 10

Profit Planning Using Master Budgets

In this chapter the focus is on profit planning as one of the systems that aid managers in achieving the overall goals of the company. The topics covered are the purposes of budgeting, the overall budgeting framework, and the steps in preparing a master budget.

Purposes and Benefits of Profit Planning

Profit planning is one of the most important functions in any organization. In a business profits just don't happen; careful planning is required to guide all parts of the organization toward its strategic long- and short-term goals. A budget is simply a detailed, quantified financial plan of action that depicts how the organization will acquire resources of different types and how these resources are to be used during a specific period of time, usually 1 year. The major purposes of profit planning are:

- **Providing a written plan of action that facilitates proactive management**. Diverse elements of the organization are guided toward a common set of goals and profit objectives. Managers are forced to develop a set of actions ahead of time and quantify them in financial terms.

- **Facilitating communication and coordination**, particularly in complex organizational structures. Profit planning provides the means for top management to make lower management levels aware of the organization's overall goals and profit objectives. Similarly, it provides lower-level managers the opportunity to participate in the budgeting process by providing input on what the profit and cost objectives should be. This communication and coordination process allows for the balancing of goals vertically from top management to lower management and horizontally by the balancing of goals across the various functions in an organization, such as production, sales, distribution, and support functions.

- **Linking management's goals and objectives to its operations**. Is the budget realistic and attainable? By preparing the budget "bottom up" the manager must think through the implication of profit objectives in terms of the underlying operations. This process not only tests the workability of the profit objectives but prods the manager to change the underlying operations to reach these objectives as well.

- **Providing a mechanism to hold managers responsible for their performance**. The various financial targets can be used as benchmarks to evaluate subsequent performance. This allows managers to evaluate the effectiveness and efficiency of managers and subunits in the organization. This will be discussed in subsequent chapters.

The Behavioral Aspects of Profit Planning and Budgeting

Profit planning is a process that affects human behavior. In this context, management should use the process to motivate all participants in the organization to undertake actions that achieve the overall goals of the organization. If successful, this will result in the goals of individuals and subunits of the organization meshing

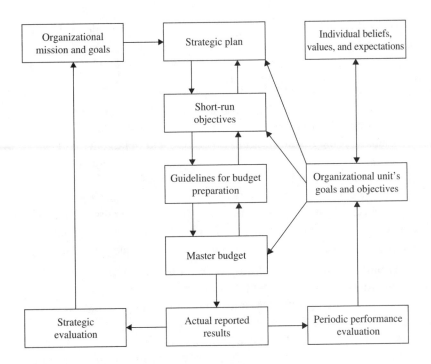

Figure 10-1   Goal congruence in the budget process.

with those of top management. This idea is known as **goal congruence**, which is summarized in Figure 10-1.

Long-range, strategic planning starts 12 to 18 months in advance of the next operating year by senior management. From 6 to 3 months before the next year, management translates the overall strategic goals into annual objectives, such as project objectives for the coming year. From these objectives budget guidelines are prepared and forwarded to lower levels of the organization. Each subunit prepares its budget based on managers' assessments of short-run plans needed by the subunit to achieve the overall objectives for the next operating year. The individual participant's goals, expectations, and values are embodied in these potential plans.

When the budget is submitted to the next higher level a process of negotiation should result in an acceptable budget that is agreed upon by both higher and lower management levels. The budget then becomes a device to motivate all levels of the organization to achieve the overall goals and objectives of the organization.

Once the year begins the budget becomes a benchmark to compare actual performance. Significant variances from the budget should be investigated and corrective action taken where necessary by each organizational unit. After each budget year ends the cycle commences again. The budget results should feed into strategic evaluation, where the organizational mission, goals, and strategic plans are adjusted as necessary.

From this discussion and the graph in Figure 10-1, several **behavioral factors** relating to profit planning and budgeting can be inferred:

- **Use a participative approach.** Behavioral science has found that allowing individuals to participate in the budgeting process results in their "internalizing" the resulting profit objectives and believing them to be their own. Participation is best achieved by preparing the budget from the bottom up and allowing the various elements to negotiate their units objectives into the final budget plan. Budgeting works best through this process and works worst when it is imposed "top down" and used as a club to pressure employees into achieving the profit objectives. Management should employ a positive approach when using a profit planning process.

- **Top management must support and participate in the budgeting process.** This involves two aspects: (1) being involved in setting the goals and negotiating the final profit plan, and holding lower-level managers responsible for achieving the adopted profit plan when it is finalized. If lower managers observe that top management shows little interest in the budgeting process, they will most likely consider it unimportant. This will severely weaken its usefulness in guiding the organization.

- **Set realistic targets.** Management should set revenue and cost targets to be "tight" but attainable. If the targets are too tight, the participants will become discouraged. If they are too easy, the participants will become apathetic and not work effectively toward achieving the underlying goals of the budget.

- **Make budgets understandable.** The terminology, format, and amount of detail should be such that participants understand the budgets. Obscure terms, confusing formats, and excessive details will help torpedo the profit planning process.

Budgeting Obstacles

- **Budgets must be flexible.** Outcomes don't always agree with the plan because conditions may change. Thus, the budget may need to be updated during the year to address any significant changes in conditions. In addition, if budgets are used for performance evaluation, changes in conditions need to be taken into consideration when judging performance. To accommodate changing conditions some companies use a **rolling budget**. A rolling budget is always current as of a specific period. For example, a 4-quarter rolling budget is kept relatively current by adding a new quarter and dropping the most recent quarter each 3-month period. A rolling budget forces management to think about the next 12 months each time it prepares for the new quarter.

- **Budgets are based on estimates.** Budget numbers should never be taken as actual data. They are based on a projected set of conditions. If conditions change, the budget numbers are no longer valid and the budget may need to be changed.

- **Budgets should be agreed upon and accepted by all participants.** Without the support of everyone who has a stake in the budgeting process, the outcome will be less likely to succeed.

- **Budgets Contain Budgetary Slack.** Organizations are composed of humans and humans may underestimate revenues and overestimate costs. This is often done so that the individual can more easily "beat the budget." Also, in budgeting for fixed costs, lower managers may assume the organizational hierarchy will cut their requests for resource allocation, and may therefore overstate their needs. Management can offset budgetary slack by providing incentives for those who more accurately predict their revenues and costs. Also, management should use the budget in a positive way—not "beating lower managers over the head" when they don't meet expectations.

The Master Budget Framework

Figure 10-2 depicts the individual interconnecting budgets that make up the master budget.

Steps in Preparing the Master Budget

The preparation of the master budget is somewhat mechanical in nature in that it follows a set routine of procedures and methods to arrive at the final product. While there may be variations from business to business, the steps in this section are typical of what are used in most organizations. An extended illustration is used that includes these steps and related formulas to prepare each of the budgets. The illustration uses a manufacturing company, since it has the most complicated of all budgets. The master budget for service and merchandising companies can be easily adapted from the illustration below.

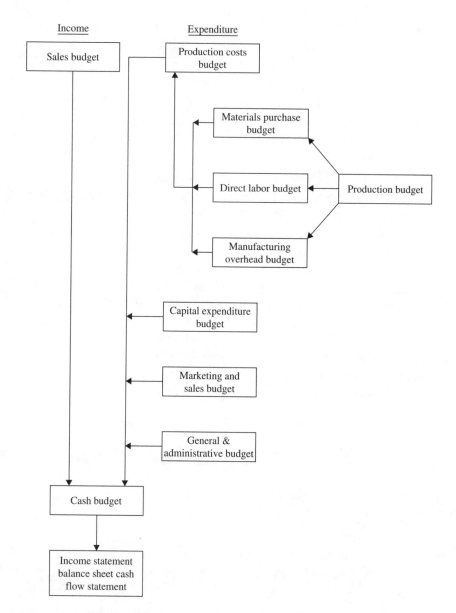

Figure 10-2   The master budget relationships.

Illustration

To exemplify the manufacturing case the Thai-Plus Teak Chair Company will be used.[1] The Thai-Plus Teak Chair Company makes and sells high-quality teak lawn chairs to distributors and large home improvement retailers. It manufactures several types of chairs that require the same basic amount of teak lumber but may vary in style and shape. The company has been steadily losing money over the past 3 years, and has established a long-range planning system that culminates in a master budget for the coming year with the expectation of improving its profit situation. The controller has been asked to prepare a master budget for the first time for the fourth quarter of 20XX. Since the budget preparation is being performed in August 20XX, the ending balance sheet for September 30, 20XX has to be estimated; it is presented in Exhibit 10-1.

The controller has established the following **budget assumptions** for preparation of the master budget:

- Numbers for sales are estimated to be 6,000, 6,300, and 5,400 for October, November, and December, respectively.

- The sales price is estimated to be $400 per chair.

- The ending balance of finished goods is estimated to be 1,100, 1,000, and 800 units for October, November, and December, respectively. The company has an inventory control model that assists in developing these numbers.

- The beginning inventory of finished goods at October 1 was 1,000 units at a unit cost of $340.

- A minimum of 1,500 standard units of teak lumber is required at the end of each period.

- The purchase of teak lumber is in a standard unit of 8″× 5 ½″× ½″ each and costs $50 each.

- Four units of lumber are required for each finished chair.

- One and a half hours of labor are required for each chair at an average labor cost of $15 per hour.

- The company uses the process cost system and the weighted-average method.

---

[1] While the budget illustration is prepared manually, in this illustration most large companies have a computerized financial planning model that consists of many mathematical interactions between the budget components from the various organizational components. Smaller companies may use computer spreadsheets, such as Excel, to prepare their budgets. The spreadsheet has an assumption section at its beginning, where the major inputs are stated. As each budget is prepared, the relevant input(s) is "pulled" into the spreadsheet and the budget is computed based on that assumption. This allows the analysts to assume different scenarios ("what if") and to recompute different results at the push of a key.

- The cash collection patterns for sales and accounts receivable are as follows:
  - 20% of sales are for cash, 80% are on credit; of the 80% credit sales:
    - 40% take a 2% discount, by paying during the first half of the month of sale
    - 60% do not take the discount
  - Of the 60% not taking the discount:
    - 20% pay in the second half of month of sale
    - 50% in the month following sale
    - 29% in second month following sale
    - 1% are uncollectible
- The cash disbursements pattern for purchases (accounts payable) are as follows:
  - All purchases of lumber are assumed to be on credit and credited to accounts payable.
  - A discount of 2% is given, if Thai-Plus pays for each month's purchases within the month of purchase. 40% of purchases are paid within this period.
  - Thai-Plus must pay the remaining amount of purchases within 30 days and no discount is received.
  - The $780,000 accounts payable balance in Exhibit 10-1 represents 60% of September purchases.
  - A minimum cash balance of $100,000 must be maintained.

Exhibit 10-1.   Estimated Balance Sheet, September 30, 20XX
Thai-Plus Chair Company
Balance Sheet
for the Period Ending September 30, 20XX

Assets			Liabilities & Stockholders Equity	
Current Assets			**Current Liabilities**	
Cash		$100,000	Accounts payable	$780,000
Accounts receivable	$1,070,400			
Less:				
Allowance for uncollectible accts	(19,680)	1,050,720	Current liabilities	$780,000
Inventories				
Teak lumber inventory (1,500 units)	$75,000			

Exhibit 10-1. (Continued)					
Work in process		0			
Finished goods (1,000 units)		340,000	455,000		
Total current assets			$1,565,720	Stockholders equity	
				Common stock	$2,945,720	
Plant, property and equipment	$3,500,000			Retained earnings	640,000	3,585,720
Less:					
Accumulated depreciation	(700,000)		2,800,000		
Total assets			$4,365,720	Total Liabilities & Stockholders Equity	$4,365,720

Step 1: The Sales Budget

The sales budget is the first schedule to be prepared as it is the foundation for the preparation of several of the subsequent budgets. This budget is prepared in units and dollars and the units are based on a sales forecast by the sales department. Thai-Plus uses a conference of salespersons to develop a composite forecast based on conditions in the various sales territories. The sales forecast and budget are shown in Exhibit 10-2.

Exhibit 10-2. Sales Budget for Quarter Ending December 31, 20XX				
	October	November	December	Total
Sales in units	6,000	6,300	5,400	17,700
Sales in dollars	$2,400,000	$2,520,000	$2,160,000	$7,080,000

Step 2: The Production Budget

The sales budget is the basis for the production budget. The production budget can be expressed in a formula:

(Sales in units) + (Desired ending finished goods inventory) = Total units required

(Total units required) – (Expected beginning inventory) = Units to be produced

An adequate ending inventory of finished goods must be in stock to ensure that customer demands for the next month are met. This quantity is based on inventory control methods established by management. Production managers have estimated the ending inventories as shown in Exhibit 10-3.

Exhibit 10-3. Production Budget for Quarter Ending December 31, 20XX				
	October	November	December	Total
Sales in units (from Exhibit 10-2)	6,000	6,300	5,400	17,700
+ Desired ending inventory	1,100	1,000	800	2,900
= Total needed	7,100	7,300	6,200	20,600
– Beginning inventory	1,000	1,100	1,000	3,100
= units to be produced	6,100	6,200	5,200	17,500

Step 3: The Raw Materials Purchases Budget

The raw materials budget is necessary to ensure adequate materials are available to meet the production needs on a timely basis. The desired ending inventory is based on management's inventory control policies. Production needs four units of lumber for each finished chair. Thai-Plus has instituted **Just-In-Time (JIT)** inventory procedures with suppliers to keep inventory at a minimum. The raw materials budget can be expressed as a formula:

What Is Just-In-Time (JIT)?

JIT is a process of purchasing, receiving, and placing inventory into production just when it is needed. This cuts the amount of inventory to be held in stock, thus reducing inventory investment and storage costs. This requires strong contractual ties and coordination with vendors to assure that materials are received when required.

(Raw materials required for production) + (Desired ending inventory of raw materials) = (total raw materials required) – Expected beginning inventory of raw materials) = Raw materials required to be purchased

The Thai-Plus Purchases Budget is shown in Exhibit 10-4.

Exhibit 10-4.   Raw Materials Purchases Budget for Quarter Ending December 31, 20XX

	October	November	December	Total
Production in units (from Exhibit 10-3)	6,100	6,200	5,200	17,500
Lumber needed per finished chair	×4	×4	×4	×4
Units required for production	24,400	24,800	20,800	70,000
+ Desired ending inventory	1,500	1,500	1,500	4,500
Total units of lumber required	25,900	26,300	22,300	74,500
– beginning inventory	1,500	1,500	1,500	4,500
Lumber units to be purchased	24,400	24,800	20,800	70,000
× Price per unit	×$50	×$50	×$50	×$50
Total cost of lumber purchase	$1,220,000	$1,240,000	$1,040,000	$3,500,000

Step 4: The Direct Labor Budget

The production department estimates the number of hours that is required to complete one finished chair. Some companies may use a standard costing system (see Chapter 12), in which case the estimated hours is the standard hours per finished unit. The average cost per hour includes salary, fringe benefits, and payroll taxes. The direct labor budget is based on the production budget and can be expressed in the following formula:

(Units to be produced) × (number of direct labor hours required for one finished unit) = (Number of direct labor hours required) × (Direct labor cost per hour) = Total budgeted direct labor cost

The Direct Labor Budget for Thai-Plus is shown in Exhibit 10-5.

Exhibit 10-5.   Direct Labor Budget for Quarter Ending December 31, 20XX

	October	November	December	Total
Production in units (from Exhibit 10-3)	6,100	6,200	5,200	17,500
Direct labor needed per finished chair	×1.5	×1.5	×1.5	×1.5
Total hours required for production	9,150	9,300	7,800	26,250
× Price per hour	×$15	×$15	×$15	×$15
Total direct labor cost	$137,250	$139,500	$117,000	$393,750

Step 5: The Factory Overhead Budget

In developing the factory overhead budget, management uses direct labor hours to allocate overhead. The fixed and variable cost components of each cost item must be separated using techniques described in Chapter 7. The controller has separated these costs and developed the prediction formula shown in Exhibit 10-6. The overhead cost for each month is the total fixed cost plus the unit variable cost times the number of direct hours.

Exhibit 10-6.	Factory Overhead Budget for Quarter Ending December 31, 20XX					
	Prediction Formula					
	Total Fixed Cost (TFC)	**Unit Variable Cost (UVC)**	**October**	**November**	**December**	**Total**
Number of direct labor hours (Exhibit 10-5)			9,150	9,300	7,800	26,250
Overhead item:						
Depreciation	$200,000	0	$200,000	$200,000	$200,000	$600,000
Indirect material	0	14	128,100	130,200	109,200	367,500
Indirect labor	37,500	5	83,250	84,000	76,500	243,750
Utilities	25,000	10	116,500	118,000	103,000	337,500
Property tax	7,500	0	7,500	7,500	7,500	22,500
Insurance	5,000	0	5,000	5,000	5,000	15,000
Maintenance	25,000	20	208,000	211,000	181,000	600,000
Total cost	$300,000	$49	$748,350	$755,700	$682,200	$2,186,250
Less depreciation			($200,000)	($200,000)	($200,000)	($200,000)
Cash outflow			$548,350	$555,700	$482,200	$1,586,250

Step 6: The Selling, General, and Administrative (SG&A) Budget

The SG&A budget is prepared after budget estimates are submitted by the marketing and administrative departments. As done in the factory overhead budget, the fixed and variable costs must be separated using techniques described in Chapter 7.

The controller has separated these costs and developed the formula shown in Exhibit 10-7. The total SG&A costs for each month are the total fixed cost plus the unit variable cost times the number of sales units.

Exhibit 10-7. Selling, General, and Administrative Budget for Quarter Ending December 31, 20XX

| | Prediction Formula | | | | | |
	Total Fixed Cost (TFC)	Unit Variable Cost (UVC)	October	November	December	Total
Total sales forecast (Exhibit 10-2)			$2,400,000	$2,520,000	$2,160,000	$7,080,000
SG&A item:						
Depreciation	50,000	0	50,000	50,000	50,000	150,000
Supplies	0	0.01	24,000	25,200	21,600	70,800
Miscellaneous	10,000	0.01	12,400	12,520	12,160	37,080
Salaries:						
Sales	15,000	0.04	111,000	115,800	101,400	328,200
Administrative	150,000		150,000	150,000	150,000	450,000
Total costs	$225,000	$0.06	$347,400	$353,520	$335,160	$1,036,080
Less depreciation			($50,000)	($50,000)	($50,000)	($150,000)
Cash outflow			$297,400	$303,520	$285,160	$886,080

Step 7: The Cash Collection Budget for Quarter Ending December 31, 20XX

The cash collection budget is prepared by evaluating cash collection patterns resulting from total sales. The collection pattern is determined through an evaluation of payment patterns and projecting those into the next 3 months by considering any change in conditions that may affect this pattern. The payment patterns were determined under the budget assumptions section listed at the beginning of the illustration.

In order to prepare this budget, the controller of Thai-Plus must use the sales data from August and September, 20XX to project collections into the fourth quarter. The August sales were $2,100,000 and the September sales were $2,000,000. The cash collections budget for Thai-Plus is shown in Exhibit 10-8.

Exhibit 10-8. Cash Collections Budget from Sales for the Quarter Ending December 31, 20XX

From:	October	November	December	Total	Discount	Uncollectible
August 20XX sales:						
$2,100,000(0.8)(0.6)(0.29)	$292,320			$292,320		
$2,100,000(0.8)(0.6)(0.01)						$10,080
September 20XX sales:						
$2,000,000(0.8)(0.6)(0.5)	480,000			$480,000		
$2,000,000(0.8)(0.6)(0.29)		$278,400		278,400		
$2,000,000(0.8)(0.6)(0.01)						$9,600
October 20XX sales:						
$2,400,000(0.2)	$480,000			$480,000		
$2,400,000(0.8)(0.4)(0.98)	752,640[a]			752,640	15,360	
$2,400,000(0.8)(0.6)(0.2)	230,400			230,400		
$2,400,000(0.8)(0.6)(0.5)		576,000		576,000		
$2,400,000(0.8)(0.6)(0.29)			334,080	334,080		
$2,400,000(0.8)(0.6)(0.01)						11,520
November 20XX						
$2,520,000(0.2)		504,000		504,000		
$2,520,000(0.8)(0.4)(0.98)		790,272[a]		790,272	16,218	
$2,520,000(0.8)(0.6)(0.2)		241,920		241,920		
$2,520,000(0.8)(0.6)(0.5)			604,800	604,800		
December 20XX						
$2,160,000(0.2)			432,000	432,000		
$2,160,000(0.8)(0.4)(0.98)			677,376[a]	677,376	13,824	
$2,160,000(0.8)(0.6)(0.2)			207,360	207,360		
Totals	$2,235,360	$2,390,592	$2,255,616	$6,881,568	$45,312	$31,200

[a]Net of discount to determine cash flow. The gross amount for accrual purposes can be determined by dividing the net amount by 0.98, i.e., 100% − 0.02.

Step 8: Determination of Accounts Receivable, Allowance for Uncollectible Accounts, and Sales Discounts Account Balances

In order to prepare the pro forma financial statements at the end of the budgeting process, the accounts receivable, allowance for uncollectible accounts, and sales discounts account balances must be projected to the end of the quarter. These balances are based on the accrual method of accounting in accord with GAAP; therefore, the credit to accounts receivable for cash collections must be converted back to the original sales amount that was debited to the accounts receivable (see footnote *a* to Exhibit 10-8). In addition, for analysis expediency, all sales (including cash sales) are debited to accounts receivable and then cash sales are credited immediately while credit sales are credited as collected. The analysis of the accounts receivable account is shown in Exhibit 10-9.

Exhibit 10-9. Analysis of Accounts Receivable	Debit	Credit
9/30/20XX Balance	$1,070,400	
October 20XX sales (Exhibit 10-2)	2,400,000	
November 20XX sales (Exhibit 10-2)	2,520,000	
December 20XX sales (Exhibit 10-2)	2,160,000	
Collections in October from beginning A/R ($292,320 + $480,000)		772,320
Cash sales in October (Exhibit 10-8)		480,000
Credit collections subject to discount (80%) (cash received $752,640) (Exhibit 10-8)		768,000
Cash collections not subject to discount (20%) (Exhibit 10-8)		230,400
Collections in November from beginning A/R (Exhibit 10-8)		278,400
Cash sales in November (Exhibit 10-8)		504,000
Collections in November from October sales (Exhibit 10-8)		576,000
Credit collections subject to discount (Exhibit 10-8) (cash received $790,272)		806,400
Credit collections not subject to discount (Exhibit 10-8)		241,920
Cash sales in December (Exhibit 10-8)		432,000
Collections in December from October sales (Exhibit 10-8)		334,080
Collections in December from November sales (Exhibit 10-8)		604,800
Credit collections subject to discount (Exhibit 10-8) (cash received, $677,376)		691,200
Credit collections not subject to discount (Exhibit 10-8)		207,360
Totals	$8,150,400	$6,926,880
12/31/20XX Balance	$1,223,520	

The analysis of the allowance for uncollectible accounts is shown in Exhibit 10-10.

Exhibit 10-10. Analysis of Allowance for Uncollectible Accounts		
	Debit	**Credit**
9/30/20XX Balance		$19,680
October estimate of uncollectibles (Exhibit 10-8)		11,520
November estimate of uncollectibles (Exhibit 10-8)		12,096
December estimate of uncollectibles (Exhibit 10-8)		10,368
12/31/20XX Balance		$53,664

The analysis of the Sales Discounts account is shown in Exhibit 10-11.

Exhibit 10-11. Analysis of Sales Discounts		
	Debit	**Credit**
October estimate of discounts (Exhibit 10-8)	$15,360	
November estimate of discounts (Exhibit 10-8)	16,128	
December estimate of discounts (Exhibit 10-8)	13,824	
12/31/20XX Balance	$45,312	

Step 9: Cash Disbursements Budget for Quarter Ending December 31, 20XX

The payment pattern for purchases is outlined in the budget assumptions section above. The cash disbursements budget is based on the purchases information shown in Exhibit 10-4. The cash disbursement budget is shown in Exhibit 10-12.

Exhibit 10-12. Cash Disbursement Budget for Purchases, the Quarter Ending December 31, 20XX					
Payment for:	**October**	**November**	**December**	**Total**	**Discount**
September 20XX purchases: 60%) (Exhibit 10-1)	780,000			780,000	
October 20XX purchases (Exhibit 10-4):					
$1,220,000(0.4)(0.98)	478,240[a]			478,240	9,760
$1,220,000(0.6)		732,000		732,000	

Exhibit 10-12.   *(Continued)*

November 20XX purchases (Exhibit 10-4)					
$1,240,000(0.40)(0.98)	486,080[a]			486,080	9,920
$1,240,000 (0.6)			744,000	744,000	
December 20XX purchases (Exhibit 10-4)					
$1,040,000(0.4)(0.98)	_____	_____	407,680[a]	407,680	8,320
Total disbursements	$1,258,240	$1,218,080	$1,151,680	$3,628,000	$28,000

[a]Net of discount to determine cash flow. The gross amount of purchases for accrual purposes can be determined by dividing the net amount by 0.98, i.e., 100% – 0.02.

Step 10: Determination of Accounts Payable and Purchase Discounts Account Balances

In order to prepare the pro forma financial statements at the end of the budgeting process, the accounts payable and purchases discounts account balances must be projected to the end of the quarter. These balances are based on the accrual method of accounting in accord with GAAP; therefore, the debit to accounts payable for cash payments must be converted back to the original purchase amount that was credited to the accounts payable (see footnote *a* to Exhibit 10-12). The analysis of the accounts payable account is shown in Exhibit 10-13.

Exhibit 10-13.   Analysis of Accounts Payable

	Debit	Credit
Balance at 9/30/20XX (Exhibit 10-1)		$780,000
October purchases (Exhibit 10-4)		1,220,000
November purchases (Exhibit 10-4)		1,240,000
December purchases (Exhibit 10-4)		1,040,000
October payments for September purchases (60%) (Exhibit 10-12)	780,000	
October payments for September purchases (Exhibit 10-12) subject to discount (cash paid $478,240)	488,000	
November payments for October purchases (Exhibit 10-12)	732,000	
		(Continued)

Exhibit 10-13. *(Continuted)*		
November payments for November purchases subject to a discount (cash paid $486,080) (Exhibit 10-12)	496,000	
December payments for November purchases (Exhibit 10-12)	744,000	
December payments for December purchases (Exhibit 10-12) (Cash paid $407,680)	416,000	
Totals	$3,656,000	$4,280,000
12/31/20XX Balance	$624,000	

Step 11: Determination of the Purchases Discount Account Balance

The Purchases Discount account balance is determined in Exhibit 10-14.

Exhibit 10-14. Analysis of Purchases Discount Account		
	Debit	**Credit**
October discounts (Exhibit 10-12)		$9,760
November discounts (Exhibit 10-12)		9,920
December discounts (Exhibit 10-12)		8,320
12/31/20XX Balance		$28,000

Step 12: The Capital Expenditures Budget

During the long-term planning process Thai-Plus management decided on investing in additional trucks and to upgrade its computer system. The capital expenditures budget is shown in Exhibit 10-15.

Exhibit 10-15. Capital Expenditures Budget for Quarter Ending December 31, 20XX				
	October	**November**	**December**	**Total**
Purchase of trucks	$100,000	0	0	$100,000
Purchase of computer system upgrades	0	0	$20,000	20,000
Totals	$100,000	0	$20,000	$120,000

Step 13: Expected Cash Budget for the Quarter Ending 12/31/20XX

Now that the cash collections from sales and the cash disbursements for purchases have been determined, the expected cash budget can be prepared. The company requires that any excess cash in a given month be temporarily invested on a short-term basis, and any cash deficiency be covered with a short-term loan. The company has a requirement that a minimum cash balance of $100,000 be maintained. The cash flow statement is shown in Exhibit 10-16.

Exhibit 10-16. Expected Cash Budget for the Quarter Ending December 31, 20XX				
	October	November	December	Total
RECEIPTS				
Beginning cash balance (Exhibit 10-1)	$100,000	$100,120	$100,000	$100,000
Cash collections (Exhibit 10-8)	2,235,360	2,390,592	2,255,616	6,881,568
Cash available before financing activities	$2,335,360	$2,490,712	$2,355,616	$6,981,568
DISBURSEMENTS				
Purchases of materials (Exhibit 10-12)	$1,258,240	$1,218,080	$1,151,680	$3,628,000
Direct labor payroll (Exhibit 10-5)	137,250	139,500	117,000	393,750
Factory overhead costs (excluding depreciation) (Exhibit 10-6)	548,350	555,700	482,200	586,250
SG&A expenses (excluding depreciation) (Exhibit 10-7)	297,400	303,520	285,160	886,080
Total cash disbursements	$2,241,240	$2,216,800	$2,036,040	$6,494,080
Cash excess (deficit)	$94,120	$273,912	$319,576	$487,488[a]
Minimum balance required	(100,000)	(100,000)	(100,000)	(100,000)
Cash available (required)	($5,880)	$173,912	$219576	$387,488
FINANCING				
Loans (repayments)[b]	$106,000	($106,000)	0	0
Sell (purchase) investments	0	(67,912)	(199,000)	(266,912)
Purchased trucks	(100,000)	0	0	(100,000)
Purchased computers	0	0	(20,000)	(20,000)
Net planned financing	$6,000	($173,912)	($219,000)	($386,912)
Ending cash balance	$100,120	$100,000	$100576	$100,576

[a]Totals horizontally will not agree with totals vertically because beginning cash is counted more than once.
[b]Loans made in $1,000 denominations.

Step 14: Prepare Pro Forma Cost of Goods Manufactured Statement for the Quarter Ending December 31, 20XX

Prior to preparation of the balance sheet, the statement of cost of goods manufactured must be prepared. The statement is shown in Exhibit 10-17.

Exhibit 10-17. Pro Forma Cost of Goods Manufactured Statement for Quarter Ending December 31, 20XX		
Beginning work in process		0[a]
Cost of raw materials used:		
Beginning raw materials balance (Exhibit 10-1)	$75,000	
Net purchases of raw materials (Exhibits 10-13, 10-14)	3,472,000	
Total raw materials available for production	$3,547,000	
Ending raw materials balance	75,000[b]	
Cost of raw materials used (Exhibit 10-4)	$3,472,000	
Cost of factory direct labor (Exhibit 10-5)	393,750	
Cost factory overhead (Exhibit 10-6)	2,186,250	
Total manufacturing costs		$6,052,000
Ending work in process		0
Cost of goods manufactured		$6,052,000

[a]For illustration purposes, the beginning and ending work in process inventories are assumed to be zero.
[b]Minimum balance required; see the assumptions section at the beginning of this illustration.

Step 15: Prepare Pro Forma Income Statement for Quarter Ending December 31, 20XX

The projected income statement for Thai-Plus is presented in Exhibit 10-18. This statement is prepared using the accrual accounting method in accord with GAAP.

Exhibit 10-18.   Pro Forma Income Statement
Thai-Plus Chair Company
October 1–December 31, 20XX

Sales		$7,080,000
Less: Sales discounts		(45,312)
Net sales		$7,034,688
Cost of goods sold:		
Finished goods inventory, 9/30/20XX (Exhibit 10-1)	340,000	
Cost of goods manufactured (Exhibit 10-17)	6,052,000	
Cost of goods available for sale	6,392,000	
Less: Finished goods inventory 12/31/20XX[a]	276,800	6,115,200
Income from operations		919,488
Bad debt expense[b]	33,984	
SG&A Expenses (Exhibit10-7)	1,036,080	1,070,064
		(150,576)
Interest revenue[c]		1,335
Income before taxes		(149,241)
Income taxes (assume rate of 40%) (refund)		59,696
Net Income		($89,545)

---

[a]Finished goods in units:

Beginning finished goods inventory	1,000
Units produced (Exhibit 10-3)	17,500
Units available for sale	18,500
Sales (Exhibit 10-2)	17,700
Ending finished goods inventory	800
Cost per unit ($6,052,000/17,500)*	×$346
Ending finished goods inventory	$276,800

[b]Bad debt expense:

Total sales	$7,080,000
× Percent of credit sales	0.80
Credit sales	$5,664,000
× Percent not taking discount	×0.60
Possible bad debts	$3,398,400
× Percent estimated uncollectible	×0.01
Estimated bad debts	$33,984

[c]Interest revenue ($266,913 × .06 × (30/360)) = 1,335

*Since the beginning and ending inventories are the same, the unit cost is based solely on the production costs during the current period.

Step 16: Prepare Pro Forma Balance Sheet for Quarter Ending December 31, 20XX

The pro forma balance is prepared next and is shown in Exhibit 10-19.

Exhibit 10-19. Estimated Balance Sheet, September 30, 20XX
Thai-Plus Chair Company
Balance Sheet
for the Period Ending December 31, 20XX

Assets			Liabilities & Stockholders Equity		
Current Assets			**Current Liabilities**		
Cash		$100,576	Accounts payable		$624,000
Interest receivable		1,335			
Income tax refund receivable		59,696			
Accounts receivable	$1,223,520				
Less:					
Allowance for uncollectible accts	(53,664)	1,169,856	Current liabilities		$624,000
Investment		266,912			
Inventories					
Teak lumber inventory (1,500 units)	$75,000				
Finished goods (800 × $346) units)	276,800	351,800			
Total current assets		$1,950,175	Stockholders equity		
			Common stock	$2,945,720	
Plant, property, and equipment	$3,620,000[a]		Retained earnings	550,455[c]	3,496,175
Less:					
Accumulated depreciation	(1,450,000)[b]	2,170,000			
Total assets		$4,120,175	Total Liabilities & Stockholders Equity		$4,120,175

[a]Plant, property, and equipment:
Beginning balance (Exhibit 10-1)	$3,500,000
Purchases of trucks & computers	120,000
Ending balance	$3,620,000

[b]Accumulated depreciation:
Beginning balance (Exhibit 10-1)	$700,000
Factory depreciation (Exhibit 10-6)	600,000
SG&A depreciation (Exhibit 10-7)	150,000
	$1,450,000

[c]Retaining earnings:
Beginning balance (Exhibit 10-1)	$640,000
Net loss (Exhibit 10-18)	(89,545)
Ending balance	$550,455

Step 17: Prepare the Pro Forma Cash Flow Statement

The final budget schedule is the pro forma cash flow statement, which is shown in Exhibit 10-20. Data from the cash budget, income statement, and the balance sheet feed into this statement. The direct method (using direct cash flows) was used to prepare this cash flow statement. Another approach, the indirect method, starts with net income on an accrual basis and adjusts each item to arrive at the cash basis. For example, depreciation, which does not involve cash, would be added back to net income. Either method is acceptable for external reporting but many internal managers prefer the direct method, since it provides more information on the source of cash flows.

Exhibit 10-20.
Thai-Plus Chair Company
Pro Forma Cash Flow Statement
for the Quarter Ending December 31, 20XX

OPERATING ACTIVITIES			
Cash collections from sales (Exhibit 10-8)		$6,881,568	
Cash payments			
For manufacturing inventory:			
Raw materials (Exhibit 10-12)	$3,628,000		
Manufacturing payroll (Exhibit 10-6)	393,750		
Manufacturing overhead (Exhibit 10-6)	1,586,250	(5,608,000)	
For nonmanufacturing costs:			
Salaries and wages (Exhibit 10-7)	$778,200		
Supplies (Exhibit 10-7)	70,800		
Miscellaneous	37,080	(886,080)	
Net cash inflow from operations			$387,488
INVESTING ACTIVITIES			
Purchase of trucks and computers (Exhibit 10-16)		$120,000	
Investments in marketable securities		266,912	
Net cash outflow from investing activities			386,912
Net increase in cash			$576

Budget Gap

One of the purposes of budgeting is to guide operations to achieve the profit goal. When the master budget is completed top management should compare the resulting prospective profit to the objectives that were set in the planning process. When there is a negative difference between the profit objective and the profit determined after all of the budgeting steps has been completed, management has a **budget gap**. A critical step for management is to find ways to close this gap. For example, the cost-volume-profit model discussed in Chapter 7 could be used to evaluate ways to improve effectiveness and efficiency. This includes changing sales prices, improving productivity, cutting discretionary fixed costs, or employing better purchasing procedures.

Activity-Based Budgeting

Some companies have extended activity-based management to the budgeting process and labeled it **activity-based budgeting** (ABB). This extension focuses on budgeting overhead costs projected to be consumed by activities that produce and sell products. By computing the budget at the activity level, the budget analyst is able to more accurately estimate costs for that activity.

The application of budgeting to activities follows the steps explained in Chapter 6, except the process is reversed by starting at the activity level and classifying its budget overhead costs into cost hierarchies: unit-level costs, batch-level costs, product-level costs, and facility-level costs (see Chapter 6).

Summary

This chapter presents master budgets as an important tool for planning and decision making. In later chapters the budget will used as a control device to evaluate performance. This chapter explained the purposes, benefits, and limitations of budgets. It then provided an overview of the budgeting process and the relationships among its various elements. The process starts with a sales forecast and sales budget, which form the foundation for the remaining budgets. Next, the production budget is prepared, outlining the production quantities needed to meet the sales forecast. This becomes the basis for budgets of materials, labor, and overhead needs in the factory. Outside the factory, operational budgets are prepared for the sales, general, and administrative functions. Once all of the individual budgets are prepared, a set of pro forma financial statements are prepared that depict the financial performance and financial conditions that will exist, if the company completes its planned operations successfully.

Practice Problems

Use the following information for problems 10-1 through 10-3:

The Clean Hand Company produces a liquid soap for use in dispensers in business restrooms. The sales department has estimated the sales in gallons during the second quarter of 20XX as shown in the following table:

Month	Total Sales
April	$9,000
May	$10,500
June	$7,500

The inventory on hand April 1st was 4,100 gallons. The ending finished goods inventory is budgeted at 30% of the next month's sales. The soap sells for $15 per gallon. Each gallon has a full cost of $12 per gallon. The sales department estimates that July sales will be 8,500 gallons.

10-1 What is the sales budget for May in dollars?

A. $120,700

B. $157,500

C. $171,000

D. $144,000

10-2 Clean Hand's production budget would show how many gallons to be produced in April?

A. 9,950

B. 12,150

C. 8,050

D. 13,100

10-3 How many gallons should be produced in June?

A. 7,800

B. 5,200

C. 5,950

D. 8,050

10-4 Which of the following would be the correct sequence in preparing a master budget?

A. Sales, cash, materials

B. Production, sales, cash

C. Sales, balance sheet, income statement

D. Sales, production, purchases

Use the following information for questions 10-5 through 10-7:

The John Company is preparing its budget for the last 6 months of 20XX. The sales department has estimated the following sales.

July	$100,000	October	$100,000
August	$110,000	November	$90,000
September	$120,000	December	$105,000

The controller projects the following cash collection pattern for sales:

70% of sales are collected in the month of the sale transactions.

20% of sales are collected in the month following the sale transactions.

8% of sales are collected in the second month following the sale transactions.

2% of sales are uncollectible.

10-5 Cash collections for the month of September are:

A. $114,000

B. $116,000

C. $105,000

D. $107,800

10-6 What is the ending balance of accounts receivable for September? Assume that the write-offs occur on the last day of the second month following the sale transaction.

A. $55,000

B. $47,000

C. $44,800

D. $50,000

10-7 How much uncollectible accounts receivable would be written off at the end of September?

A. $2,200

B. $2,000

C. $8,000

D. $2,400

Use the following information for questions 10-8 through 10-9:

XYZ Industries produces T-shirts of various colors and sizes. These shirts are sold to distributors and large retail chain stores. XYZ has developed the unit costs displayed in the table below for the production of one T-shirt. Each T-shirt requires approximately the same amount of material and labor. XYZ purchases pre-dyed cloth for the shirts; therefore, no further treatment is required. XYZ has a normal capacity to produce 5,000 shirts per month over the next year.

Cost Item	Quantity Per Shirt	Cost Per Unit of Input
Direct material	Two square yards	$3 per yard
Direct labor	½ hour	$15.00 per hour
Variable overhead	½ hour	$20.00 per hour
Fixed overhead	–	150% of direct labor cost

10-8 XYZ expects to produce 4,800 units during the next month. What is the total amount of direct labor budgeted for that month?

A. $72,000

B. $48,000

C. $28,800

D. $36,000

10-9 What is the total material cost included in the budget, if the 4,800 units are produced?

A. $33,000

B. $22,000

C. $28,800

D. $50,000

10-10 Handy Wholesale Company is preparing its budget for the next month. The sales forecast is for $1,000,000 in sales. The costs of goods sold are expected to be 35% of sales. Because of favorable negotiation, Handy pays for all purchases at the beginning of the next month after purchase. Next month's beginning inventory is projected to be $60,000 and Handy requires an ending inventory of $50,000. The company projects an accounts payable balance of $300,000 for the end of this month. What is the amount of cash that should be budgeted to pay for purchases during the next month?

A. $300,000

B. $340,000

C. $350,000

D. $400,000

Solutions to Practice Problems

10-1 B

$$10,500 \times \$15 = \$157,500$$

10-2 C

$$[9,000 + (10,500 \times .30)] - 4,100 = 8,050 \text{ gallons}$$

10-3 A

$$7,500 + (8,500 \times 0.3) - (7,500 \times 0.3) = 7,800$$

10-4 D

10-5 A

$$(0.70 \times \$120,000) + (0.20 \times \$110,000) + (0.08 \times \$100,000) = \$114,000$$

10-6 B

$$[\$120,000 \times (1.00 - 0.70)] + [\$110,000 \times (1.00 - 0.70 - 0.20)] = \$47,000$$

10-7 B

$$\$100,000 \times 0.02 = \$2,000$$

10-8 D

$$4,800 \times \tfrac{1}{2} \times \$15 = \$36,000$$

10-9 C

$$\$3 \times 2 \text{ yards} \times 4,800 = \$28,800$$

10-10 A

Since the company pays for all purchases the following month, only the beginning accounts payable would be due.

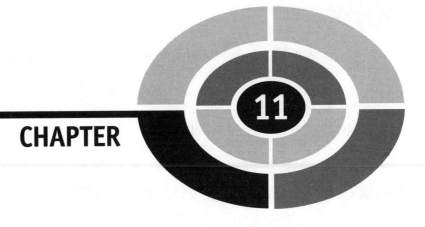

Planning and Performance Evaluation: Using Flexible Budgets

This chapter describes flexible budgeting as a tool for planning and controlling overhead costs. It will explore flexible budgeting for planning purposes, including activity-based budgets (ABB); a general model for financial performance evaluation using flexible budgeting; and flexible budgeting for control purposes.

A **flexible budget** is a tool for planning and controlling overhead costs in manufacturing, merchandising, and service organizations. For planning purposes, it is prepared *ex ante* (before the fact) by projecting both variable and fixed cost over the budget period. For control purposes it is prepared *ex post* (after the fact) by adjusting the budget to the output actually achieved.

Flexible Budgets for Planning

A flexible budget, as defined above, can be better understood by comparing it to a static budget. A **static budget** is a detailed plan of revenues and expenses projections based on *one level* of activity. It ignores the impact of changing volume levels on revenues and costs. Generally, the overall master budget is prepared using the static budget model. A **flexible budget**, on the other hand, adjusts costs for any level of activity within the relevant range of activity for an operating period. The total flexible budget is normally presented in the **contribution margin** statement format, and includes fixed costs so that both contribution margin income and operating income can be presented.

Illustration

Exhibit 11-1 is an example of the static budget for planning purposes.

Exhibit 11-1. Static Budget	
Revenues (100,000 units sold)	$1,000,000
Less: Variable costs (based on 100,000 units sold):	
Raw materials	100,000
Direct labor	200,000
Variable manufacturing overhead	150,000
Variable selling, general, and administrative costs	80,000
Total variable costs	$530,000
Contribution margin	$470,000
Less: Fixed costs	
Fixed manufacturing costs	200,000
Fixed selling, general, and administrative costs	150,000
Total fixed costs	$350,000
Net operating income	$120,000

In Exhibit 11-1 the variable costs are separated from fixed costs but the variable costs are based on one level of production, 100,000 units. This budget is not helpful to management since it does not consider the impact of possible volume changes on projections.

The flexible budget, on the other hand, is a detailed plan of revenues and expense projections based on various levels of production or sales volume. The projected levels of volume by management are estimates. Exhibit 11-2 recasts the static budget of Exhibit 11-1 into a flexible budget. The total flexible budget formula is $TC = \$350,000 + \$5.30X$, where TC = total cost and X = volume. Many companies will build flexible budget formulas into their financial planning models using spreadsheets or other software, which makes it easy to recompute the budget with different hypothetical numbers.

Exhibit 11-2. Flexible Budget[a]			
Number of units sold	99,000	100,000	101,000
Revenues @ $10 per unit	$990,000	$1,000,000	$1,010,000
Less: Variable costs:			
Raw materials @ $1.00 per finished unit	99,000	100,000	101,000
Direct labor @ $2.00/per finished unit	198,000	200,000	202,000
Variable manufacturing overhead @ $1.50/ unit	148,500	150,000	151,500
Variable selling, general, and administrative costs @ $.080/per finished unit	79,200	80,000	80,800
Total variable costs @ $5.30 per finished unit	$524,700	$530,000	$535,300
Contribution margin	$465,300	$470,000	$474,700
Less: Fixed costs			
Fixed manufacturing costs	200,000	200,000	200,000
Fixed selling, general, and administrative costs	150,000	150,000	150,000
Total fixed costs	$350,000	$350,000	$350,000
Net operating income	$115,300	$120,000	$124,700

[a]In this illustration the flexible budget is applied to the company as a whole, including both manufacturing costs and SG&A expenses but it can also be used separately, for manufacturing overhead only, for example.

Flexible Budgets for Activities and Planning of Overhead Costs

In Chapter 10 we referred to activity-based budgeting (ABB). ABB is really a variation of a flexible budget for overhead in that it "flexes" the overhead costs of a given activity based on the volume of each cost driver at that activity's level. (Thus it is sometimes referred to as an **activity-based flexible budget**.) Recall that in activity-based costing, manufacturing and nonmanufacturing overhead costs are first allocated to activities using resource drivers, then the activity's costs are allocated to cost objects (products, services, and/or customers) using a cost driver. These costs are categorized by cost hierarchy: unit-level costs, batch-level costs, product-level costs, and facility-level costs.

In activity-based budgeting the process is just the reverse. A budget is prepared at the activity level based on the consumption of overhead by product or services or the customers to be served. Thus, the focus is on the customer's product and service needs. This is contrast to the traditional budget process, which focuses on the cost elements and general ledger accounts (as shown in Exhibit 11-2). As applied to overhead costs, ABB results in multiple cost drivers being used, which should result in more accurate budgeting of the related costs.

Illustration

Best Markets Wholesale is a distributor of nonalcoholic beverages and snacks. The controller is preparing its master budget for April 20X5. Last year it installed an activity-based costing (ABC) system, which included activity-based budgeting. The ABC system has five activities:

1. *Purchasing.* The cost driver is the number of purchase orders (batch level costs).
2. *Receiving.* The cost driver is the number of deliveries (batch level costs).
3. *Warehouse storage.* The cost driver is the number of hours (output level costs).
4. *Shipping.* The cost driver is the number of shipments/deliveries to supermarkets (batch level costs).
5. *Customer support.* The cost driver is the number of customers (output level costs).

Best Market sells three different types of items: fruit drinks, colas, and snacks. The cost driver rates and quantity of cost drivers projected for April 20X5 is summarized in Exhibit 11-3.

Exhibit 11-3. Projected Activity Rates and Cost Driver Volume for Best Market

Activity and Driver	Cost Driver Rates		April 20X5 Budgeted Volume of Cost Driver		
	20X4 Actual Rate(a)	April 20X5 Budgeted Rate[a]	Fruit Drinks	Colas	Snacks
Purchasing (per purchase order)	$50.00	$55.00	20	22	30
Receiving (per delivery from vendor)	$40.00	$45.00	18	20	28
Warehouse storing (per hour)	$18.00	$20.00	100	140	60
Shipping (per delivery to supermarkets)	$10.00	$12.00	80	84	95
Customer support (per customer)	$8.00	$8.20	100	120	90

[a]The individual overhead costs (budgeted and actual) have been allocated to each activity using resource drivers. The individual activity and cost driver rates were computed by dividing the total costs of each activity by each cost driver. (See Chapter 6 for detailed allocation procedures.)

An activity-based budget for each activity is prepared for April 20X5 in Exhibit 11-4.

Exhibit 11-4. Best Market Activity Based Budget for Overhead Costs for April 20X5

Activity	Cost Hierarchy	Fruit Drinks	Colas	Snacks	Total
Purchasing (per purchase order) $55 × 20; × 22; × 30	Batch level	$1,100	$1,210	$1,650	$3,960
Receiving (per delivery from vendor) $45 × 18; × 20; × 28	Batch level	810	900	1,260	2,970
Warehouse storing (per hour) $20 × 100; × 140; × 60	Output level	2,000	2,800	1,200	6,000
Shipping (per delivery to supermarkets) $12 × 80; × 84; × 95	Output level	960	1,008	1,140	3,108
Customer support (per customer) $8.20 × 100; × 120; × 90	Output level	820	984	738	2,542
Total flexible budget costs		$5,690	$6,902	$5,988	$18,580

Exhibit 11-4 shows the advantage of using activities with different cost drivers for each to budget overhead costs. It demonstrates how different products require different amounts of resources. Using a single cost driver such as labor hours or sales would not have accounted for these differences, since a cost driver assumes the same use of resources across activities by the products sold.

General Model for Evaluating Financial Performance

Before flexible budgeting is considered for control purposes, a model for evaluating financial performance—which includes flexible budgeting—will be described. This model is depicted in Figure 11-1.

Looking at Figure 11-1, we see that the type and level of budget is tied to the level of responsibility (the **responsibility center** manager). At the top of the organization, the master budget is aggregated at the overall revenue and cost level. Senior managers are responsible to the board of directors and stockholders for meeting stated financial goals and objectives. They receive performance reports that portray the overall operating income broken down into total revenues and costs.

What Is a Responsibility Center?

It is an organizational unit in which the manager is held responsible for the performance of the unit. Responsibility centers are further defined and described in Chapter 14.

As reporting moves down the organization the performance reports are prepared as flexible budgets and successively broken down into more detailed revenues and costs then sent to the responsible managers on a regular basis. Figure 11-1 only covers performance measures tied to master and flexible budgets. Other performance measures, such as benchmarking, return on investment, and residual income are discussed in Chapter 14. The most detailed reports are at the lower management level and are shown at the bottom of the reporting hierarchy. These detailed reports are the subject of Chapter 12, where departmental variance analysis is described in detail.

Evaluating financial performance in a business

(1) Level of analysis— responsibility	(2) Item	(3) Budget benchmark	(4) Actual results	(5) Variance (3) – (4) F = Favorable U = Unfavorable
		Master budget	Actual results	Master budget variance
Level responsibility: CEO and senior management	Total budgeted operating income	$ XXX	$ XXX	$XXX (3) - (4)
Level of responsibility: CEO and senior management	Units sold	XXX	XXX	XXX
	Sales	$XXX	$XXX	$XXX
	Variable costs	(XXX)	(XXX)	(XXX)
	Contribution margin	$XXX	$XXX	$XXX
	Fixed costs	(XXX)	(XXX)	(XXX)
	Operating income	$XXX	$XXX	$XXX
		Flexible budget	Actual results	Flexible budget Variance (3) – (4)
Level of responsibility: Middle management (divisions or business units)	Units sold	XXX	XXX	-0-
	Sales	$XXX	$XXX	$XXX
	Variable costs	(XXX)	(XXX)	(XXX)
	Marketing & Sales	XXX	XXX	XXX
	Production	XXX	XXX	XXX
	Others	XXX	XXX	XXX
	Contribution margin	$XXX	$XXX	$XXX
	Fixed costs	(XXX)	(XXX)	(XXX)
	Operating income	$XXX	$XXX	$XXX
		Flexible budget	Master budget	Sales volume variances (3) – (4)
Level of responsibility: Middle management (sales regions or business units)	Units sold	XXX	XXX	XXX
	Sales	$XXX	$XXX	$XXX
	Variable costs(a)	(XXX)	(XXX)	(XXX)
	Contribution margin	$XXX	$XXX	$XXX
	Fixed costs	(XXX)	(XXX)	(XXX)
	Operating income	$XXX	$XXX	$XXX

Level of responsibility: Lower management (departments or cost centers)

(a) May be broken down into department or responsibility centers.

(Detailed sales prices variances)	(Detailed sales volume variances)	(Detailed cost variances) (b)

(b) Costs variances are covered in Chapter 12 and sales variances are covered in Chapter 13.

Figure 11-1 Evaluating financial performance in a business.

Flexible Budgets for Control

Flexible budgets for control purposes are prepared using the volume actually achieved. Thus, they compare actual results to the budget as it would have appeared had that actual volume level been used for planning during the period. What this does is filter out any variance due solely to difference in volume between the static budget and the actual volume achieved. Variable manufactured overhead is controlled at the departmental level with cost reports breaking total variable overhead down into individual line items. Fixed overhead is controlled at the acquisition stage through capital expenditure analysis as described in Chapter 8.

A question often asked is what measure of volume should be used in constructing the flexible budget. This question relates to whether the measure should be an *output* measure or an *input* measure. If the company produces only one product or if a performance report is designed for senior management, the volume of product output is the one normally used. At the senior management level, output volume is normally used due to aggregation of revenues and costs at that level. Also, senior managers are interested in the impact of a sales output different from that embodied in profit objectives. However, when the company produces more than one product, input measures are often the best measures to use.

Why are input measures of volume better than output measures in multiproduct production? Because, multiple products likely will require differing amounts of inputs of overhead. Thus, an input measure that is associated with that product's consumption of overhead will likely provide a more accurate measure of that use. For example, a product that requires a machine-intensive production process, compared with another product that requires a labor-intensive production process, should use machine hours as the cost driver. The other product should use labor hours. Using two different cost drivers would provide a more accurate costing of products than using an output measure or just one input measure alone to capture the related costs. In activity-based costing there are multiple cost drivers relating to that activity's consumption of resources.

Flexible Budgeting in Action

Illustration of Flexible Budget for Control at the Senior Management Level

Assume Best Cut is a small company that manufactures scissors for sale to large office suppliers. The company uses a flexible budget and for September 20X5 projected sales of 30,000 units, a unit variable cost per pair of scissors of $2.00

each, and total fixed costs of $50,000. The company projected a sales price of $6 per pair of scissors. The actual results for September 20X5 were total variable costs of $56,550 and actual fixed costs of $49,000. The company actually produced 29,000 pairs of scissors are sold them at an average price of $5.90. Prepare a performance report to be sent to the president of the company.

Solution

The solution is shown in Exhibit 11-5. The columns in Figure 11-1 have been recast for computational purposes. The total master budget variance for operating income is $4,450. But this is not very informative. By breaking the total budget variance down further, senior and business unit managers will be able to have a clearer picture of what caused the total variances. For example, the sales flexible budget variance is $2,900U, which is due to the actual sales price being less than the budgeted sales price ($5.90 – $6.00) × 29,000 units. The total sales volume variance exists because the actual sales and production volumes missed the master budget target by 1,000 units. Generally, senior managers will be most interested in the overall income variance and will leave the analysis for more detailed variances to lower management. In Chapters 12 and 13 it will be shown that the flexible budget variances can be broken down further into price, efficiency, and other variances for lower level managers to more fully determine the exact cause of total master budget variance.

Exhibit 11-5. Best Cut Flexible Budget					
	Actual Results	**Flexible Budget Variance**	**Flexible Budget**	**Sales Volume Variance**	**Master Budget**
Sales	$171,100[a]	$2,900U	$174,000[b]	$6,000U	$180,000[c]
Less: Variable costs	56,550[d]	1,450F	58,000[e]	2,000F	60,000[f]
Contribution margin	$114,550	$1,450U	$116,000	$4,000U	$120,000
Less: Fixed costs	49,000	1,000F	50,000	0	50,000
Operating income	$65,550	$450U	$66,000	$4,000U	$70,000

[a] 29,000 × $5.90
[b] 29,000 × $6.00
[c] 30,000 × $6.00
[d] Given in problem description ($56,550 ÷ 29,000 = $1.95)
[e] 29,000 × $2.00
[f] 30,000 × $2.00

Total master (static) budget bariance $4,450U

Determining the Cause of Flexible Budget Variances

A very important task in variance analysis is to understand the cause of the variance and use this information to improve the related process. As we described in Figure 11-1, all performance reports should be sent to the responsible manager to provide feedback on actual performance compared with the budgeted objective. Each manager should then be responsible for discovering why the variance arose and take corrective action and, above all, learn from mistakes or deficiencies in the system processes. In many cases the cause may lie in two or more interrelated functions. For example, a production cost variance could be related to the purchasing department's failure to order input materials on time, which necessitated the purchase of materials on a rush basis, resulting in higher prices and shipping charges. Other interrelated causes could be inadequate training, inadequate product design, mistakes in setups, and inadequate coordination between the sales department and the production department on the number of units to be produced.

Only significant variances should be investigated. Companies may set a percentage trigger level as to when to investigate variances, such as a 3% difference between the budget and the actual results. Other companies let managers use their judgment as to when to investigate. Significant favorable variances should be investigated as carefully as unfavorable ones, because a significant favorable variance may signal poor estimates in the budgeting process or other major problems.

Activity-Based Flexible Budgeting and Variance Analysis

Earlier in this chapter activity-based budgeting (ABB) for planning was discussed and illustrated. It was shown that ABB provides more accurate budgeting of overhead resource consumption by individual products. It should make sense then that the ABB-prepared budget would provide better benchmarks for comparison to actual performance than traditional overhead flexible budgets. Why? There are three reasons: (1) the flexible budget assumes that all costs are at the unit output-level. ABB aggregates costs into a four-tier cost hierarchy (unit output–level costs, batch-level costs, product-level costs, and facility-level costs) that provides more accuracy in predicting resource consumption. (2) Flexible budgets normally use departmental or plant-wide allocation rates, particularly for manufacturing overhead. ABB uses a rate for each activity based on the appropriate cost driver for that activity. As Exhibit 11-4 demonstrated, this provides a more accurate reflection of resource consumption by products and is a better model for comparing actual costs. This motivates managers to manage the cost driver, which will result in better control of related resource usage. (3) By breaking the overhead costs down into activities with an appropriate cost driver, the resulting budget better links costs to the responsible manager.

Illustration

To illustrate the use of ABB for performance evaluation, the Best Market Wholesale illustration embodied in Exhibit 11-3 will be used. Assume the actual performance data for Best Market as summarized in Exhibit 11-6.

Exhibit 11-6.	Actual Overhead Costs and Volume for April 20X5				
		Volume of Cost Driver			
Activity	Total Actual Costs	Fruit Drinks	Colas	Snacks	Total Volume
Purchase orders	$4,080	23	20	28	71
Deliveries	3,150	24	18	26	68
Labor	5,750	105	130	58	293
Shipments	2,900	83	79	90	252
Customers	2,550	105	112	86	303

A performance report using the activity-based flexible budget is displayed in Exhibit 11-7.

Exhibit 11-7.	Activity Performance Report for April 20X5				
	Cost Driver Budgeted Rates and Actual Volume		April 20X5 Flexible Budget Variances		
	(1)	(2)	(3)	(4)	(5)
Activity and Driver	April 20X5 Budgeted Rate	Total Actual Activity Volume (From Ex. 11-6)	Total Flexible Budget for Activity (1) × (2)	Total Actual Costs of Activity[a] (Ex. 11-6)	Flexible Budget Activity Variances (3)–(4)
Purchasing (per purchase order)	$55.00	71	$3,905	$4,080	$175U
Receiving (per delivery from vendor)	$45.00	68	3,060	3,150	90U
					(Continued)

Exhibit 11-7. *(Continued)*					
Warehouse storing (per hour)	$20.00	293	5,860	5,750	110F
Shipping (per delivery to supermarkets)	$12.00	252	3,024	2,900	124F
Customer support (per customer)	$8.20	303	2,485	2,550	65U
Total Flexible Budget Variance	–	–	$18,334	$18,430	96U

[a]The actual individual overhead cost elements were allocated to each activity using resource drivers. (See Chapter 6 for detailed allocation procedures.)

The performance report in Exhibit 11-7 illustrates the flexible budget variance for each activity and a total flexible budget variance for all activities. The total flexible budget variances were caused by higher spending than was projected in the budget. This is true because the budget was adjusted to the actual volume achieved, thus filtering out the effects of any volume variance.

What is the advantage of performance reporting at the activity level? If the performance report were only for the total flexible budget, the variance would have been an unfavorable budget of $195. This would have obscured the fact that two of the activities had a favorable variance and the total unfavorable variances were actually higher than is indicated by the $195. Thus, reporting variances at the activity level provide more information.

A more important variance is the volume variance relating to the individual cost drivers, since management should control the cost driver under an activity-based management system. This variance will be covered in Chapter 12.

Summary

This chapter explained the concept of overhead flexible budgeting for planning purposes by showing that overhead costs are separated into their variable and fixed elements and the total budget can be computed at different levels of projected volume. For control purposes, it was shown that flexible budgets were superior to static budgets because they adjust the budget to the volume actually achieved. It was demonstrated how activity-based budgeting can be used at the activity level, thus providing more accuracy to the budget figures. Next, a general model of performance evaluation was introduced. This model was applied to flexible and activity-based budgets for controlling overhead costs using variance analysis. Finally, it was emphasized that variances should be traced to their underlying causes. Once the underlying cause is determined, it is most important that managers take corrective action to alleviate it.

Practice Problems

11-1 Which of the following statements about flexible budgets is *not* true?

A. A flexible budget is superior to a static budget.

B. A flexible budget includes overhead costs.

C. A flexible budget is not based on one particular level of activity.

D. All of the above statements are true.

Use the following information for questions 11-2 through 11-4:

Quick Air produces industrial fans for sale to distributors. The fans sell for an average price of $70.00 each. Each fan has an estimated raw material cost of $18.00 and labor cost of $16.00 and production requires one hour per fan. The company expects to produce 2,000 units during the coming month and 25,000 during the coming year. The company has a highly automated production process. Manufacturing overhead costs are expected to be $36,000 for the next month and $425,000 for the next year and are allocated based on direct labor hours. Of the total overhead cost, 10% is variable. Sales volume may vary significantly from month to month throughout the year.

11-2 What is the budgeted manufacturing overhead rate?

A. $17.00 per unit

B. $16.00 per unit

C. $18.00 per unit

D. None of the above

11-3 What is the total manufacturing flexible budget for 24,000 units, 25,000 units, and 26,000 units, respectively?

A. $856,800, $892,500, $928,200, respectively

B. $1,239,300, $1,275,000, $1,310,700, respectively

C. $1,224,000, $1,275,000, $1,326,000, respectively

D. None of the above

11-4 What is the flexible budget formula for manufacturing overhead?

A. TC $= \$425,000 + \$1.70X$

B. TC $= \$382,500 + \$35.70X$

C. TC $= \$382,500 + \$1.70X$

D. None of the above

Use the following information for questions 11-5 through 11-8:

The Better Rite Company manufactures custom mechanical pencils and sells them in sets to two office supply companies. The budgeted and actual selling price for a set of pencils is $8.00. The budgeted and actual data for Better Rite are displayed in the table below:

	Budgeted	Actual
Sets produced and sold	100,000	105,000
Variable costs:		
Raw materials	$275,000	$294,000
Direct labor	50,000	60,000
Variable manufacturing overhead	75,000	80,000
Variable selling, general, and administrative costs	25,000	27,000
Fixed manufacturing costs	125,000	126,000
Fixed selling, general, and administrative costs	75,000	77,000

11-5 What is the actual operating income for Better Rite?

A. $379,000

B. $175,000

C. $193,750

D. $176,000

11-6 What is the master (static) budgeted operating income for Better Rite?

A. $175,000

B. $176,000

C. $193,750

D. $379,000

11-7 What is the flexible budget variance for Better Rite?

A. $18,750U

B. $17,750U

C. $14,750U

D. None of the above

11-8 What is the master budget variance for Better Rite?

A. $17,750U

B. $18,750U

C. $1,000F

D. $4,000F

11-9 Which of the following statements about activity-based flexible budgeting system are *true*?

A. It can be used for manufacturing and nonmanufacturing costs.

B. It uses multiple cost drivers.

C. It can also be used as the basis for a flexible budget for planning and control purposes.

D. All of the above

11-10 Johnson Manufacturing requires a new setup each time a job is processed through the cutting department. The setup activity has a $27.00 rate per setup. The activity-based budget for the next month showed 100 setups for this activity. The actual costs for this activity were $2,900 at the end of the month. What was the activity variance?

A. $0

B. $200U

C. $100U

D. None of the above

Solutions to Practice Problems

11-1 D

11-2 A

The overhead rate should be computed on an annual basis, due to the seasonal fluctuations.

Variable overhead rate = $(0.10 \times \$425,000) \div 25,000$ units = $1.70

Fixed overhead rate = $\$425,000 \times (1.00 - 0.10) \div 25,000 = \$15.30$

Budgeted manufacturing overhead rate = $17.00

11-3 B

The solution is computed in the table below:

Number of units to be produced	24,000	25,000	26,000
Raw materials @ $18.00/unit	$432,000	$450,000	$468,000
Direct labor @ $16.00/unit	384,000	400,000	416,000
Variable manufacturing overhead @ $1.70/unit	40,800	42,500	44,200
Total variable costs @ $35.70 per finished unit	$856,800	$892,500	$928,200
Fixed manufacturing costs ($425,000 × 0.90)	382,500	382,500	382,500
Total manufacturing flexible budget	$1,239,300	$1,275,000	$1,310,700

11-4 C

Variable overhead rate = $(0.10 \times \$425,000) \div 25,000$ units = $1.70

Total fixed costs = $(1.00 - 0.10) \times \$425,000 = \$382,500$

11-5 D (See table below)

11-6 A (See table below)

11-7 B (See table below)

11-8 C

$175,000 budgeted – $176,000 actual = $1,000F

Solution to Questions 11-5 Through 11-8					
	Actual Results[a]	Flexible Budget Variance	Flexible Budget	Sales Volume Variances	Master Budget
Sets sold	105,000		105,000		100,000
Sales @$8	$840,000	–	$840,000	$40,000F	$800,000
Less: Variable costs[b]					
Raw materials @$2.75	$294,000	$5,250U	$288,750	$13,750U	$275,000
Direct labor @$0.50	60,000	7,500U	52,500	2,500U	50,000
Variable manufacturing overhead @$0.75	80,000	1,250U	78,750	3,750U	75,000
Variable SG&A expenses @$0.25	27,000	750U	26,250	1,250U	25,000
Total variable expenses	$461,000	$14,750U	$446,250	$21,250U	$425,000
Contribution margin	$379,000	$14,750U	$393,750	$18,750F	$375,000
Less: Fixed costs					
Manufacturing overhead	$126,000	$1,000U	$125,000	0	$125,000
SG&A expenses	77,000	2,000U	75,000	0	75,000
Total fixed costs	$203,000	$3,000U	$200,000	0	$200,000
Operating income	$176,000	$17,750U	$193,750	$18,750F	$175,000

[a]Actual costs results were given. Total actual sales = $8 × 105,000 = $840,000
[b]Each unit variable cost shown is the *budgeted* unit variable cost determined by dividing the total budgeted variable cost by the units budgeted.

11-9 D

11-10 B $27 × 100 setups = $2,700 budgeted less $2,900 actual = $200U

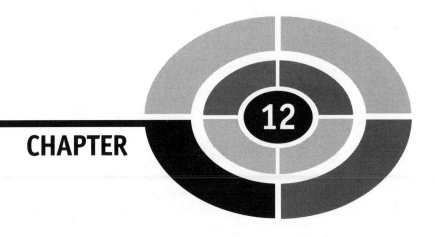

Performance Evaluation: Standard Costing and Variances Analysis

This chapter presents standard costing as a method for performance measurement, cost control, and for costing products into inventory in a manufacturing company. The topics covered are: The concept of a standard; the advantages and criticisms of standard costing; how standards are used in performance measure and variance

analysis; investigating variances; using standards in product costing; and end of period adjustments to close the variance accounts.

What Is a Standard?

A **standard** is a predetermined criterion or benchmark against which actual performance can be compared. It can be thought of as the expected use of resources by an organization in normal operations. A **standard cost** is the cost of one unit of product output in materials, labor, and overhead. Thus, it is a unit concept as compared to a budget benchmark, which is a total concept. Also, a budget is thought of as the expected cost of operations for a set period of time—normally one year—whereas a standard is based on what the cost and usage of an input into production *should* be under effective and efficient operations. In this sense, standards do not relate to time as budgets do but they must be reviewed periodically for currency. Standards can be used with budgets to determine the cost of operations for a specified period.

In setting standards, management must decide at what level they should be set.

Ideal Standards

Ideal standards are set at a level of ideal, or perfect, operations. This means that inputs are acquired at the lowest possible price, used in production at a level of perfect efficiency in operations, and products are produced at a perfect level of quality. While a few managers believe that standards should be set at this level to motivate workers, most managers and behavioral scientists believe such standards actually discourage workers from performing at their best. Ideal standards may motivate workers to focus only on meeting the cost standards, thus going to the extent of reducing the quality of output, which in the long run could result in higher costs because of defects and customer dissatisfaction.

Practical Standards

Practical standards provide a more reasonable benchmark in motivating employees. These have often been defined as "tight, but attainable." They are set to be operative under normal operations, including allowances for breakdowns, normal waste, downtime for breaks, vacations, and other normal disruption of operations.

Advantages of Standard Costing

Actual performance very rarely turns out to be exactly what was planned. Even when overall performance appears close to that which was planned, there can be smaller components of performance that offset significantly what was planned. Thus, management needs a system for evaluating both the overall performance, like that provided by flexible budgets, and for "mining" the details of cost down to the lowest subcomponent so that each element can be isolated, measured, and evaluated. Cost standards aid in this process by providing several advantages. A standard cost system:

- Provides an effective benchmark and overall framework for comparing and evaluating the cost of operations
- Facilitates management by exception
- Is very useful in setting long range cost-plus pricing
- Lowers recordkeeping costs by using predetermined values when recording cost transactions
- Provides a more accurate measurement of inventory

Criticisms of Standard Costing

While cost standards are used by most large businesses in the United States and throughout the world, there is growing criticism of this system's use. Critics say that standard cost systems:

- Are out of touch with today's new manufacturing environment, because standards are
  - Too inventory focused. Just-in-time inventory methods have reduced inventories to near-zero level, thus reducing the need for an expensive standard cost system.
  - Focused too much on labor. With the increased use of automated manufacturing processes, labor is becoming a smaller part of manufacturing costs.
  - Less effective than other approaches that can attain the same objective, such as target costing, activity-based costing, and continuous improvement methodology.
- Focused too much on cost control and give little attention to control of quality.

- Very expensive to install and to keep current, particularly in a business environment where there are short product life-cycles.

- Creating cost variances that are untimely and too aggregated to provide enough information for continuous improvement.

Standard Costing in Performance Evaluation

In Chapter 11 a model of performance evaluation was presented in Figure 11-1. Embodied in this model is the premise that performance evaluation involves using a predetermined measure of performance (a budget or a standard), a system for measuring and collecting actual performance, making a comparison between the predetermined measure, and reporting variances to the responsible manager. Standard costing and variance analysis are still widely used as an important component of this process. They have three basic objectives:

- **Evaluating the effectiveness of operations.** This involves comparing output to the production or sales budget. In sales, effectiveness requires comparing the budgeted quantity to the actual quantity, which provides the sales volume variance. In manufacturing, effectiveness requires comparing the budgeted production quantity (production quotas) to the actual quantity produced, which aids in evaluating the effective utilization of capacity. Thus, volume variances are used to evaluate effectiveness of operations.

- **Evaluating the economy of operations.** This involves measurements that ensure inputs are purchased for production at the lowest price. As will be shown later in this chapter, evaluating economy is primarily done through the material price variances.

- **Evaluating the efficiency of operations.** This involves measurements that compare outputs to inputs, which measure the efficiency of material, labor, and overhead usage in operations. As will be shown later in this chapter, this is done through the material, labor, and overhead efficiency variances. In order to compare inputs and outputs in the same dimension, it will be necessary to convert output units into input units. This is done through the use of the standard quantity allowed (if a standard cost system is not used, the budgeted quantity would be used). For example, if a finished unit has a standard requiring 2 pounds of a raw material per finished unit and there were 1,000 pounds used to produce 490 finished units, then the standard quantity allowed would be 980 ($2 \times 490 = 980$). This means that 1,000 pounds were actually used when 980 pounds should have been used to produce the 490 finished units.

Who Is Responsible for Setting Standards?

Purchasing

Purchasing managers are responsible for acquiring materials at the lowest cost and with high enough quality to meet production needs. Therefore, they should be the leaders in setting price standards for materials. A **bill of materials** is established showing the amount of materials, labor, and overhead required for one finished unit of product. Purchasing will estimate the price of materials based on the economic order quantity, available discounts, and information on material availability.

Bill of Materials

A document that contains information on product materials based on specifications of the quality and quantity needed for production.

Industrial Engineering

Internal industrial engineers or external consulting engineers should prepare the bill of materials for materials and the amount of labor required for one unit of finished goods. They should consult with production managers on the types and quantities of materials required and any allowances for scrap, shrinkage, and waste. They should also work with production managers in conducting time and motion studies and test runs to establish the time standards required to produce one unit of finished goods.

Human Resources

Human resources managers can provide input to the managerial accountant on the availability of required workers, salary and wage trends, and costs of benefits. Management accountants should work with production in determining how the mix of skill levels will affect the final amount and wage rate of labor required for one finished unit of product. In setting labor wage rates, production will assist in computing an average rate in a given department based on the mix of worker skill levels required.

Management Accountant

The management accountant acts as the facilitator of the standard costing process by providing cost information, data analysis, and approving of and monitoring the standards as they are completed. As described in the previous paragraph, the accountant may be responsible for finalizing the labor price rate standards based on input from production and human resources. Finally, the management accountant may determine the allocation rates for indirect costs (overhead) based on input from production managers.

Using Standard Costing in Material and Labor Cost Variance Analysis

Standard cost variance analysis is a further breakdown of flexible budget variances discussed in Chapter 11 and depicted at the bottom of Figure 11-1. Also, standard cost variances are reported to departmental managers as shown at the bottom of Figure 11-1.

Looking at Figure 12-1, the top row [1] reflects the total costs—budgeted and actual—that would be reported to the department manager as described in Chapter 11. The second row [2] displays totals broken down into the price and efficiency variances in a formula format. And the bottom row [3] shows the total flexible budget variance as described in Chapter 11. In effect, the diagram in Figure 12-1 breaks

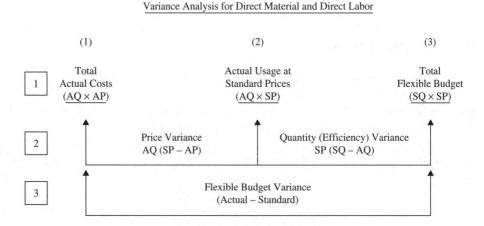

Figure 12-1   Variance analysis for direct material and direct labor.

down the total flexible budget variance into the price and quantity or efficiency variances.

Illustration

The Picture Frame Company produces large picture frames for sale to museums and auction houses at $55.00 each. It uses a standard cost system that contains the following standard for one of its most popular frames:

Standard per Unit of Finished Product:		
Lumber, 4 linear feet units	2 @ $6 each unit	$12.00/finished unit
Direct labor	½ hour @ $20/hour	$10.00/finished unit
Manufacturing Overhead:[1]		
Variable:	½ machine hour (MH)	
	@$10 MH	$ 5.00/finished unit
Fixed	½ machine hour (MH)	
	@$15.00 per MH	$ 7.50/finished unit
Total standard manufacturing cost per finished unit		$ 34.50
Budgeted Data for June 20X5:		
• Finished units	3,000	
• Machine hours	1,500	
• Variable overhead	$15,000	
• Fixed overhead	$22,500	
Purchasing Data for June 20X5:		
• Units of lumber purchased:	6,000 for $35,400	
• **Production Data for June 20X5:**		
• Finished frames produced:	2,900	
• Units of lumber used:	6,000	
• Total actual machine hours:	740	
• Total wages paid for factory workers:	$30,810 for 1,580 hours	
• Actual variable overhead:	$15,500	
• Actual fixed overhead:	$23,500	

[1] How to compute overhead rates was explained in Chapter 4.

The graphic approach for material variances for the Picture Frame Company are computed in Figure 12-2.

> **Formula Approach for Material Variances:**
>
> Price variance = $(AQ \times AP) - (AQ \times SP) = AQ(SP - AP) = 6,000(\$6.00 - 5.90) = \$600F$
>
> Quantity variance = $(AQ \times SP) - (SQ \times SP) = SP(SQ - AQ)$
>
> $\$6[(2,900 \times 2) - 6,000] = \$6(5,800 - 6,000) = \$1,200U$

The graphic approach for direct labor variances for the Picture Frame Company are computed in Figure 12-3.

> **Formula Approach for Labor Variances:**
>
> Rate variance = $(AQ \times AR) - (AQ \times SR) = AQ(SR - AR) = (\$20.00 - \$19.50) \times 1,580 \text{ hours} = \$790F$
>
> Efficiency variance = $(AQ \times SR) - (SQ \times SR) = SR(SQ - AQ) = \$20.00[(2,900 \times 1/2) - 1,580] = \$2,600U$

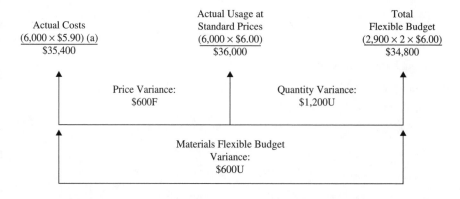

Direct Material Variance Analysis Report for the Picture Frame Company

Direct Material Variances:

	Actual Costs $(6,000 \times \$5.90)$ (a) $\$35,400$	Actual Usage at Standard Prices $(6,000 \times \$6.00)$ $\$36,000$	Total Flexible Budget $(2,900 \times 2 \times \$6.00)$ $\$34,800$

Price Variance: $\$600F$

Quantity Variance: $\$1,200U$

Materials Flexible Budget Variance: $\$600U$

(a) $\$35,400 \div 6,000$ actual units = $\$5.90$

Figure 12-2 Direct materials variance analysis for the Picture Frame Company.

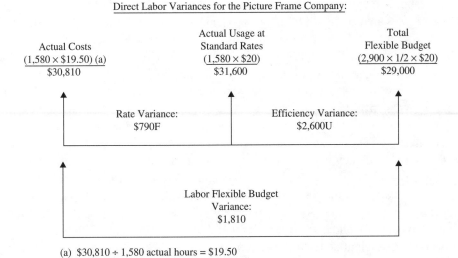

Direct Labor Variances for the Picture Frame Company:

| Actual Costs
(1,580 × $19.50) (a)
$30,810 | Actual Usage at
Standard Rates
(1,580 × $20)
$31,600 | Total
Flexible Budget
(2,900 × 1/2 × $20)
$29,000 |

Rate Variance:
$790F

Efficiency Variance:
$2,600U

Labor Flexible Budget
Variance:
$1,810

(a) $30,810 ÷ 1,580 actual hours = $19.50

Figure 12-3   Direct labor variances for the Picture Frame Company.

Causes of Direct Material and Direct Labor Variances

The material price variance is normally the responsibility of the purchasing manager and should be computed at the point of purchase. A favorable price variance could be caused by the following: the purchasing manager used more effective purchasing practices, such as buying a larger quantity than planned that resulted in a greater discounthan expected; market forces caused an unexpected drop in prices; or the standard could be outdated.

On the other hand, unfavorable material price variances could be caused by unexpected inflationary pressures; an unexpected change in specification by production that resulted in a price increase; the purchasing manager using ineffective purchasing practices; production required a rush order (in which case the production manager may be responsible for the unfavorable price variance); or the standard could be outdated.

The material quantity variance is normally the responsibility of production managers and should be computed at the point of issuance into production based on the bill of materials. Unfavorable quantity variances could be caused by inefficient worker practices; poor quality of material purchased; inferior machinery; and poor supervision practices. Favorable quantity variances could be caused by more efficient worker and supervisory practices; higher quality of materials purchased; and the purchase of more efficient machinery during the period.

The labor rate variance is also the responsibility of the production manager because the labor rates are usually set for the year. The labor rate is the average of the standard rate of workers in a department or activity. Thus, a favorable or unfavorable rate variance relates to the mix of worker assignments in the workplace. If a higher-skilled worker with a higher labor pay rate is assigned to a job that requires a worker with a lower skill rate, then there will be an unfavorable rate variance. If the opposite assignment occurs, then there will be a favorable rate variance. Further, overtime requirements will result in an unfavorable labor rate variance, and this is controlled by the production manager. Of course, any variance could be caused by outdated standards.

The labor efficiency variance is an indication of the efficiency or productivity of labor in the production process. A favorable labor efficiency variance could be caused by better supervision of workers; improvements in skill level due to more training; increased speed by workers due to motivational methods; and installation of more efficient machinery and equipment. Unfavorable labor efficiency variances could be caused by insufficient demand or machine breakdowns, resulting in idle time; poorly trained or supervised workers; poorly motivated workers; failure by purchasing to acquire adequate materials, resulting in idle time; and outdated standards.

Variable Manufacturing Overhead Variances

Variable overhead is controlled using one of two approaches: (1) flexible budgets and variance analysis with a focus on the variable overhead cost driver. Using this approach, departmental budget reports will break down total overhead costs into individual line items. The responsibility center manager then focuses on controlling each of these individual costs. (2) Flexible activity-based budgets with a focus on controlling the cost driver for each activity or the cost-hierarchy level. Controlling overhead using activity-based budgets was covered in Chapter 11. This chapter focuses on variable overhead variance analysis.

Variable overhead variance analysis breaks down the total flexible budget into the variable overhead efficiency variance and the variable overhead spending variance.

- **Variable manufacturing overhead efficiency variance** is the difference between the flexible budget based on actual input of the cost driver and the flexible budget based on standard units allowed of the cost driver times the budgeted variable overhead rate per unit (see Figure 12-4).

- **Variable manufacturing overhead spending variance** is the difference between the actual variable overhead and the budgeted variable overhead based on the actual quantity of the cost driver times the budgeted variable overhead rate (see Figure 12-4).

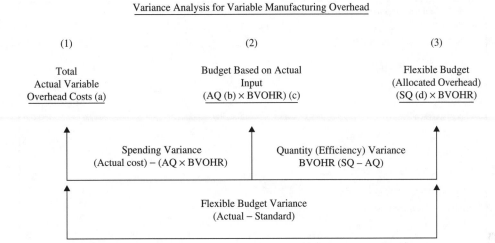

Figure 12-4 text content:

Variance Analysis for Variable Manufacturing Overhead

(1)	(2)	(3)
Total Actual Variable Overhead Costs (a)	Budget Based on Actual Input (AQ (b) × BVOHR) (c)	Flexible Budget (Allocated Overhead) (SQ (d) × BVOHR)

Spending Variance
(Actual cost) − (AQ × BVOHR)

Quantity (Efficiency) Variance
BVOHR (SQ − AQ)

Flexible Budget Variance
(Actual − Standard)

Figure 12-4   Variance analysis for variable manufacturing overhead.

For some, the overhead variances may be difficult to understand. This is because overhead is allocated to products (cost objects) using a budgeted quantity of the allocation base, not a budgeted quantity of the underlying variable overhead (see Chapter 4). Also, in computing the overhead rate, individual variable overhead cost items are aggregated (plantwide, departmentally, or by activity) and divided by the base (or cost driver). That is, an allocation rate is *not* computed for each individual overhead cost item.

A framework for variable overhead variance analysis is shown in Figure 12-4.

Illustration

The Picture Frame Company illustration from above is continued. Relevant portions are recopied below.

Standard per One Unit of Finished Product:		
Lumber, 4 linear feet units	2 @ $6 each unit	$12.00/finished unit
Direct labor	½ hour @ $20/hour	$10.00/finished unit
Manufacturing Overhead:		
Variable:	½ machine hour (MH)	
	@$10 MH	$ 5.00/finished unit
Fixed	½ machine hour (MH)	
	@$15.00 per MH	$ 7.50/finished unit
	(Based on 3,000 units)	
		(*Continued*)

Total standard manufacturing cost per finished unit	$34.50

Budgeted Data for June 20X5:

- Finished units · · · · · · · · · · · · · · · · · 3,000
- Machine hours · · · · · · · · · · · · · · · · · 1,500
- Variable overhead · · · · · · · · · · · · · $15,000
- Fixed overhead · · · · · · · · · · · · · · · $22,500

Purchasing Data for June 20X5:

- Lumber purchased: 6,000 units for $35,400

Production Data for June 20X5:

- Finished frames produced: 2,900
- Units of lumber used: 6,000
- Total actual machine hours: 1,425
- Total wages paid for factory workers: $30,810 for 1,580 hours
- Actual variable overhead: $15,500
- Actual fixed overhead: $23,500

The variable overhead variances for the Picture Frame Company are computed in Figure 12-5:

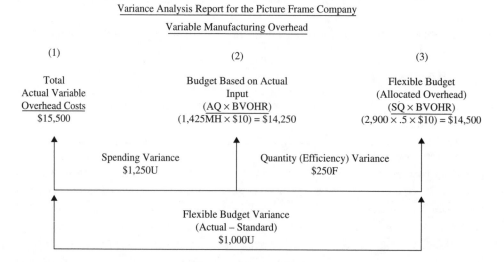

Figure 12-5   Variance analysis report for the Picture Frame Company, variable manufacturing overhead.

Explanation and Causes of Variable Manufacturing Overhead Variances

The difference between the flexible budget (column 3) and the budgeted overhead based on the actual quantity of the cost driver (column 2) is the variable overhead efficiency variance. Calling it this is really a misnomer. Why? Because this variance is due solely to the efficient or inefficient use of the cost driver or allocation base used to determine the predetermined overhead rate. Stated another way, this variance measures the effect of using a greater or lower amount of the actual input of the cost driver than the standard allowed. If direct labor hours are used as the cost driver, then the direct labor variance in hours will be the same as the variable overhead variance in hours.

Why the Variable Overhead Efficiency Variance Is Not Called Something Else

Although the variable overhead efficiency variance does not directly show the variance of the variable overhead compared to the actual one in the budget, it does suggest such a variance. If the cost driver, such as machine hours, is higher than what was budgeted, it is assumed that inefficient use of machine hours resulted in inefficient use of related variable overhead. For example, electricity use would be higher than expected because the machines operated longer than expected. This gives production managers a signal to review the use of individual overhead items in more detail.

The difference between the actual variable overhead and the budgeted variable overhead based on the actual quantity of the cost driver is the variable overhead spending variance. The major cause of the spending variance usually lies in fluctuations in prices of the underlying overhead items. Some examples: utility costs may increase more than foreseen when computing the budgeted overhead rate; repairs and maintenance were higher or lower than expected; and indirect materials were higher or lower than the estimate used to compute the predetermined overhead rate. This variance may also be caused by shrinkage or waste in some of the individual variable overhead items. Also, since the predetermined (or budgeted) overhead rate was computed using the budgeted quantity of a cost driver or allocation base and the actual quantity of that cost driver was used to compute column 2 above, there could be some more inefficiency in the spending variance that was not accounted for under the efficiency variance.

The total flexible budget variance is a measure of the combined effects of both the spending and efficiency variances.

Fixed Manufacturing Overhead Variances

Before fixed manufacturing overhead variances are covered, the nature of **fixed costs** will be discussed. Fixed costs are "big ticket" items, such as machinery, computer systems, and buildings. They constitute the **production capacity** of a business and management is responsible for the effective utilization of this capacity. The decision to purchase fixed manufacturing assets is made and controlled by senior management during the strategic planning stage using capital expenditure analysis (see Chapter 8). Once these costs are incurred they are known as **committed fixed costs** in that they do not fluctuate by volume of production or sales activity nor can management change these amounts recorded in the accounts (unless, of course, they decided to dispose of an asset).

The goal of management is always to *utilize capacity* to the greatest extent possible by increasing sales and production. As pointed out earlier in this book, the greater the amount of production, the more fixed costs will be spread over units of production, thus lowering the unit fixed cost. Therefore, the definition of capacity is important in setting the predetermined overhead rate for fixed overhead. There are four definitions of capacity in a business.

Theoretical Capacity

Requires the perfect utilization of fixed assets. There are no machine breakdowns, no inefficiency, and no breaks or holidays. Of course, it is unrealistic for management to define capacity in this way when setting their planning and control options.

Practical Capacity

Starts with theoretical capacity and subtracts the effects of normal interruptions such as idle time, breakdowns, and holidays. This is essentially an engineering definition in that it is related to using the engineering capabilities of the fixed facilities involved.

Normal Capacity

Relates to long-range plans for production based on company growth, market forces, and the like. It considers the capacity needs for a period of time lasting between 5 to

10 years. Thus, this definition of capacity will likely be similar to or less than practical capacity at times, due to normal business cycles.

Expected Capacity

Is based on the forecasted sales and production levels for the next operating period, usually 1 year. This is a short-run concept and is not used for the planning of long-range fixed asset needs. However, it is very useful in determining capacity levels that will be used in the master budget. It is also useful for estimating how much unused capacity is available for alternative uses, e.g., special order production.

The previous discussion underscores the importance of defining capacity in terms of volume level when computing the predetermined overhead rate. This definition affects the amount of fixed overhead allocated to products. Variable overhead is virtually unaffected by the capacity definition, because it is adjusted on the basis of changed volume level.

A framework for evaluating the utilization of fixed overhead is presented in Figure 12-6.

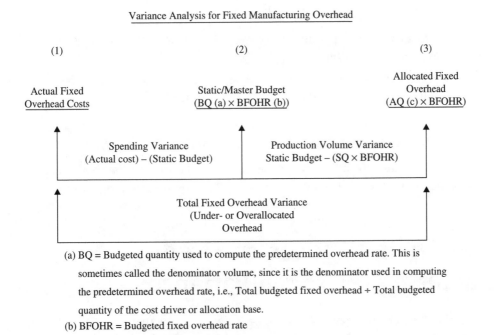

Variance Analysis for Fixed Manufacturing Overhead

(a) BQ = Budgeted quantity used to compute the predetermined overhead rate. This is sometimes called the denominator volume, since it is the denominator used in computing the predetermined overhead rate, i.e., Total budgeted fixed overhead ÷ Total budgeted quantity of the cost driver or allocation base.

(b) BFOHR = Budgeted fixed overhead rate

(c) AQ = Allowed input quantity of cost driver for actual finished output

Figure 12-6 Variance analysis for fixed manufacturing overhead.

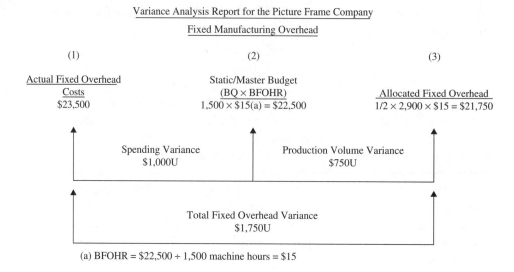

Variance Analysis Report for the Picture Frame Company
Fixed Manufacturing Overhead

(1)

Actual Fixed Overhead
Costs
$23,500

(2)

Static/Master Budget
(BQ × BFOHR)
1,500 × $15(a) = $22,500

(3)

Allocated Fixed Overhead
1/2 × 2,900 × $15 = $21,750

Spending Variance
$1,000U

Production Volume Variance
$750U

Total Fixed Overhead Variance
$1,750U

(a) BFOHR = $22,500 ÷ 1,500 machine hours = $15

Figure 12-7 Variance analysis report for the Picture Frame Company, fixed manufacturing overhead.

The variances in Figure 12-6 can be summarized as follows:

- **Fixed overhead spending variance** is how much actual fixed costs exceeded the master or static budget.
- **Fixed overhead production volume variance** is the difference between budgeted overhead and allocated fixed overhead.

Illustration of fixed overhead variances

The fixed manufacturing overhead variances for the Picture Frame Company are computed in Figure 12-7.

Explanation and Causes of Fixed Manufacturing Overhead Variances

The **fixed overhead spending variance** is how much actual fixed costs exceeded the master or static budget. This is a pure budgetary variance in that it explains how much, more or less, the business invested in fixed overhead items than were budgeted. It has no relationship to volume. In the Picture Frame Company the actual fixed overhead exceeded the master budget by $1,000, an unfavorable variance.

The **production volume variance** is the difference between budgeted and allocated fixed overhead. In this case, the static budget is used because fixed overhead cannot be "flexed" like variable overhead. This variance arises solely because the actual level of production (measured by the cost allocation base volume or cost driver volume) differed from the static budgeted volume used in computing the predetermined (budgeted) fixed overhead rate. Thus, it measures the extent of productive capacity utilization. In the Picture Frame Company the budgeted quantity used to compute the budgeted overhead rate was 1,500 machine hours. However, the budgeted quantity of machine hours allowed for the actual output of 2,900 finished units was 1,450 machine hours (2,900 × ½). Thus, the company used its facilities 50 hours less than was expected. Measured in dollar terms, this is 50 machine hours times $15 equals $750 unfavorable variance.

Some managers and accountants have argued that the volume variance is of very little use, since it is largely a noncontrollable variance. Why? The *numerator* in computing the budgeted fixed overhead rate is set by decisions in the capital budgeting process; nothing can be done to change these costs. The *denominator* may be difficult to control because it is based largely on sales volume. Thus, the sales and production volume variance may have more to say about what is happening in the market than with production utilization. If too much emphasis is placed on the production volume variance, it could have a dysfunctional effect. For example, too much emphasis may motivate the production manager to schedule more production than is necessary to utilize capacity, and this would result in an unnecessary increase in inventory levels. The increase in inventory carrying costs would result in unjustifiable expenses to the company as a whole. So managers should be held responsible for controlling inventory levels along with effective capacity utilization.

The difference between the total actual fixed manufacturing overhead and the allocated amount is the amount of underallocated or overallocated fixed overhead.

Different Approaches for Analyzing Manufacturing

The overhead variance analysis covered above is the most detailed analysis of total overhead in that it separates variable and fixed overhead and computes the following variances:

- Variable and fixed overhead spending variance
- Variable overhead efficiency variance

- Fixed overhead production volume variance
- Variable and fixed overhead budget variance

This format is sometimes called a **four-way analysis** of total manufacturing overhead. Some companies do not go to the expense of aggregating costs, which would allow a four-way analysis to be performed. Three other approaches are outlined in Figure 12-8. The data from the Picture Frame Company are used to illustrate.

Levels and Types of Manufacturing Overhead Variance Analysis

Levels	Type of Variance		
One-Way	Total Overhead Variance = (Total actual manufacturing overhead) − (Total budgeted manufacturing overhead) ($15,500 + $23,500) − ($14,500 + $21,750) = $2,750U		
Two-Way	(a) Flexible Budget Variance = (Total OH) − [(SQ (b) × BVOHR) + BFOH] ($15,500 + $23,500) − [(2,900 × .5 × $10) + $22,500] = $2,000		(c) Production Volume Variance = (Static Budget) − Allocated Overhead (BQ (d) × BFOHR) − (SQ (e) × BFOHR) (1,500 × $15) − (2,900 × .5 × $15) = $750U
Three-Way	(f) Spending Variance (VOH + FOH Spending Variances) $1,250U + $1,000U = $2,250U	(g) Efficiency Variance (AQ × BVOHR) − (SQ × BVOHR) (1,425MH × $10) − (2,900 × .5 × $10) = $250F	(h) Production Volume Variance $750U

(a) Pertains to total overhead.

(b) SQ = Budgeted quantity allowed for the actual finished output.

(c) Pertains to fixed overhead only.

(d) BQ = Budgeted quantity used to compute the predetermined overhead rate. This is sometimes called the

   denominator volume, since it is the denominator used in computing the predetermined overhead rate, i.e.,

   Total budgeted fixed overhead ÷ Total budgeted quantity of cost driver or allocation base.

(e) SQ = Allowed input quantity of cost driver for actual finished output.

(f) Pertains to both variable and fixed overhead.

(g) Pertains to variable overhead only.

(h) Pertains to fixed overhead only.

Figure 12-8   Levels and types of manufacturing overhead variance analysis.

Cost Variances in the General Ledger

The cost flow in Figure 5-1 in Chapter 5 depicted the flow of actual manufacturing costs through the general ledger. The flow of costs is the same in a standard cost system, except that accounts must be added for the cost variances in the system. There are different ways to do this. Theoretically, the cost variance should be computed at the earliest possible point in the cost flow. This allows managers to take corrective action as quickly as possible if there is a significant variance. Some companies, however, elect to compute costs at standard whenever production is completed, and compute all variances at that time.

Illustration

Using the rationale of computing the variances at the earliest point in the cost flow the following **journal entries** would be made, using the Picture Frame Company example. The relevant data for variances computed earlier are reproduced below for these journal entries.

Standard per One Unit of Finished Product:		
Lumber, 4 linear feet units	2 @ $6 each unit	$12.00/finished unit
Direct labor	½ hour @ $20/hour	$10.00/finished unit
Manufacturing Overhead:[1]		
Variable:	½ machine hour (MH)	
	@$10 MH	$ 5.00/finished unit
Fixed	½ machine hour (MH)	
	@$15.00 per MH	$ 7.50/finished unit
	(Based on 3,000 units)	
Total standard manufacturing cost per finished unit		$ 34.50
Budgeted Data for June 20X5:		
• Finished units	3,000	
• Machine hours	1,500	
• Variable overhead	$15,000	
• Fixed overhead	$22,500	

[1] The overhead rates were computed as explained in Chapter 4.   *(Continued)*

Purchasing Data for June 20X5:

- Lumber purchased: 6,000 for $35,400

Production Data for June 20X5:

- Finished frames produced: 2,900

- Units of lumber used: 6,000

- Total actual machine hours: 740

- Total wages paid for factory workers: $30,810 for 1,580 hours

- Actual variable overhead: $15,500

- Actual fixed overhead: $23,500

- **Raw materials received from vendor.** Debit the raw material inventory at the standard price per item times the actual quantity purchased. The raw materials price variance account would be debited if there is an unfavorable variance and credited if there is a favorable one.

Raw materials	Dr.	36,000
Materials price variance	Cr.	600
Accounts payable	Cr.	35,400

- **Raw materials issued to production.** Debit the work in process inventory for the standard quantity allowed based on the bill of materials. The credit to raw materials inventory is for the actual quantity issued to production times the standard price per item.

Work in process inventory	Dr.	34,800
Materials quantity variance	Dr.	1,200
Raw materials inventory	Cr.	36,000

- **Payroll is paid.** For the labor rate and efficiency variances, debit work in process inventory for the standard hours allowed, times the equivalent units started in production, times the standard wage rate. Credit wages payable for the amount actually paid to employees.

Work in process inventory	Dr	29,000
Labor efficiency variance	Dr.	2,600
Labor rate variance	Cr.	790
Wages payable	Cr.	30,810

- **Various manufacturing overhead purchases and computations during the period.** Many companies will separate variable overhead from fixed overhead as it is entered into the accounts. Others enter total overhead initially and separate variable from fixed overhead later, using separate computations, which are not entered into the accounts. In this illustration, overhead variances have been entered into the accounts.

Variable manufacturing overhead control	Dr.	15,500
Fixed manufacturing overhead control	Dr.	23,500
Accounts payable and other accounts	Cr.	39,000

- **Manufacturing overhead is allocated.** Most companies create an overhead allocated account when overhead is allocated. This account is an offset to the manufacturing overhead control account. The variable or fixed manufacturing overhead allocated accounts are debited when allocation is made. To do this, the standard quantity allowed is multiplied by the predetermined (budgeted) overhead rate. The variable or fixed manufacturing overhead control account is credited for the actual variable overhead. First, the variable manufacturing overhead entries are made:

Variable manufacturing overhead allocated	Dr.	14,500
Variable manufacturing overhead spending variance	Dr.	1,250
Variable manufacturing overhead efficiency variance	Cr.	250
Variable manufacturing overhead control	Cr.	15,500

Next, the fixed manufacturing overhead entries are made:

Fixed manufacturing overhead allocated	Dr.	21,750
Fixed manufacturing overhead spending variance	Dr.	1,000
Fixed manufacturing overhead production volume variance	Dr.	750
Fixed manufacturing overhead control	Cr.	23,500

Disposition of Cost Variances

Since the variance accounts are temporary accounts, end of the period adjustments are required to close out these accounts. Many companies simply close them to the cost of goods sold account. Depending on the amount of the variances, this procedure could result in the inventory balances being significantly overvalued or undervalued. Theoretically, the variance balances should be proportionately pro-rated among the accounts in which the related standard costs reside at the end of the period, based on the amount of standard costs in the ending balances. Alternatively, the physical number of units in each account could be used.

The material price variance affects the most accounts since it is entered at the time of purchase. Therefore, its balance should be prorated based on the ending balances of raw materials, raw materials usage variance, work in process, finished goods, and cost of goods sold accounts. To illustrate, assume the following *partial* balances in the XYZ Manufacturing Company at the end of 20X5, all valued at standard costs:

	Debit	Credit
Raw materials price variance		$6,000
Raw materials inventory	$15,000	
Raw materials quantity variance	5,000	
Work in process inventory	20,000	
Finished goods inventory	30,000	
Cost of goods sold	130,000	

Based on the ending balances above, the following percentage ratios are computed by dividing the amount of each item by the total amount of all items. These ratios are used to prorate the raw materials price variance:

Raw materials inventory	7.5%
Raw materials quantity variance	2.5
Work in process inventory	10.0
Finished goods inventory	15.0
Cost of goods sold	65.0
Total	100.0%

The following journal entries would be made:

Raw materials price variance	6,000	
Raw materials inventory		450
Raw materials quantity variance		150
Work in process inventory		600
Finished goods inventory		900
Cost of goods sold		3,900

The remaining raw material, labor, and overhead variances should be prorated based on the standard cost balances in work in process, finished goods, and cost of goods sold accounts, after making the above entries.

Summary

A standard is defined as what the cost of one finished product should be based on industrial engineering studies of effective purchasing and efficient production. A standard cost system enters the cost of material into the raw material account at standard times the actual quantity. Raw material is entered into work in process at standard prices times the standard quantity allowed for units started. Similarly, labor is entered into work in process at standard prices times standard quantities allowed. Variable and fixed overhead are entered into work in process at the predetermined (budgeted) overhead rate times the standard quantity allowed.

The advantages of a standard cost system are: it provides effective benchmarks for use in variance analysis; it facilitates management by exception, it aids in the long range pricing of products, and it saves expenses and times in recordkeeping.

Standard costing is very useful in evaluating the performance of economy, effectiveness, and efficiency of operations. The variances from the standard costs should be reported to the manager, who has the responsibility for controlling the related costs. Variances should always be evaluated to determine if more than one function has responsibility for their occurrence.

The material price variance is used to evaluate the economy of purchases. The material quantity variance is used to evaluate the efficiency of material usage in production. The labor price variance is used to evaluate the assignment mix of workers in production. The labor efficiency variance is used to evaluate how efficiently labor is used in production. The overhead spending variances are used to evaluate overhead spending practices. The overhead efficiency variance is used to evaluate the efficient use of the cost driver or base used to allocate overhead to work in process. Finally, the

production volume variance provides an indication of how effective production capacity was.

The variance accounts are temporary and should be closed to the accounts in which the related standard costs reside at the end of the period.

Practice Problems

The following information pertains to questions 12-1 through 12-7:

The Foam Pillow Company manufactures high-quality orthopedic foam pillows for sale to specialty stores. Foam material is purchased in 18" × 30" standard units. The company uses a standard cost system and isolates the cost variances at the earliest point in the manufacturing process. The standard for one pillow (MH = Machine Hour) is as follows:

Cost Category	Standard Input	Standard Input Cost
Direct Materials	1 unit	$8.00
Direct Labor	¼ hour @ $16/hour	4.00
Variable Overhead Rate	¼ MH @ $12/MH	3.00
Fixed Overhead Rate	¼ MH @ $20/MH	5.00

The table below shows budgeted and actual data for October 20X5.

Budgeted Data for October 20X5:	
Number of finished units	10,000
Number of machine hours	2,500
Total variable overhead	$30,000
Total fixed overhead	$50,000
Actual Production Data for October 20X5:	
Pillows produced	9,800
Total cost of raw materials purchased and used (9,700 units)	$79,000
Total actual machine hours	2,550
Total wages paid to factory workers (2,700 hours)	$41,600
Total variable overhead	$32,000
Total fixed overhead	$49,000

12-1 What is the total overhead budget variance?

    A. $1,000F

    B. $1,000U

    C. $1,200F

    D. $1,600U

12-2 What are the direct material price and direct labor rate variances, respectively?

    A. $1,000F and $1,600U

    B. $1,000U and $1,600F

    C. $1,400U and $1,600F

    D. $1,541U and $1,400F

12-3 What are the direct material and direct labor quantity and efficiency variances, respectively?

    A. $4,000F and $800U

    B. $2,443F and $3,081U

    C. $800F and $2,400U

    D. None of the above

12-4 What is the variable overhead spending variance?

    A. $2,000U

    B. $1,400U

    C. $2,400U

    D. None of the above

12-5 What is the variable overhead efficiency variance?

    A. $150U

    B. $600U

    C. $2,000U

    D. $1,200U

12-6 What is the fixed overhead spending variance?

    A. $2,000U

    B. $1,000F

    C. $500U

    D. None of the above

12-7 What is the fixed overhead production volume variance?

    A. $1,000F

    B. $2,000U

    C. $1,000U

    D. None of the above

The following information pertains to questions 12-8 through 12-9:

The Jelco Company had the following *partial* trial balances at the end of the current year:

Direct materials price variance	Dr.	$10,000
Direct materials efficiency variance	Dr.	10,000
Direct materials inventory	Dr.	70,000
Cost of goods sold	Dr.	500,000
Work in process inventory	Dr.	100,000
Finished goods inventory	Dr.	120,000
Variable overhead variance	Cr.	20,000

The company prorates the ending balances in the appropriate accounts using the appropriate ending balance.

12-8 How much is the balance in work-in-process inventory after proration?

    A. $99,879

    B. $105,000

    C. $105,016

    D. None of the above

12-9 How much is in the direct materials inventory after proration?

    A. $71,750

    B. $73,750

    C. $89,522

    D. $70,875

12-10 Which of the following is not an advantage of a standard cost system?

    A. It is focused on inventory valuation.

    B. It facilitates management by exception.

    C. It provides effective benchmarks for performance evaluation.

    D. It may assist in long-term cost-plus pricing.

Solutions to Practice Problems

12-1 D

Budgeted variable overhead = $(9,800 \times \frac{1}{4})$ $12.00 = $29,400

Budgeted fixed overhead = $50,000 (fixed amount)

Total budgeted overhead – Total actual overhead = Total budget variance

($29,400 + 50,000) – ($32,000 + 49,000) = $1,600U

12-2 C

Direct materials and direct labor price variances = (SP – AP)AQ

[$8.00 – ($79,000/9,700 units)]9,700 = $1,400U (rounded)

[$16.00 – ($41,600/2,700 hrs)]2,700 = $1,600F (rounded)

12-3 A

Direct material quantity and direct labor efficiency variance = (SQ allowed – AQ)SP

Direct material: [(9,800 × 1) – 9,700]$8.00 = $800F

Direct labor: [(9,800 × $\frac{1}{4}$) – 2,700]$16.00 = $4,000U

12-4 B

Variable overhead spending variance = (Total actual variable overhead) – (AQ × BVOHR)

$32,000 – (2,550 × $12) = $1,400U

12-5 D

Variable overhead efficiency variance = (AQ – SQ)BVOHR

[$2,550 – (9,800 × $\frac{1}{4}$)]$12 = $1,200U

12-6 B

Fixed overhead spending variance = Actual fixed costs – Budgeted fixed costs

$49,000 – $50,000 = $1,000F

Or $49,000 – (2,500 × $20) = $1,000F

12-7 C

Fixed overhead production volume variance = (BQ – SQ)BFOHR

[2,500 – (9,800 × 0.25)]$20 = $1,000U

Or [$50,000 – (9,800 × 0.25)] = $1,000U

12-8 A

Compute ratios:		
Direct material quantity variance	$10,000	(0.0125)
Direct materials inventory	70,000	(0.0875)
Cost of goods sold	500,000	(0.625)
Work in process inventory	100,000	(0.125)
Finished goods inventory	120,000	0.150
Total	$800,000	(1.00)

Direct material price variance prorated to direct material quantity variance:

$0.0125 \times \$10,000 = \$125.00$

Direct material price variance prorated to work in process:

$\$10,000 \times 0.125 = \$1,250$

Direct material quantity variance prorated to work in process:

$(\$10,000 + \$125) \times 0.1389 = \$1,407$ (rounded)

Variable overhead variance prorated to work in process:

$\$20,000 \times 0.1389 = \$2,778$

Ending work in process balance:

$\$100,000 + \$1,407 + \$1,250 - \$2,778 = \$99,879$

Note: The variable overhead variance is subtracted since it was favorable.

12-9 D

The Direct Materials Inventory is adjusted for only the price variance; none of the other variances is adjusted to Direct Materials. Therefore, the solution should be:

$10,000 price variance × ($70,000/$800,000) (see first part of solution for 12-8) = $875; $70,000 + $875 = $70,875

12-10 A

Performance Evaluation: Sales Variances and the Balanced Scorecard

In this chapter the subject of performance evaluation is continued by examining sales variances in assessing a company's performance, including sales volume, sales mix, sales quantity, market share, and market-size variances. Also, the balanced scorecard is explained as a method to aid management in formulating,

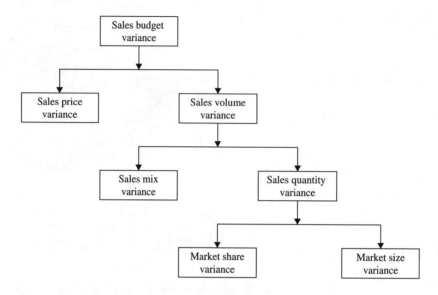

Figure 13-1   A framework for sales variance analysis.

achieving, and evaluating strategy, while there is a brief overview of other performance evaluation systems, such as Six Sigma and benchmarking.

Sales Variances

In Chapter 11 (Figure 11-1) an overall framework for evaluating financial performance was introduced. Chapters 11 and 12 were devoted to evaluating the cost performance side of a business, with very little attention given to sales performance. In this chapter the sales side of a business will be considered by presenting sales variance analysis that focuses on a specific underlying characteristic of sales performance. This analysis will aid management in uncovering the cause of any significant difference between actual performance and expectations embodied in the sales forecast. A framework for evaluating sales performance is depicted in Figure 13-1.

Illustration

The Strider Shoe Company data will be used to illustrate different sales variances. Strider had the following budget and actual data for 20X5:

Budget Sales and Contribution Margin Data for the Strider Shoe Company Sales Department

Shoe A:	10,000 pairs @ $30/unit	$300,000
	Variable cost @ $20/unit	$200,000
	Contribution margin	$100,000

Shoe B:	12,000 pairs @ $40/unit	$480,000
	Variable cost @ $28/unit	$336,000
	Contribution margin	$144,000

| | Estimated area market volume | 200,000 pairs |
| | Budgeted market share (22,000 ÷ 200,000) | 11% |

Actual Sales and Contribution Margin Data for the Strider Shoe Company Sales Department

Shoe A:	10,500 pairs @ $32/pair	$336,000
	Variable cost @ $21/pair	$220,500
	Contribution margin	$115,500

Shoe B:	11,200 pairs @ $39/pair	$436,800
	Variable cost @ $29/pair	$324,800
	Contribution margin	$112,000

| | Actual area market volume | 210,000 pairs |
| | Actual market share (21,700 ÷ 200,000) | 10.85 % |

Sales Mix for the Strider Shoe Company:

	Volume		Mix	
Budget	**Actual**		**Budget**	**Actual**
Shoe A 10,000	10,500		45.455%	48.387%
Shoe B 12,000	11,200		54.545%	51.613%
Total 22,000	21,700		100.0%	100.0%

Total Sales Budget Variance

The total **sales budget variance** is the difference between the total sales budget (budgeted sale price × budgeted volume) and the total actual sales (actual sale price × actual volume). This sales budget is the same as that used in the master budget that was discussed in Chapter 11. The total sales budget can be broken down into sales of individual products and variances computed for each product, depending on the evaluation objectives of a business.

Using the above data, the total sales budget variance for Strider Shoe is computed as follows:

	Actual Sales	Budgeted Sales	Variance
Shoe A	$336,000	$300,000	$36,000F
Shoe B	$436,800	$480,000	$43,200U
Total	$772,800	$780,000	$7,200U

The $7,200 unfavorable variance (less than 1% of budget) is relatively insignificant and suggests that Strider's sales performance was satisfactory. However, this total does not provide the complete picture. This insignificant variance could mask significant underlying variances by individual products. Thus, the total variance needs to be broken down into more detailed variances in order to completely evaluate the sales performance.

Moreover, the above analysis focused on total budgeted sales and actual sales dollars. Some companies choose to focus on contribution margin to show the performance results of both sales and related variable costs. Such companies prepare a flexible budget for the sales function that includes both sales and a deduction for variable costs to arrive at the contribution for the sales function. The contribution margins (CM) for Strider Shoe are computed above and are summarized below:

	Actual CM	Budgeted CM	Total CM Variance
Shoe A CM	$115,500	$100,000	$15,500F
Shoe B CM	$112,000	$144,000	$32,000U
Total CM	$227,500	$244,000	$16,500U

The total contribution margin variance broken down reveals that the contribution margin variance is much larger than the total sales variance. This detail shows that the actual variable costs were likely significantly higher than budgeted. Thus, this method provides more information than does the sales variances alone. An alternative to computing the contribution margin variances in aggregated form is to prepare a flexible budget statement for the sales function being measured that displays total sales less individual items of variable costs that computes the total contribution margin, and computing the total variances for each.

Sales Price Variance

To provide more insight into the causes of the total sales variances, the latter can be broken down into the sales price variance and the sales volume variance. The sales price variance is the difference between the budgeted sales price and the actual sales price times the actual sales volume. In a formula format it is:

$$SPV = (BSP - ASP)ASV, \text{ where:}$$

> SPV = Sales price variance
>
> ASP = Actual sales price
>
> BSP = Budgeted sales price
>
> ASV = Actual sales volume

Using the data from the Strider Shoe Company:

Shoe A: SPV = ($30 – $32) × 10,500 =	$21,000F
Shoe B: SPV = ($40 – $39) × 11,200 =	$11,200U
Total sales price variance	$ 9,800F

The total sales price variance is favorable but it masks the fact that the individual shoe sales had wide differences in pricing performance. Thus, breaking the sales down by type of shoe provides more information to management to fully evaluate sales pricing performance.

Why Does the Sales Price Variance Look Like a Flexible Budget Variance?

The sale price variance is sometimes called the *flexible budget variance*, since the budgeted and actual prices are multiplied by the actual sales volume. However, this flexible budget is different from the cost flexible budget discussed in Chapter 11 because it is based on *outputs*, whereas the cost flexible budget is based on *inputs*.

As an alternative or supplement to the sale price variance, some companies value the sales price variance by multiplying the actual volume times the budgeted contribution margin per unit, less the actual volume times the actual contribution margin per unit. This is also called the flexible budget variance.

Sales Volume Variance

The sales volume variance is the difference between the budgeted sales volume in the master budget and the actual sales volume times the budgeted sales price. It is necessary to hold the price at the budgeted level in order to isolate the variance between budgeted and actual volume. The sales volume variance in formula format is:

SVV = (BSV – ASV) BSP, where:

SVV = Sales volume variance

BSV = Budgeted sales volume

BSP = Budgeted sales price

Using the data from Strider Shoe:

Shoe A SVV = (10,000 – 10,500)$30 =	$15,000F
Shoe B SVV = (12,000 – 11,200)$40 =	$32,000U
Total sales volume variance	$17,000U

The results show that Strider Shoe sold significantly more of Shoe A than budgeted and significantly less of Shoe B than budgeted. There is no apparent relationship between the price variances and the volume variances. Thus, management needs to fully investigate the market forces that caused these significant variances.

As an alternative or supplement to the sale volume variance, some companies value the sales volume variance by multiplying the actual volume minus the master budget sales volume times the budgeted contribution margin per unit.

Sales Mix Variance

The sales mix variance (SMV) is very useful in evaluating whether the company is meeting its market niche target stated in its strategic goals. This variance focuses on the effects of sales mix change between the budgeted and actual. The sales mix variance can best be shown in a formula format:

$$SMV^a = BSP^a \times (ASM^a - BSM^a) \times ASV^t, \text{ where:}$$

SMV^a = Sales mix variance for product A

BSP^a = Budgeted sales price for product A

BSM^a = Budgeted sales mix for product A

ASM^a = Actual sales mix for product A

ASV^t = Actual sales volume for *all* products

Using the data from Strider Shoe Company, the company's sales mix variances are computed as follows:

Shoe A: $30 \times (0.48387 - 0.45455) \times 21,700 =$	19,087F
Shoe B: $40 \times (0.51613 - 0.54545) \times 21,700 =$	25,450U
Total sales mix variance	$6,363U

The Strider Shoe's unfavorable SMV shows that the sales mix of the two products was significantly different from the master budget. The company should focus on the total sales mix and find the cause of this significant difference.

As an alternative or supplement to the sale mix variance, some companies value the sales mix variance by multiplying the actual sale mix percentage minus the master budget sales mix percentage, times the actual units of all products sold times the budgeted contribution margin per unit.

Sales Quantity Variance

The sales quantity variance (SQV) is the difference between the sales units of all products in the master budget and the actual sales units of all products sold, times the budgeted sales price of an individual product times the budgeted sales proportion for the same product. In effect, this computation holds constant the sales price and sales mix effects and isolates the *overall* sales quantity variance. In formula format:

$$SQV^a = BSP^a \times (ASQ^t - BSQ^t) \times BSM^a, \text{ where:}$$

SQV^a = Sales quantity variance for product A

BSP^a = Budgeted sales price for product A

ASQ^t = Actual sales quantity for all products

BSV^t = Budgeted sales quantity for all products

BSM^a = Budgeted sales mix for product A

For Strider Shoe the BQV is computed as follows:

Shoe A: SQV = $30 × (21,700 − 22,000) × .45455 = \$4,091U$

Shoe B: SQV = $40 × (21,700 − 22,000) × 0.54545 = \underline{\$6,545U}$

Total sales quantity variance \qquad \underline{\underline{\$10,637U}} (Rounded)

The SQV for Strider Shoe shows the effects of total sales volume for all products failing to meet the total budgeted goals for all products set in the master budget. Why did the actual sales volume differ from the budgeted sales volume? Was it due to a decrease in the market size during the period, over which the company has no control? Or was it due to the loss of market share, over which the company does have some control? The answer to the latter two questions can be discerned by breaking the sales quantity variance down into market size variance and market share variance.

As an alternative or supplement to the sale quantity variance, some companies value the sales quantity variance by multiplying the actual sale units of all products sold minus the master budget units of all products sold, times the master budget sales mix percentage times the budgeted contribution margin per unit.

Sales Market Share Variance

The sales market share variance (MSV) is the difference between the actual company market share proportion and the budgeted company market share proportion times the actual market size in sales units, times the budgeted weighted average sales price. In the formula format:

SMSV = BWASP × (AMSP − BMSP) × AMSV, where:

SMSV = Sales market share variance

BWASP = Budgeted weighted average sales price

AMSP = Actual market share proportion

BMSP = Budgeted market share proportion

AMSV = Actual total market share volume

Using the data from Strider Shoe, we first must compute the BWASP:

Total pairs of Shoe A and Shoe B budgeted = (10,000 + 12,000) = 22,000 pairs

BWASP = ($30 × 10,000 pairs) + ($40 × 12,000 pairs) ÷ 22,000 = $780,000 ÷ 22,000 = $35.454

Next, the SMSV is computed for Strider Shoe:

SMSV = $35.454 × (0.103333 − 0.110000) × 210,000 pairs = $49,639U (Rounded)

From the budgeted and actual data from above, Strider's market size actually increased from 200,000 budgeted pairs of shoes to 210,000 pairs. However, Strider's market share was lower than budgeted, 10.3333% vs. 11.0000%, and resulted in an unfavorable market share variance. This requires an investigation into why Strider's marketing strategies were not working as planned.

Sales Market Size Variance

The sales market size variance (SMSV) is the difference between the actual total area market size in volume minus the budgeted total area market size in volume times the budgeted weighted average sales price, times the budgeted market share proportion. In formula format:

SMSV = BWASP × (AMSV − BMSV) × BMSP, where:

    SMSV = Sales market share variance

    BWASP = Budgeted weighted average sales price

    AMSV = Actual total area market share volume

    BMSV = Budgeted total area market share volume

    BMSP = Budgeted area market share proportion

Using the data from Strider Shoe the variance is computed:

SMSV = $35.454 × (210,000 − 200,000) × 0.11 = $30,002F (Rounded)

The SMSV was favorable because the total actual area market size exceeded expectations. However, from the market share variance above, it was shown that Strider did not maintain its market share expectations in face of the area market expansion.

Figure 13-2 shows a summary of the sales variances for the Strider Shoe Company.

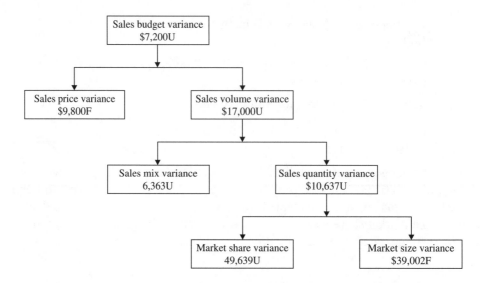

Figure 13-2   Summary of Strider Shoe sales variance analysis.

Evaluating the Success of a Strategic Initiative

Up to this point, this book has been primarily concerned with financial measures of revenues and costs. While financial measures are very important to evaluate *past* performance, many managers argue that they are not "forward looking" enough to influence and evaluate the success of strategic initiatives. Similar to their namesake in economics, financial measures may be thought of as historical or **lag indicators**, since they are an excellent way of assessing whether the organization has achieved its *past* goals, i.e., they are very useful in measuring outcomes. However, they are not very useful in aiding management to identify potential future outcomes or indicators of the organization's ability to meet its future strategic goals. These indicators can be thought of as **lead indicators** and are largely nonfinancial in nature.

Lead indicators are similar to key factors of success that organizations historically used to influence and evaluate the success of strategic planning; they also are largely nonfinancial in nature. They concern areas such as customer loyalty and satisfaction, productivity, and employee knowledge and skill capabilities. Lead indicators are early measures of outcomes of management and employee activities that allow managers to identify opportunities, predict problems, and help prevent mistakes. For example, early measurement of employee training and capabilities could predict or signal final outcomes in later strategic areas such as customer satisfaction, sales, and operating income growth. Since lead indicators influence activities in subsequent links of the **value chain**, they may be used at a later stage as lag indicators to measure outcomes of management activities.

What Is a Value Chain?

It is a linked sequence of operations or processes that add value or usefulness to a product or service from the start of the chain through each link to delivery to the customer. For example, in a manufacturing company the chain would contain research and development, design, physical resource acquisition, production, marketing, distribution, and customer service.

Balancing Financial and Nonfinancial Success Factors

As discussed above, the key factors that lead to strategic success in a business are not limited to financial issues alone. Fully measuring the success of strategic initiatives requires the balancing of nonfinancial measures with those of a financial nature. This balancing act was developed in the 1990s as the **balanced scorecard** concept, which has become a powerful tool in managing strategy creation, execution, and evaluation.

The balanced scorecard was first developed at Analog Devices, Inc. in the late 1980s. However, it was left to Robert S. Kaplan and David P. Norton to develop the balanced scorecard theory in the 1990s and extend its application to organizations of all types, from manufacturing to service businesses, and from governmental to other nonprofit organizations. It has been adopted by hundreds of organizations worldwide and is considered one of the most significant advances of the late 20th century for measuring organizational performance.

The balanced scorecard approach is similar to the Hoshin Planning approach that was developed in Japan, and which is also an organization-wide strategic planning system. Hoshin focuses management's attention on the key areas that are necessary for the organization's overall success and communicates strategic policy to all organizational participants.

Broadly speaking, the balanced scorecard is a strategic evaluation tool to help an organization recognize and meet its responsibilities to its major stakeholders: employees, customers, suppliers, stockholders, and the community. Under the balanced

scorecard, the organization's management fulfills its responsibilities by (1) deciding how to add value to each of these stakeholder groups; (2) developing lead indicators that drive strategic initiatives and create value in each link of the value chain; and (3) developing a system for an ongoing monitoring of these indicators and their results, to assess strategic success.

Some Guidelines for Adopting the Balanced Scorecard

The following factors should be carefully considered when adopting and implementing the balanced scorecard:

- *Focus on strategy*. Focusing the system on strategy will help ensure that the measurement system is more "forward looking" than the traditional financial measurement system; that the system focuses on cause and effect, or which measures will influence the desired strategic change; and that it helps motivate employees to think and act in fundamentally different ways, as to focus on learning, improving, and innovating, for example.

- *Size of company matters*. Due to the large expense in implementing the balanced scorecard, larger companies benefit more from this tool than do smaller companies. However, smaller companies could start a balanced scorecard using spreadsheets.

- *Consider outside consultants*. Companies that do not have the inside expertise using this concept should consider experienced outside consultants. In addition to advice, many consultants have software that can be adapted to various organizations.

- *An employee "contract" is essential*. As with most new concepts that affect human behavior, the balanced scorecard concept must be sold to the organizational participants and their acceptance must be gained before undertaking its implementation. Supervisors can play an important role by meeting with employees and discussing the balanced scorecard system, explaining the potential measures, and gaining input from employees.

- *Upfront training is also critical*. Successful implementation of the balanced scorecard requires extensive training before it is implemented. A shortcut in training will result in a shortcut in success.

- *Use a participatory approach.* Develop expectations and measures with key supervisors. If consultants are used, employees must not be squeezed out of the scorecard design and implementation. Key supervisors and employees must be involved to ensure acceptance of the balanced scorecard approach.

- *Tips for selecting measures of performance:*

  - They should embody desired results in terms of achievement—customer satisfaction, achieving process objectives, and meeting overall revenue and cost objectives.

  - They should be relevant, objective, quantitative, timely, and simple.

  - They should include effectiveness and efficiency measures. Effectiveness measures relate to desired output or outcome, such as quantity targets, desired quality level, completion date, and accuracy. Efficiency measures relate to output in terms of input required to produce one unit: labor, materials, and other costs.

- *Obtain measures and targets from outside the company.* In addition to measures from outside consultants, trade associations may have several performance measures, including benchmark measures of best practices. Internet research may also be helpful in finding competitive measures and targets.

- *Target levels should be challenging but achievable.* A target that is too high and unachievable will be dysfunctional by creating frustration, and will result in lower morale. A very low target will also be dysfunctional by creating apathy towards the target and the system.

- *Go slow.* Companies should consider testing this concept in selected area(s) of the organization to find "bugs" in software and other problem areas. Testing also helps to reduce the employee learning curve.

Measuring the Key Success Areas

The key areas of the balanced scorecard as conceived by Kaplan and Norton (cited above) are summarized in the framework depicted in Figure 13-3. Each of these areas will be discussed next.

Vision and Strategy

A vision is a leadership aspiration for an exalted future state of the organization that significantly challenges organizational participants. This high aspiration encompasses the shared core values and purposes of what the organization wants to become. Strategy translates the vision into broad goals and communicates them to everyone in the organization. It then plans to obtain the resources for achieving the created goals. The four key areas in the balanced scorecard assist management in achieving its vision, goals, and strategies.

Learning and Innovation

In today's rapidly changing technology both the organization and its employees must continuously be motivated to improve their knowledge and skills. Managers must also grow a strong positive corporate culture for learning, innovation, improvement, and growth. Training employees is a very expensive investment and requires the business to have strong policies in place to attract, motivate, and retain its human resources. A successful business will go beyond mere training to mentor or coach employees on internal business processes that lead to improved customer satisfaction and increased market growth.

Organizational "learning" is also very important to the balanced scorecard and relates to organizational improvement and innovation. A successful business will learn new ways to enhance revenue, find new markets, and develop new products and services to meet customer needs.

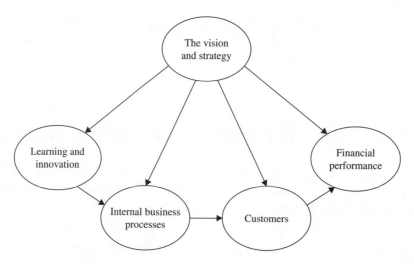

Figure 13-3   Key areas of the balanced scorecard.

Learning and Innovation Measures of Performance

Exhibit 13-1 lists typical strategies for a business and its employees to learn and innovate. It includes lead and lag measures of performance that are tied to the sample strategic goals. These measures are not necessarily all inclusive but are meant to provide a sample of measures that could be used.

Exhibit 13-1. Learning and Innovation Performance Measures		
Strategic Goals	**Lead Indicators**	**Lag Indicators[a]**
Develop employee skills that result in product or service innovation that meets customer satisfaction	Number of new products or services in the development pipeline	Number of cutting-edge products or services introduced into the market
	Amount of sales from new revenue initiatives	Product or service cycle time
	Percentage of employees participating in the employee suggestion program	Percentage of employees trained in process and quality improvement
	Number of adopted suggestions per employee	Percentage of employees at specified skill levels
	Average savings or revenue enhancement per employee suggestion	Number of hours of training (in house or external) per employee
		Number of new patents or copyrights
Recruit and retain educated, trained, and motivated employees to meet strategic skill objectives	Education level index of employees	Employee turnover index
		Employee retention index
	Employee survey that results in an employee satisfaction index	Amount or percentage of sales dollars spent on employee training
[a]The lag indicators do not necessarily match or relate to a specific lead indicator.		

Internal Business Processes

The second key area of the balanced scorecard focuses on internal business processes. A **business process** is a set of activities and methodologies needed to achieve a business objective or output. Internal business processes focus on:

- New and innovative products and services that meet customer requirements.
- Producing products and services at the lowest possible cost.
- Having the highest possible level of quality.
- Products and services that arrive at market ahead of the competition.

Successful companies will have at least four major internal business processes that lead to customer satisfaction and value, such as:

- *Product or service innovation processes.* A successful company must anticipate customer requirements and have a pipeline of new products or services to satisfy these requirements. To ensure success, this requires strategic decisions on how to organize the creative process and how much research and development to spend on new product or service development. Innovation also involves finding creative ways to increase revenues, such as new markets and new customer segments.

- *Customer management processes.* All successful companies have learned that the customer must be the major focus in strategic planning and execution. Internal processes should focus on excellent customer relations and customer service.

- *Supply chain management processes.* This involves managing inbound logistics and outsourcing activities. Strong supplier relations are critical in acquiring needed resources for product or service creation. This is particularly true when the company uses a just-in-time inventory system. Careful attention must be given to quality of the resources received and the timeliness of supply. With respect to outsourcing, attention must be given to supplier capabilities, quality of resources provided, and performance of the provider.

- *Employee productivity and improvement processes.* Successful companies will have processes in place that ensure a high employee output, level of quality, and level of efficiency. In addition, they will create continuous improvements activities and provide incentives to their employees for suggestions on process improvements.

Internal Business Process Performance Measures

Exhibit 13-2 provides a sample of strategic initiatives for initiating and improving internal business processes and the related lead and lag indicators for measuring success.

Exhibit 13-2.   Business Process Performance Measures

Strategic Goals	Lead Indicators	Lag Indicators
Develop cutting-edge products or services	Average time to develop a new product or service	Revenue from each new product or service
	Percentage of sales from new products or services	Percentage of sales from new products
	Cycle time required to introduce new product or service to market	Number of new patents
Develop strong working relations with customers and provide world class customer service	Amount of training per employee on resolving customers service calls	Percentage of products or services delivered on time
		Number of customer complaints
		Average time required to satisfy customer complaint
	Employee suggestions that anticipate customers needs	Average time from receipt of employee suggestions to successful adoption
	Customer feedback and suggestions on improving product and service quality	Customer loyalty ratings
		Number of customer service calls answered within x-seconds
		Average time from the receipt of defective product to the repair of the product
	Measures of product quality	Number of rejects
		Number of recalls
Develop strong working relations with suppliers that ensure high quality receipt of materials and other services	Supplier certification	Supplier performance ratings
	Supplier cycle time	On-time delivery performance by suppliers
		Number of defects in delivered materials from supplier
		Number of customer complaints from outsourced deliveries

(Continued)

Exhibit 13-2. *(Continued)*		
Maximize employee effectiveness and efficiency and minimize operational problems	Average training hours per employee to improve on-the-job skills	Average labor input for units of output (productivity)
	Policies and procedures detailing employee suggestions for process improvements	Number of employee suggestions
		Amount of savings from employee suggestions
	Cycle time in hiring and training new employees	Percentage of total products produced with quality defects
	Quality of product production	Manufacturing down time
		Number of products with unfavorable efficiency variances
	Quality of product deliveries	Time required to process customer order from time of call to time of shipment
		Percentage of total deliveries to customers that are on time

Customer Focus

As stated above, the customer is the major focus in setting strategy, which poses the following questions: What are the targeted markets, the strategies for reaching these markets, and the measures for assessing success? How does the company retain the customer's loyalty? What products and services satisfy customer requirements for utility, price, and quality? In a nutshell, who are the company's customers, and what are their needs and expectations?

Customer Performance Measures

Exhibit 13-3 lists examples of strategies for acquiring and retaining customers and the related lead indicators and lag indicators for evaluating the success in achieving these strategies.

Exhibit 13-3.   Customer Focus Performance Measures

Strategic Goals	Lead Indicators	Lag Indicators
Increase market share by a certain percentage	Potential new customers in market	Market share in given market area or industry
		Number of new customers and related sales dollars
		Relevant sales variances discussed earlier in this chapter
	Policies and procedures detailing employee suggestions for future needs of customers	Number of new employee suggestions for improving customer focus and service
		Number of employee suggestions adopted for improving customer focus and service
	Product or service price compared to competitors	Customer survey ratings on price and service
Increase customer satisfaction	Customer survey responses	Number of customer complaints
		Product returns as a percentage of sales
	Interviews with focus groups	Interview results that indicate customer dissatisfaction
Increase customer loyalty and retention	Customer feedback on employee service, responsiveness to complaints, and product quality	Customer satisfaction rating or index
	Number and disposition of customer suggestions for product or service improvement	
	Research on product and company image	Survey indexes from external consultants, e.g., J.D. Power Consultants
	Customer loyalty and retention	Percentage of sales revenue from repeat customers
		Percentage of customers retained from previous year

Financial Performance

The ultimate success of any strategy is whether it results in increased shareholder value. Changes in shareholder value are embedded in the financial goals and performance of the business. These revolve around such measures as profitability, return on investment, and increase market share. These measures have traditionally been the cornerstone of a business's strategy, since they are quantifiable and easily understood by most managers and the company's stakeholders. Financial performance has two major focus points: How well have the company's revenue growth strategies worked? And how well has the company managed its productivity, costs, and asset utilization?

Financial Performance Measures

Exhibit 13-4 lists examples of overall financial strategies to grow a profitable business. Included are the lead indicators and lag indicators for evaluating the success in achieving these strategies.

Exhibit 13-4. Financial Performance Measures		
Strategic Goals	**Lead Indicators**	**Lag Indicators**
Increase return on investment by a specified percent	Economic Value Added (EVA) (covered in Chapter 14)	Return on investment (ROI) (covered in Chapter 14)
		Residual income
		EVA®
	Amount of unused capacity available to achieve strategic goals	Estimated dollar amount of excess capacity using Activity-Based Costing (see Chapter 6)
Increase profitability by a specified percent	Revenue-to-cost ratio	Increase in revenues
	Benchmark results compared to "best practice" peer companies	Overall profitability
		Customer profitability
		Increase in market share
		Various sales variance presented earlier in this chapter
		Various cost and productivity variances presented in Chapters 11 and 12
		Industry-specific measures such as net interest margin in banks

Six Sigma and the Balanced Scorecard

Six Sigma is a quality improvement methodology whose objective is to eliminate defects in any aspect that affects customer satisfaction. This methodology has been used by such companies as General Electric, Motorola, and Bank of America to significantly improve customer quality within their organizations. The premise of Six Sigma is that by measuring defects in a process, a company can develop ways to eliminate them and practically achieve "zero defects."

Six Sigma works like this: every process, every human will sometimes perform at variance from what is expected. In statistics, "sigma" is the symbol for the standard deviation, a measure of variation from the mean. The objective of Six Sigma is:

- *Quantifying the customer's expectation* (called "specification limits").

- *Quantifying whether the company got it right.* This involves quantifying the organization's performance in the same dimension as the specification limit.

- *Quantifying success.* This involves comparing results to the spec, and using the analysis to take corrective action. Under Six Sigma, success is defined as an organization achieving six standard deviations between the mean performance of the process and the specification limit. The standard measure for Six Sigma is 3.4 errors per million, or one error or defect in a population of 300,000.

Six sigma can be used with the balanced scorecard by providing a more rigorous measurement system based on statistics. The balanced scorecard's underlying objective is to add value to each link in the value chain through strategic initiatives. The Six Sigma methodology can be used to quantify the impact and cause of defects or results that vary from expectation. In many organizations this means a measure of quality that strives for near perfection.

Six Sigma in Action

Two companies that have implemented the Six Sigma methodology are **Bank of America** and General Electric. Bank of America (BAC) has used the Six Sigma approach to significantly improve customer satisfaction. BAC's philosophy is a relentless focus on the customer to ensure that each person has a "delightful" and pleasant banking experience. Further, the company strives to ensure that the customer relations experience is applied consistently across the entire bank. To measure its success, a customer satisfaction survey is administered to customers using a 10-point scale. BAC's goal is to have 90% of its customers rate its service at a 9 or

10 on a 10-point scale of the customer satisfaction dimension. After 3 years of using Six Sigma, the percentage of customers rating BAC at 9 or 10 has gone from 42% to 52%. In addition, the methodology has aided BAC to significantly reduce product delivery times and problem resolution times in dozens of areas across the entire bank.

General Electric

General Electric (GE) strives to delight the customer by providing high performance, reliability, competitive prices, on-time delivery, service, clear and correct transaction processing and more; apply outside-in thinking by looking at the business from the customer's perspective, not the company's; and implement leadership commitment by involving all employees in the process. GE provides opportunities and incentives for employees to focus their talents and energies on satisfying customers.

Performance Dashboard

Some companies have developed **performance computer "dashboards"** on a real-time basis, reporting a key set of performance metrics (six to ten) that provide a "quick look" summary of mission-critical information to management. The set could include balanced scorecard metrics, Six Sigma metrics, or other key performance measures. For example, General Electric provides every participant in a Six Sigma project or deployment—from the CEO to a factory floor worker—with his or her own dashboard of summaries for his or her area of responsibility.

Benchmarking

Another methodology for evaluating organizational performance is benchmarking. Benchmarking developed during the 1990s as a methodology for measuring how well a business process, business unit, or even a corporation has performed compared with similar organizations in its industry or class. Benchmarks represent **best practice performance measures** either internal or external to the organization. Internally, businesses take measures from a business unit, division, or administrative function that has excellent performance in specific areas. Best practice measures representing this performance are then benchmarked and used to motivate and evaluate employees in other similar functions within the company. Any unit, function, or process is a candidate for benchmarking. For example, some large banks have benchmarked several key factors relating to customer service with the goal of becoming "world class" in these areas.

Best Practice Performance Measures

These are process or system measures identified by research or experience in a business, nonprofit, or governmental organization that represent exceptional performance and have been widely recognized as "best" by peer organizations.

External benchmarks of "best practice" used by competitors or even unrelated industries compare similar metrics of performance in the company. Competitive benchmarking occurs when an organization's processes are compared with best practices of another "best practice" company or companies within the industry. Some companies partner with other corporations in developing benchmarking projects as a source of benchmarks. Others turn to trade associations and consulting firms that specialize in this field and have a repository of "best practice" benchmarks. Also, nationwide benchmarking exchanges have been created to share benchmarks among its members and other professionals.

Like the balanced scorecard, a benchmarking system requires considerable expense and top management commitment. It also requires:

- Careful planning
- Employee participation and "buy-in"
- Careful selection of benchmarks
- Choosing a partner company or another source of "best in class" benchmarks
- A data collection and reporting system
- Procedures for evaluation and assessment by responsible managers
- Plans for improvement to eliminate shortcomings
- Follow-up to ensure that corrections for improvement have been made

Summary

This chapter has presented several variances as methods for evaluating the performance of the sales side of the business; sales volume, sales mix, sales quantity, market share, and market-size variances. These variances were shown to be useful in determining underlying causal factors for performance that vary from expectations. The balanced scorecard was presented as a methodology for influencing and assessing the success in achieving strategic goals. While traditional financial measures of performance are excellent for assessing financial performance, they are lag indicators in that they only measure past performance. The balanced scorecard "balances" these lag indicators with lead indicators that influence the creation of strategies and then assist in the measuring and assessing of success in achieving them. The balanced scorecard is divided into four areas: learning and growth, internal business systems, customer focus, and financial. Two other performance measurement systems covered were Six Sigma and benchmarking. Six Sigma is directed at measuring and improving customer satisfaction. It is directed at eliminating defects or performance that deviate from the mean. The goal is to improve customer satisfaction to six "sigmas" or six standard deviations from the mean. Benchmarking methodology is directed at measuring how well a business process, business unit, or even a corporation is performing compared to a similar organization or "best practice" organization in its industry or class. Benchmarks can be best practice performance measures that are developed internally or externally to the organization.

Practice Problems

The following information pertains to problems 13-1 through 13-6:
The Rufus Company manufactures two products, X and Y. Rufus reported the following information for the month of July 20X5:

	Product X	**Product Y**
Budgeted units	9,000	16,000
Actual units sold	11,000	15,000
Actual selling price	$40	$70
Budgeted selling price	$42	$65
Actual industry volume	325,000	
Actual market share	0.08	
	(26,000/325,000)	
Budgeted industry volume	294,000	
Budgeted market share	0.085	
	(25,000/294,000)	

13-1 What is the total sales variance?

    A. $62,000F

    B. $53,000F

    C. $53,000U

    D. $65,000F

13-2 What is the total sales volume variance?

    A. $19,000F

    B. $10,000F

    C. $10,000U

    D. $21,000F

13-3 What is the total sales mix variance?

    A. $33,579U

    B. $47,260U

    C. $38,440U

    D. $37,730U

13-4 What is the sales quantity variance?

    A. $113,440F

    B. $59,200F

    C. $56,720F

    D. None of the above

13-5 What is the sales market size variance?

    A. $149,457F (Rounded)

    B. $140,666F (Rounded)

    C. $143,772F (Rounded)

    D. None of the above

13-6 What is the sales market share variance?

    A. $83,378U (Rounded)

    B. $91,845F (Rounded)

    C. $83,378F (Rounded)

    D. $92,170U (Rounded)

13-7 A balanced scorecard measures performance in four areas of an organization, one of which is customer focus. Which of the following is a measure of customer satisfaction?

A. Sales market share

B. Percentage of customers retained from previous year

C. Hours of sales training

D. Cycle time for introduction of new service

13-8 A balanced scorecard measures performance in four areas of an organization, one of which is learning and growth. Which of the following is a measure of learning and growth in an organization?

A. Number of defects in processing a customer transaction

B. Percentage of customers retained from previous year

C. Number of hours training on job skills

D. Time required to complete a job order

13-9 Which of the following would *not* be a measure of performance from the internal business process perspective?

A. Number of new customers

B. Time lost due to errors

C. Quality of work in a manufacturing operation

D. Time to complete a job order

13-10 Which of the following is *not* a lead indicator?

A. Percentage of employees retained from previous year

B. Quality of production

C. Employee capability assessment

D. Market share achieved by a sales region

13-11 Which of the following is *not* a performance measure from the financial perspective?

A. Revenue per employee

B. Customer satisfaction index

C. Cost reduction per business unit

D. Increased operating income from productivity gains

13-12 Which of the following is *not* true about the balanced scorecard?

- A. The balanced scorecard is a system that uses only qualitative measures of performance.

- B. The company should sell the balanced scorecard to employees and gain their acceptance before implementing it.

- C. The balanced scorecard is very useful in motivating employees to work toward achieving the company's strategy.

- D. Employees should be effectively trained before implementing the balanced scorecard.

Solutions to Practice Problems

13-1 B

Sales price variance = (ASP – BSP) ASV

Product X = ($40 – 42)11,000 units = $22,000U

Product Y = ($70 – 65)15,000 units = $75,000F

Total sales price variance = ($22,000U + $75,000F) = $53,000F

13-2 A

Sales volume variance = (ASV – BSV) BSP

Product X = (11,000 – 9,000)$42 = $84,000F

Product Y = (15,000 – 16,000)$65 = $65,000U

Total sales volume variance = ($84,000F + $65,000U) = $19,000F

13-3 D

$SMV^a = BSP^a \times (ASM^a - BSM^a) \times ASV^t$, where:

   SMV^a = Sales mix variance for product A

   BSP^a = Budgeted sales price for product A

   BSM^a = Budgeted sales mix for product A

   ASM^a = Actual sales mix for product A

   ASV^t = Actual sales volume for *all* products

First, compute the proportions:

Actual Volume Proportion			Budgeted Volume Proportion	
X	11,000	42.31%	9,000	36.0%
Y	15,000	57.69%	16,000	64.0%
Total	26,000	100.0%	25,000	100.0%

Product X = $42 (0.4231 − 0.3600) 26,000 = $68,905F

Product Y = $65 (0.5769 − 0.6400) 26,000 = $106,639U

Total sales mix variance = $68,905F + $106,639U = $37,730U (rounded)

13-4 C

$SQV^a = BSP^a \times (ASQ^t - BSQ^t) \times BSM^a$, where:

SQV^a = Sales quantity variance for product A

BSP^a = Budgeted sales price for product A

ASQ^t = Actual sales quantity for all products

BSV^t = Budgeted sales quantity for all products

BSM^a = Budgeted sales mix for product A

Product X = $42 (26,000 − 25,000) 0.36 = $15,120F

Product Y = $65 (26,000 − 25,000) 0.64 = $41,600F

Total sales quantity variance = $15,120 + $41,600F = $56,720F

13-5 A

$SMSV = BWASP \times (AMSV - BMSV) \times BMSP$, where:

$SMSV$ = Sales market share variance

$BWASP$ = Budgeted weighted average sales price

$AMSV$ = Actual total area market share volume

$BMSV$ = Budgeted total area market share volume

$BMSP$ = Budgeted area market share proportion

First, the budgeted weighted average sales price (BWASP) is computed:

Product X $42 × 9,000 = $378,000

Product Y $65 × 16,000 = $1,040,000

Total budgeted revenue = $378,000 + $1,040,000 = $1,418,000

BWASP = $1,418,000/25,000 = $56.72

SMSV = $56.72 (325,000 − 294,000) 0.085 = $149,457F (rounded)

13-6 D

$$SMSV = BWASP \times (AMSP - BMSP) \times AMSV, \text{ where:}$$

SMSV = Sales market share variance

BWASP = Budgeted weighted average sales price

AMSP = Actual market share proportion

BMSP = Budgeted market share proportion

AMSV = Actual total market share volume

$$SMSV = \$56.72 \, (0.080 - 0.085) \, 325,000 = \$92,845U \text{ (Rounded)}$$

13-7 B

13-8 C

13-9 A

13-10 D

13-11 B

13-12 A

Performance Evaluation in Decentralized Companies

This chapter describes decision making when a company decentralizes its operations into segments—called responsibility centers—and assigns responsibility for each segment to a manager. Specifically, the chapter will cover the nature of decentralization, types of responsibility centers, performance evaluation measures, and transfer pricing.

Nature of Decentralization

The goal of most business leaders is to grow their company's markets and customer base in order to improve profitability and meet their responsibilities to the company's stockholders. When the company is first organized, it is likely to be small and its decision making vested in one person or in a very small number of people. As the business grows it becomes more complex and often dispersed geographically, making centralized management more difficult and ineffective. At some point in its growth, a company will likely begin to consider decentralizing its management.

Decentralization is a means of moving decision making away from central management and closer to its point of service or action. While decentralization is usually associated with a multiple-division—often multinational—company, it really occurs any time higher management assigns responsibility for managing a subunit to a lower level in the organization. Decentralization is a fancy way of saying that a senior manager is too busy performing high-level responsibilities to effectively manage a lower-level organizational unit and delegates the job to someone else. What kinds of responsibilities are delegated? Basically, the manager delegates authority and responsibility to plan and control the operations of the unit to which he or she has been assigned. This may involve managing costs only, managing costs and revenues, or managing revenues, costs, and assigned capital assets. The units involved vary widely and may be a sales department, bank branch, production plant, restaurant, division, or even a separate company owned by the headquarters company. This chapter will specifically discuss performance evaluation in the most decentralized organization structure: profit and investment centers.

What is Delegation of Authority and Responsibility?

Delegation simply means assigning authority and responsibility to a person or persons to act on behalf of another person for a fixed purpose. In organizational decentralization, it means assigning the management responsibility of an organizational unit to someone along with the necessary authority to effectively accomplish the job.

Advantages of Decentralization

There are a number of benefits to decentralization.

- Decentralization allows senior management more time to make strategic decisions that affect the entire organization.

- It enables management to respond faster to opportunities and problems relating to customers, suppliers, employees, and a changing local environment.

- It provides a training ground for future managers. Increased responsibility provides experience for managers who aspire to senior-level positions.

- It increases motivation in lower-level managers by allowing individual discretion and initiative.

- It allows the assignment of individuals with management skills to an organizational unit that needs a new manager.

Disadvantages of Decentralization

There are also drawbacks to decentralization.

- Decentralization may lead to dysfunctional decision making. That is, the lower-level manager may make decisions that are not congruent with the goals of senior managers of the overall organization. This occurs when the goals, values, or commitments of the individual manager are at variance with those of the overall organization.

What Is Goal Congruency and Its Relationship to Motivation?

Perfect goal congruency simply means that *all* employees are motivated to work toward the same result. Of course, this never happens. Practically, it means coordination of the personal and group goals of subordinates and superiors with those of the organization. There are three levels of goals: organizational goals, which usually relate to maximization of profit in some form; group goals, which usually relate to mutual commitment to shared values and ideals; and individual goals that relate to a desire or motivation to succeed, thus leading to self-esteem.

Motivation is the intent, effort, and tenacity that push or pull individuals toward a selected goal. It is important that performance measurement systems and incentives aid in motivating individual and group decision-making mesh with those of the organization. This is called **goal congruence**.

- The cost of monitoring and controlling the decisions and activities of subunit managers may far exceed the benefits. Before an organization embarks on decentralization, management must carefully consider the costs and benefits of this approach.

- Some functions, tasks, or activities may be duplicated. Decisions often faced in decentralization involve whether to centralize accounting, human resources, and other support functions or have replicate these functions at the decentralized unit.

- Decentralization may also result in conflict with other, similar, organizational units. While some competition among units is healthy, too much competition or failure to cooperate usually results in dysfunctional behavior.

Responsibility Accounting System

An overall framework for measuring performance in large organizations was depicted in Figure 11-1. You may want to review that framework at this time. What follows is a description of the responsibility accounting system that is used to measure and report on performance.

A **responsibility accounting system** is both a process and a structure. As a *process*, it is a system of measuring, collecting, and reporting data by responsibility center. The kind of information that is measured, collected, and reported, broadly speaking, includes feedback needed by the manager to plan and control his or her sphere of responsibility. Depending on the type of responsibility center (discussed below), this could include costs and/or revenues and nonfinancial information. As a *structure* it involves creating responsibility centers. The process and structure in a responsibility accounting system are further discussed in the following sections.

The Issue of Controllability

The manager should be able to control information provided to his or her responsibility centers. A **controllable cost** is one about which the manager has the authority to make decisions, such as whether to incur or change a cost; the manager is also responsible for such decisions. Including only controllable costs and revenues helps foster goal-congruent decisions. The controllability relates to the level of authority a responsibility center has and the time frame involved. Most responsibility centers have the authority to incur short-term costs. Decisions to incur long-term capital asset costs (buildings and equipment, for example) are generally made by the senior-level managerial staff during the strategic planning process. However, lower-level managers are held responsible for the effective and efficient uses of these investment assets.

Controllable revenue does not have a mirror meaning to controllable cost, since the manager who is responsible for generating revenue does not have complete control over his or her market. However, relevant managers are responsible for making decisions that influence the generation of revenue.

Managerial Evaluation Compared to Segment Evaluation

Controllable costs and controllable revenues relate to **managerial evaluation**, the personal performance of a manager based on his or her assigned responsibilities. Managerial evaluation should not be confused with **segment evaluation**, which involves the evaluation of a *segment* of an organization, that is, a business unit or a division. Segment evaluation usually involves looking at the profitability of a segment to determine whether it should be continued or discontinued. This is an important distinction because the accounting system collects *controllable* costs and revenues for managerial evaluation, and *traceable* costs or revenues for segment evaluation. A cost or revenue could be traceable but not controllable at a given level. For example, a bank considering whether to close a branch would be interested in all traceable costs, which would include fixed assets over which the branch manager would not necessarily have control. In this situation the manager could have been doing a perfectly good job of managing a branch that is in a poor market area, resulting in the branch itself performing poorly.

Responsibility Centers

As a *structure*, a responsibility accounting system involves creating responsibility centers. At several points in this book a reference has been made to responsibility centers (see Chapter 11, for example), but it was usually related to cost centers. The concept is now expanded to include all responsibility centers that are used in decentralized organizations: cost, discretionary cost, revenue, profit, and investment centers. These centers are illustrated in Figure 14-1.

Cost Center

A cost center is the smallest area of responsibility into which an operating organization is divided for control and accountability purposes and to which budget and cost reports are assigned. The sphere of responsibility relates to costs (inputs), which in

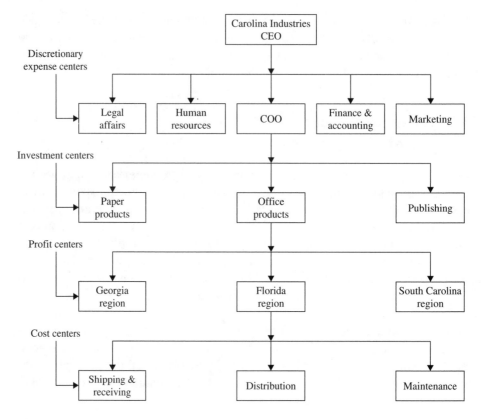

Figure 14-1   Responsibility centers.

turn relate to a defined input–output relationship. Thus, cost centers are often found in a manufacturing operation with a standard costing system and are sometimes called engineered cost centers. Performance evaluation is often in the form of flexible budgets and variance analysis, as discussed in Chapters 11 and 12. Cost centers are also found in service companies, where input–output relationship standards can be established, such as check processing in a bank.

Discretionary Expense Center

A **discretionary expense center** is usually an administrative or staff function in an organization that provides services and incurs expenses, but the center does not have an input–output relationship. In a large company these centers would include such units as advertising, legal, public relations, research and development, and accounting. Similar types of centers are found in government and large nonprofit organizations.

Why isn't there a good expense-to-output relationship? To answer this, as an example consider a legal department that handles different types of cases. It is difficult to quantify legal advice (output). While one could measure such things as number of clients, number of cases, and the like, there is little homogeneity among the various cases or clients being served. The major control devices in these organizations are usually negotiated static budgets, annual budget ceilings, and in some cases nonfinancial measures of performance such as benchmarking. Managers are responsible for not exceeding the budget and there may be penalties if this occurs. In fact, in many governmental organizations exceeding the budget is unlawful.

Revenue Centers

Revenue centers are usually sales departments or sales regions responsible for marketing and selling a product or service. The major focus of control is on maximizing sales, while the major control devices are sales budgets and sales variances that were discussed in Chapter 13. In addition to revenue, the revenue center manager would be responsible for the costs in the center and the principal control device would be a flexible budget of sales expenses.

Profit Centers

A profit center is a decentralized unit in which the manager has the responsibility and the authority to make decisions that affect both costs and revenues, which in turn affect its profitability. Profit centers are sometimes loosely called business centers and are found in all types of organizations, such as banks, restaurants, divisions, and any other organization where the manager's decisions affect both profit and expenses. Profit center managers usually have some authority to make capital investment decisions, such as making investments up to a maximum of a few thousand dollars. They do not have authority to purchase large items, such as equipment and buildings.

Principal control devices in performance evaluation are sales variance analysis, profitability targets, flexible budget variances, and other methods, such as the balanced scorecard discussed in Chapter 12. Moreover, profit centers often use a contribution margin format income statement, as depicted in Exhibit 14-1.

Exhibit 14-1. Georgia Region Income Statement Performance Report January 1 through March 31, 20X5			
	Budgeted	**Actual**	**Variance**
Revenues	$900,000	$960,000	$60,000F
Less: Variable costs:			
Cost of goods sold	200,000	220,000	20,000U
Shipping and receiving expenses	60,500	64,500	4,000U
Distribution expenses	80,000	81,440	1,440U
Total variable costs	$340,500	$365,940	$25,440U
Contribution margin	559,500	594,060	34,560F
Less: Fixed costs:			
Fixed shipping and receiving expenses	200,000	190,000	10,000F
Fixed general and administrative expenses	150,000	140,000	10,000F
Total fixed costs	$350,000	$330,000	$20,000F
Net operating income	$209,500	$264,060	$54,560F

Profit centers are organized in various ways. Some large companies divide their investment centers into geographical divisions, others by product or service. General Electric, for example, is such a large, diversified company that it has some divisions organized by region and others organized by product.

A major problem with using profit centers is how to measure profit when a center is not independent of other profit centers (in terms of revenue generation). On the revenue side, profit centers often transfer goods to other units in the organization. How should these goods be valued? This question will be addressed later under transfer pricing. On the cost side, profit centers often are allocated costs from their headquarters for costs that are common to all units. For example, discretionary expenses of headquarter functions, such as advertising and legal services, may be allocated to subsidiary units on the rationale that they benefit from the services provided by the support units, and the managers may have some influence over incurring them. Holding profit center managers responsible for these allocated costs is problematical and should be done with care, because the manager often does not have control over these allocated costs.

> ## Profit Center vs. Investment Center
>
> Investment centers are often called *profit centers*; in fact, the terms are often used interchangeably. However, technically, a profit center is not an investment center because it does not have the responsibility to acquire large capital assets.

Investment Centers

An investment center is a responsibility center in which the manager is overseeing revenues, costs, and its investment in assets. Investment centers are often called *divisions*. In this book the term *division* and *investment center* are used interchangeably. Divisional capital assets are acquired through either of two situations: Managers are granted authority to purchase assets up to a specified limit, say $500,000, or managers request assets above the specified limit by going through a capital budget process in which purchases are approved by senior management during the strategic planning process and assigned to the profit center for effective utilization of the approved capital assets.

Measuring Investment Center (Divisional) Performance

Performance evaluation in investment centers is more complex than in other responsibility centers. As stated earlier, investment center managers are responsible for revenues, expenses, and investment in capital assets, which require an expanded measurement. The expanded measures used to evaluate investment centers are return on investment (ROI), residual income (RI), and economic value added (EVA). These are often described as composite measures and are discussed in the following section.

Return on Investment (ROI)

ROI is widely used to determine whether investment center managers have generated a target rate of return on the company's investment in the division. The ROI measure is widely used because it blends all of the components of profitability (investment, revenues, and expenses) into one formula. The basic formula for this measurement is:

$$\text{ROI} = \frac{Operating\ Income}{Investment\ Center\ Assets}$$

Most companies break down this formula further:

$$ROI = \frac{Operating\ Income}{Revenue} \times \frac{Revenue}{Investment\ Center\ Assets}$$

or

$$ROI = \text{Profit margin} \times \text{asset turnover}$$

The latter formula was developed by DuPont several decades ago and is broken down into the profit margin times the investment asset turnover. The **profit margin** is a measure of the divisional manager's ability to generate revenues at the lowest cost; that is, how much of each revenue dollar goes to income. The manager will be motivated to increase sales and decrease expenses. The **investment center's asset turnover** is a measure of the investment center manager's ability to generate revenue for each dollar of asset invested in the center, or how many sales dollars are generated by each dollar in capital asset investment. The manager will be motivated to increase sales and keep investment to the necessary minimum.

To illustrate, assume that the XYZ Division has operating income of $265,000 and an investment base of $1,700,000. The ROI would be computed as follows:

$$ROI = \frac{\$265,000}{\$1,700,000} = 0.156 = 15.6\%$$

Further, assume that the XYZ Division generated sales of $1,500,000 to arrive at the $265,000 operating income; the ROI could be broken down into the profit margin ratio and the investment turnover:

$$ROI = \frac{\$265,000}{\$1,500,000} \times \frac{\$1,500,000}{\$1,700,000} = 0.177 \times 0.882 = 15.6\%$$

XYZ Division's rate of return is 15.6%, which on the surface looks good. However, breaking it down further into its profit margin of 17.7% and its asset turnover of 0.882 times provides much more useful information. An asset turnover of less than 1.0 means that the division is not generating at least one dollar of sales for each dollar of investment but is obtaining 17.7% of profit for each dollar of sales. Whether this is a good return depends on how well the division meets the targets of the measures set by senior management and how well it compares with similar companies in its industry.

Residual Income (RI)

Residual income is the amount of operating income left over after deducting a minimum capital charge based on the firm's investment base. While the ROI measure discussed above is widely used, it is not without its critics. The major argument against this measure is that it may motivate incongruent behavior by divisional managers maximizing ROI to the point of rejecting projects that exceed the target ROI set by senior management. For example, assume the following for the ABC Division:

Current division ROI:	22%
Proposed project ROI:	20%
Company minimum ROI:	15%

In the above situation the manager would be motivated to reject the proposed project because its estimated ROI (20%) doesn't exceed what the division is currently earning on its assets (22%). On the other hand, the project should be accepted for the company as a whole, because it is greater than its minimum acceptable rate of return on assets (15%).

To overcome this problem many companies use the residual income measure (RI), which is computed as follows:

$$RI = \text{Divisional operating income} - (\text{Divisional investment base} \times \text{Minimum capital charge})$$

The minimum capital charge is the minimum rate of return set by senior management based on risk and other investment opportunities foregone.

To illustrate, assume the ABC Division has an investment base of $1,500,000 and operating income of $265,000, and the overall company requires a minimum rate of return of 15%. The RI would be computed as follows:

$$RI = \$265,000 - (\$1,500,000 \times 0.15) = \$265,000 - \$225,000 = \$40,000$$

In this case, ABC had a positive RI and exceeded the expected minimum rate of return. This shows that the RI tends to motivate more goal-congruent behavior by divisional managers.

The greatest advantage of the RI measure over the ROI measure is the impact it has on divisional consideration of proposed investment projects. Using the above example of a proposed project that would earn 20%, the ABC divisional manager would be motivated to accept the project because it would increase the divisional residual income, since it is greater than the minimum rate of return expected. Thus, RI overcomes the problem of dysfunctional behavior that the ROI measure may generate.

Economic Value Added (EVA)®a

The EVA method, registered by the consulting firm Sterns and Stewart, is a variation of the residual income approach just discussed. It is based on two assumptions: (1) that both debt and equity have a cost and EVA® is designed to calculate the true *economic profit* of a company, and (2) that it will motivate management to improve EVA in one or more of three ways:

1. Invest capital in high-return projects that improve EVA
2. Increase revenues and reduce costs that lead to higher profits
3. Use fewer capital assets or less expensive capital assets

EVA has been adopted by many large companies—such as Coca-Cola, Equifax, Georgia Pacific, and Eli Lilly—and is used for several purposes:

- Setting strategic goals
- Measuring performance of the overall company or at the investment center level
- Evaluating capital budgeting projects
- Motivating managers
- Determining compensation

In its simplified form EVA is calculated as follows:

$$EVA = NOPAT - (Capital\ investment \times Weighted\ cost\ of\ capital)$$

Where

NOPAT = Net operating profit after taxes

Capital investment = the investment center's total assets minus current liabilities

Weighted average cost of capital =

$$\frac{(After\ Tax\ Cost\ of\ Debt\ Capital)(Bond\ Market\ Value\ of\ Debt) + (Cost\ of\ Equity\ Capital)(Stock\ Market\ Value\ of\ Equity)}{(Bond\ Market\ Value\ of\ Debt) + (Stock\ Market\ Value\ of\ Equity)}$$

Weighted average cost of capital: The above formula computes the overall cost of a company's sources of long-term financing computed as the average of the after-tax interest rate on the company's long term debt and required rate of return on the company's equity weighted by the respective *proportion* of debt and equity in a company's capital structure.

---

[a] Economic Value Added (EVA) is a registered trademark of Stern Stewart & Company.

The Weighted Average Cost of Capital Seems a Little Too Complicated

The best way to understand cost of capital is to think of it as the estimated minimum rate that a company must earn on its assets to satisfy investors. Often, companies will use the required ROI as the estimate of the cost of capital.

After tax cost = Interest rate on long-term debt $\times$ (1-tax rate)

Cost of equity capital = the opportunity cost to investors for an investment opportunity foregone to invest in this company

To illustrate the application of EVA, assume that the XYZ Division used above is evaluated using EVA. Use the following information:

Operating income before taxes	$265,000
Market value of long term bonds outstanding	$500,000
After-tax cost of long term debt	7%
Current tax rate	30%
Market value of common stock outstanding	$1,150,000
Estimated cost of equity capital	12%
Total assets	$1,700,000
Current assets	$50,000

Using this data, compute the EVA for XYZ.
First, compute the weighted average cost of capital:

$$\frac{[((.07 \times 1).30)\$500,000] + (.12)(1,150,000)}{(\$500,000) + (1,150,000)} = \frac{\$148,500}{\$1,650,000} = 0.09$$

Next, compute the EVA:

EVA = $265,000 − ($265,000 × 0.30) = $185,500;

$185,500 − ($1,700,000 − $50,000) × 0.09 = $162,525;

$185,500 − $148,500 = $37,000

The positive EVA signals that XYZ Company has exceeded its cost of capital and created additional value to the company and additional wealth to its shareholders. However, this measure should also be compared to the target EVA set by the company executives at the beginning of the period.

Measuring Income and the Investment Base

Three questions are often raised when the return on investment, residual income, and economic value added measures are used:

- How is income measured?
- What is included in the investment base?
- How is the investment base valued?

How Is Income Measured?

When it comes to income measurements for investment centers, there are various definitions of this divisional income:

- *Controllable income*, which is defined as contribution income (revenue less variable costs and any controllable fixed costs).

- *Traceable income*, which is defined as sales less controllable costs less traceable costs that are traced to a division but not controllable by the divisional manager. Traceable costs are capital assets purchased for a specific division.

- *Net income before taxes*, which includes deductions for traceable costs and common costs allocated by the parent company but not controllable by the division.

- *Net income after taxes* (since taxes are paid by the parent company, these are allocated taxes).

Which definition is best? As previously discussed, EVA normally uses net income after taxes (NOPAT), even though it may contain deductions for costs that are not controllable by the divisional manager. The rationale is that these assets have been provided to the manager for the division mission, so he or she should be held responsible for their effective and efficient utilization. Also, by deducting all expenses, corporate management can fully evaluate the divisional performance.

There are differences of opinion about the using return on investment or residual income. First, some argue that only controllable income should be used in ROI and RI computations for managerial evaluation and that traceable costs should only be deducted for evaluating the division itself (see the earlier discussion in this chapter on managerial vs. segment evaluation). Others argue that income before taxes and interest should be used, which results in traceable and allocated common expenses being deducted but not taxes and interest. They argue that taxes should not be deducted because these costs are related to corporate tax decisions or to tax law, and have no bearing on managerial control or the division itself. They believe interest should not be deducted because it relates to decisions made by the central headquarters, over which the divisional manager does not have control. Those in favor of this definition cite the need to be able to compare divisions or to be able to make comparisons with companies outside the corporation.

A compromise between these two positions is to deduct controllable costs and expenses to arrive at controllable income; then deduct other traceable and allocated expenses to arrive at operating income. The first could be used in the ROI and RI computations to evaluate managerial performance and the second to evaluate segment or divisional performance.

What Is Included in the Investment Base?

There are several possibilities:

- *Total assets provided to the investment center*. This inclusion is based on the argument that, when the productivity and performance of a division are evaluated, the investment base should include all capital assets provided or committed to that division. Most capital investment decisions are made at corporate headquarters during the capital budgeting process.

- *Total productive assets provided to the investment center*. This would include total assets less any asset that is not used in production, such as vacant land held for future expansion. This is based on the fact that RI is inherently a short-term performance measure, while nonoperational or nonproductive assets usually relate to the long term.

- *Total assets less current liabilities provided to the investment center*. This definition is based on the assumption that divisional managers have discretionary authority to incur short-term liabilities and should be allowed to maximize their use without a corporate policy constraint and, thereby, being held accountable for maximizing ROI or RI.

- *Allocation of centrally controlled cash and accounts receivable balances*. Companies that control working capital centrally often allocate cash and accounts receivable balances using incremental demands by divisions for these capital assets. These allocations are included in the division's investment base for segment evaluation but not for managerial evaluation. The rationale for this allocation is that by allocating working capital balances the performance measures are more comparable, since not including them would result in an artificially higher ROI, RI, or EVA than if it were not allocated. The disadvantage of this allocation is that it incurs the problem associated with transfer pricing, which is discussed next.

Which of these alternatives is best? Most corporations use total operational assets less current liabilities less any assets that are not in productive use.

Are There Other Adjustments to the Investment Base?

Yes, potentially. Some divisions or companies rely on leases more heavily than other divisions or companies. In this situation the investment base would be unusually low. To adjust for this, the leases may be capitalized and amortized to ensure that the division or company is comparable. Also, companies with large research and development and restructuring costs may take the same action.

How Is the Investment Base Valued?

Irrespective of what is included in the investment base, the question remains as to how the investment base should be valued. The alternatives are gross book value, net book value, and current value:

- *Gross book value*. This position argues that depreciation should not be deducted because net book value provides no relationship to the productivity of the capital assets, and depreciation methods are inherently arbitrary. Further, gross book value partially compensates for changing prices of assets and facilitates comparison between divisions or similar companies outside the corporation. The disadvantage of gross book value is that managers may be motivated to get rid of productive assets, since such action would result in a lower investment and a higher ROI or RI.

- *Net book value*. A deduction for depreciation provides a value that agrees with those shown on the balance sheet for external reporting, making the valuations more comparable to companies outside of the corporation. In addition, valuing the investment base using net book value is consistent with net income computations, which deducts depreciation. A disadvantage of the net book value method is that, as assets age, the ROI will partially increase each year solely because of the increase in the accumulated depreciation offset to related assets.

- *Current value*. This position argues that current costs should be used by adjusting historical costs with price indices for different classes of assets. Very few companies use this approach since it is difficult to obtain accurate current costs and this approach is expensive to implement.

Activity-Based Costing and Responsibility Accounting

ABC was described in Chapter 6, where it was shown how ABC could be used in to determine the profitability of a customer, a market segment, or a segment of the organization. As discussed in Chapter 11, a few companies have extended the use of ABC to responsibility accounting, where the focus is not only on evaluating investment centers, profit centers, and cost centers, but also on extending performance evaluation to the activities themselves. This approach allows the company to evaluate the costs of the activities and to evaluate whether the activity has added value to the product or service involved. An illustration of ABC used with responsibility accounting is presented in Chapter 11.

Transfer Pricing

Many companies have investment centers with products that are transferred entirely to other internal divisions or sold internally or externally on the open market. When sales are made to other divisions they become revenue to the selling division and purchases to the buying division. However, the effect on profit for the company overall is zero, since these transfers are eliminated when computing the overall company profit. Nevertheless, for managers held responsible for a target profit or return on its capital assets, the question of what is the correct transfer pricing is very important.

The transfer pricing mechanism should meet the following tests:

- Promote decisions by the divisional managers that are in the best interests of the overall company; that is, it should promote goal congruency

- Allow independent decision making by divisional managers with few constraints

- Provide transactional data for use in evaluating divisional performance when both revenues and expenses are involved

Transfer Pricing When There Is No External Market

When there is no external market the transferring division is a captive supplier. In this situation the transfer price is usually set at full cost or at total variable cost. In the full cost case, the transfer price equals total manufacturing costs plus total general and administrative costs (there should be no selling costs, since the transferring division is a captive supplier). In the variable cost case, the transfer price equals total manufacturing variable costs plus any variable general and administrative costs. In both cases, the transferring division is, in effect, a cost center, since there is no profit markup involved. The cost-based transfer prices should *not* be based on actual costs, as the transferring division will be able to transfer along inefficiencies to other divisions or cost centers. Therefore, the transfer price should be based on a measure of standard costs or budgeted costs. The transferring division's performance should be evaluated and controlled using standard costs and flexible budgets.

Transfer Pricing When There Is an External Market

When there is an established market for the products required by the buying division and the prices are fairly easily obtainable, **market-set pricing** is the best alternative. However, a problem develops when the producing division has excess capacity. This requires the use of relevant costing concepts that were discussed in Chapter 8.

Transfer Pricing When the Producing Division Has Excess Capacity

If the producing division has excess capacity and the idle facilities cannot be used for other purposes, then the transfer pricing should be set at the relevant cost to the company *as a whole* (usually differential or marginal costs). To illustrate setting a transfer price when there is an external market and the producer has excess capacity, assume that XYZ Manufacturing Company has two decentralized autonomous divisions: P Division and B Division. B Division purchases a component part from P Division, which is used to complete Product A for sale outside of the overall company. The component part can also be purchased from outside the company. Relevant data are as follows:

Outside market price for the component part	$60
P Division's variable costs per unit	$30
P Division's annual fixed costs	$100,000
B Division's sales price of Product A	$110
B Division's additional variable cost	$0
B Division's fixed cost	$50,000
B Division's annual production of Product A	2,000 units

Assume further that an outside supplier has offered to sell B Division the component part for $40 ($20 below P Division's price). Assuming that P Division refuses to lower its price, what is the likely outcome for the company *as a whole*?

Alternative 1: Transfer Price Set at Variable Cost of $30		
	P Division	**B Division**
Sales		
$30 × 2,000	$60,000	
$110 × 2,000		$220,000
Variable costs		
$30 × 2,000	60,000	
$30 × 2,000		60,000
Fixed costs	100,000	50,000
Divisional operating profit	($100,000)	$110,000
Overall company profit	$10,000	

Alternative 2: Seller Division Purchases Externally for $40 per Unit		
	P Division	**B Division**
Sales		
$60 × 0	0	
$110 × 2,000		$220,000
Variable costs		
$30 × 0	0	
$40 × 2,000		80,000
Fixed costs	100,000	50,000
Divisional operating profit	($100,000)	$90,000
Overall company profit (loss)	($10,000)	

Without constraint or intervention from top management, the B Division manager would be motivated to purchase the component part externally, since the P Division is not willing to lower the sales price. This results in the overall company going from a $10,000 profit, if the producer sells at its variable cost, to a $10,000 loss, if the B Division purchases externally.

Transfer Pricing When the Producing Division Can Use Idle Facilities for Other Purposes

When the producer can use the idle facilities for other purposes, the additional revenue or cost savings become relevant to the decision. In the above illustration, assume that the P Division could use the idle facilities to accept a special order that would result in a net profit of $20,000. What would be the likely outcome for the company as a whole, given that the other data remain the same?

Alternative 1: Transfer Price Set at Variable Cost of $30		
	P Division	**B Division**
Sales		
$30 × 2,000	$60,000	
$110 × 2,000		$220,000
Variable costs		
$30 × 2,000	60,000	
$30 × 2,000		60,000
Fixed costs	100,000	50,000
Divisional operating profit	($100,000)	$110,000
Overall company profit	$10,000	

Alternative 2: Seller Division Purchases Externally for $40 Per Unit		
	P Division	**B Division**
Sales		
$60 × 0	0	
$110 × 2,000		$220,000
Variable costs		
$30 × 0	0	
$40 × 2,000		80,000
Fixed costs	100,000	50,000
Net profit from special order	20,000	
Divisional operating profit	($80,000)	$90,000
Overall company profit	$10,000	

Without top management intervention the B Division would purchase the component part from the outside, and the P Division would use the idle facilities to accept its special offer. The result would be an increase in the company's overall profit of $10,000 under either alternative and the autonomy of both divisions would be preserved.

How does top management ensure that the right transfer price is used in the situation with producer excess capacity? There are no easy solutions to this problem, but there are several possibilities:

- Allow *negotiation* between the two divisions. This may lead to more congruent decisions and preserve the autonomy of the divisions.

- Establish an *arbitration board* to consider disputes over transfer pricing in this situation.

- Create *policies* on how the transfer price is to be set when there is excess capacity. If there are policy constraints that require the transfer price to be set at break-even relevant cost, the producing division may not have an incentive to produce and transfer. Accordingly, top management could let the producing division add a small markup in order to provide an incentive for the producer to produce and make the transfer.

- *Intervention by top management* to force the correct transfer price. This should be the action of last resort, because it would violate the autonomy of each division and be detrimental to the decentralization concept.

Transfer Pricing When Producing Division Has No Excess Capacity

If the producing division has no excess capacity, it should be allowed to sell to either the buying division or to the outside market. This policy guards against setting the transfer price below the producing division's opportunity cost, which is the market price that the producing division has to forego if it sells internally. The buying division should be required to buy internally, if the producing division's price is not greater than that in the market and if the quality of the products meets the buying division's specifications. However, pricing disputes will likely arise and top management should have an arbitration process ready to settle pricing disputes. The foregoing preserves the decentralized autonomy of the investment center manager.

Transfer Pricing in a Multinational Environment

Setting transfer pricing in companies that have investment centers in foreign countries becomes more complicated. Local country laws, import duties, and tax consequences become very important. This coverage is beyond the scope of this book. The reader should consult an advanced text on managerial accounting for further information on transfer pricing in a multinational environment.

A Synthesis of Performance Evaluation Methodologies

The last four chapters have covered several methodologies to evaluate performance in several settings. It would be helpful to synthesize all of these methodologies and measures as a summary of performance evaluation in organizations. This is done in Exhibit 14-2.

Exhibit 14-2. A Summary of Performance Measurement Methodologies and Measures		
Responsibility Center	**Performance Measurement Methodologies**	**Examples of Relevant Performance Measures**
Investment centers	Composite measures	• Return on investment
		• Residual income
		• Economic Value Added
	Sales targets	• Sales variance analysis
	Balanced Scorecard/Six Sigma/Benchmarking	Some examples:
		• Customer satisfaction
		• New product or service cycle time
		• Customer loyalty ratings
		• Employee suggestions
		• Supplier cycle time
		• New products in development
		• Level of employee training

Exhibit 14-2. *(Continued)*		
Expense centers	• Negotiated static budgets	• Budget and cost report variances
	• Incremental budgets	• Annual budget ceilings
	Benchmarking	• Nonfinancial performance indicators
Profit centers	Flexible budgets	• Flexible budget variances
		• Profit variances
	Sales targets	• Sales variances
Sales or revenue centers	Sales targets	• Sales variance analysis
	Flexible budgets	• Flexible budget variances
	Activity-based costing	• Cost variances
	Benchmarking	• Nonfinancial measures
Cost centers	Flexible budgets	• Budget reports
	Standard costs	• Cost variance analysis
	Activity-based costing	• Cost variances
	Quality targets	• Number of defects

Summary

This chapter has covered decentralization in large corporations that often operate in a multinational environment. Decentralization was defined as a means of more widely distributing decision making to bring it closer to the point of service or action. Decentralization has the advantages of:

- Enabling senior management to devote more time to strategic decision making that affects the entire organization
- Enabling faster response time to opportunities and problems relating to customers, suppliers, employees, and a changing local environment
- Providing a training ground for future managers
- Increasing motivation in lower managers by allowing individual discretion and initiative
- Allowing the assignment of individuals with the special skills related to the organizational unit that is to be managed

A responsibility accounting system is both a process and a structure. As a *process* it is a system of measuring, collecting, and reporting data by responsibility center. As a *structure* a responsibility accounting system involves creating responsibility centers. The types of responsibility centers are as follows:

- A *cost center* is the smallest area of responsibility into which an operating organization is divided for control and accountability purposes and to which budget and cost reports are assigned. The sphere of responsibility relates to costs (inputs), wherein the costs relate to a defined input–output relationship.

- A *discretionary cost center* is usually an administrative or staff function in an organization that incurs expenses that don't have an input–output relationship. In a large company these centers would include such units as advertising, legal, public relations, research and development, and accounting.

- A *revenue center* is usually a sales departments or sales region responsible for marketing and selling a product or service.

- A *profit center* is a decentralized unit in which the manager has the responsibility and the authority to make decisions that affect both costs and revenues that in turn affect the profitability of the assign center.

- An *investment center* is a responsibility center in which the manager is responsible for revenues, costs, and its investment in assets. Investment centers are often called divisions.

    Performance measures used to evaluate investment centers are:

- Return on investment, which is defined as $\text{ROI} = \dfrac{Operating\ Income}{Investment\ Center\ Assets}$

- Residual income, which is defined as Divisional operating income − (Divisional investment base × Minimum capital charge)

- Economic Value Added, which is defined as net operating profit after taxes (NOPAT) − (Capital investment × Cost of capital)

Two major issues in using ROI, RI, and EVA are what is to be included in the investment base and how the investment base should be measured.

When investment centers transfer or sell products to other investment centers within the company, a transfer pricing mechanism must be used that promotes goal congruence among the divisions and with the overall company. Transfer pricing can be market-based, cost-based, or negotiated. The concept of differential cost and pricing should be used in establishing transfer pricing when there is excess capacity in the producing division.

Practice Problems

14-1 Which of the following is a responsibility center?

A. Profit center

B. Cost center

C. Discretionary expense center

D. All of the above are responsibility centers

14-2 Which of the following measures is *not primarily* used to evaluate investment center performance?

A. EVA

B. Residual income

C. Net cash flow

D. Return on investment

The following information pertains to problems 14-3 through 14-7.
    The following data were constructed from the Willow Company for its Southern Division for 20X5:

Sales revenue	$3,000,000
Current assets	300,000
Total assets	2,000,000
Current liabilities	100,000
Net operating income	300,000
Land held for future use	100,000
Net income	210,000
Income tax rate	30%
Minimum return on capital	15%
Long-term debt market value	$1,500,000
Long-term debt interest rate	6%
Equity capital market value	$1,000,000
Equity capital interest rate	12%

14-3 What is the profit margin for the investment center?

A. 10.00%

B. 10.04%

C. 10.35%

D. 11.00%

14-4 What is the investment asset turnover for the investment center?

A. 1.000

B. 1.875

C. 1.400

D. 0.900

14-5 What is the return on investment (ROI) for the investment center?

A. 10.000%

B. 10.500%

C. 18.875%

D. 10.400%

14-6 What is the residual income (RI) for the investment center?

A. $60,000

B. $15,000

C. $45,000

D. $140,000

14-7 What is the economic value added (EVA) for the investment center?

A. $81,750

B. $60,000

C. $78,240

D. $70,920

14-8 The Johnstone Company is a multidivisional company. Each division has responsibility for achieving a target budget for the coming year. P Division sells a key component to Q Division and Q uses it to produce a final product. There is no external market for the component part. The company uses budgeted unit costs in preparing its master budget. The budgeted unit costs for P Division are as follows.

Direct material	$25.00 per unit
Direct labor	$22.00 per unit
Variable overhead	$12.00 per unit (based on direct labor hours)
Fixed overhead	$15.00 per unit (based on machine hours)

What is the transfer price per unit for the component based on budgeted variable cost?

A. $47

B. $59

C. $74

D. None of the above

14-9 Which of the following statements about transfer pricing is true?

A. The transfer price objective should be to merge the manager's interests with those of the overall company.

B. The transfer price should be chosen by the autonomous divisions so that the final selection should maximize both the investment center's profit and the overall company's total profit.

C. The transfer price outcome should meet the goals of the overall company.

D. All of the above are true statements.

The following information pertains to questions 14-10 through 14-12.
    The Multinational Company has two divisions, X and Y. Division X sells a component part to Division Y. Each divisional manager has responsibility for achieving a target profit for the year. The Multinational controller has provided the following data.

	Division X	Division Y
Market price of finished component	$160	
Variable cost of finished component	100	
Contribution margin	$60	
Market price of final product		$250
Variable cost:		
From Division X (one component @ $100)	$100	
Division Y	75	175
Contribution margin		$75

The variable cost of Division Y will be incurred regardless of where it purchases the components, internally or externally.

14-10 What is the maximum that Division Y should pay Division X for the component part?

A. $75

B. $100

C. $160

   D. $175

14-11 Division X has no excess capacity. What should be the transfer price?
   A. $160

   B. $100

   C. $175

   D. $75

14-12 Division X has excess capacity. What is the lowest transfer price that X will accept from Division Y?
   A. $75

   B. $175

   C. $100

   D. $160

Solutions to Practice Problems

14-1 D

14-2 C

14-3 A

Note: The following computations contain the answers to questions 14-3 through 14-5.

ROI = Profit margin × Investment asset turnover

$$\text{ROI} = \frac{Operating\ Income}{Revenue} \times \frac{Revenue}{Investment\ Center\ Assets}$$

$$\text{ROI} = \frac{\$300,000}{\$3,000,000} \times \frac{\$3,000,000}{(\$2,000,000 - \$100,000 - \$300,000)}$$

(Current liabilities and nonproductive assets are normally deducted from the investment base.)

ROI = 10.0% × 1.875 times = 18.75%

14-4 B

14-5 C

14-6 A

RI = Divisional operating income − (Divisional investment base × Minimum capital charge)

RI = $300,000 − [($2,000,000 − 300,000 − 100,000) × 0.15] = $300,000 − $240,000 = $60,000

14-7 D

First, compute the cost of capital:

$$\frac{(\textit{After Tax Cost of Debt Capital})(\textit{Bond Market Value of Debt}) + (\textit{Cost of Equity Capital})(\textit{Stock Market Value of Equity})}{(\textit{Bond Market Value of Debt}) + (\textit{Stock Market Value of Equity})}$$

$$\text{WACC} = \frac{.06 \times (1-.30)(\$1,500,000 + .12 \times \$1,000,000)}{(\$1,500,000 + \$1,000,000)} = 7.32\%$$

Next, compute the economic value added (EVA):

EVA = NOPAT − (Investment in assets × Cost of capital)

EVA = [$300,000 − (1 − 0.3)] − [($2,000,000 − $300,000 − $100,000) × .0732] = $210,000 − $139,080 = $70,920

14-8 B

$22 + 25 + 12 = $59

14-9 D

14-10 C

14-11 A

14-12 C

Final Exam

Chapter 2

Use the following information to answer questions 1 through 3.

Manufacturing costs	$3,000,000
Units manufactured	500,000
Beginning inventory in units	0
Finished units sold during the year	400,000

1. Compute the unit manufacturing cost.
   A. $6.00
   B. $7.50
   C. $3.33
   D. $8.00

2. Compute the cost of finished goods in ending inventory.

    A. $3,000,000

    B. $2,400,000

    C. $600,000

    D. $0

3. Compute the amount of cost of goods sold.

    A. $2,400,000

    B. $3,750,000

    C. $600,000

    D. $100,000

4. Which of the following formulas would determine cost of goods sold in a manufacturing entity?

    A. Cost of goods manufactured + Ending FG inventory + Beginning FG inventory = Cost of goods sold

    B. Beginning FG inventory + Ending FG inventory – Cost of goods manufactured = Cost of goods sold

    C. Beginning FG inventory – Ending FG inventory – Cost of goods manufactured = Cost of goods sold

    D. Cost of goods manufactured – Ending FG inventory + Beginning FG inventory = Cost of goods sold

5. If $200,000 of raw materials were purchased on account for the month of January, which of the following journal entries would be correct?

		Dr.	Cr.
A.	Accounts payable control	200,000	
	raw materials control		200,000
B.	Raw materials overhead control	200,000	
	accounts payable control		200,000
C.	Raw materials control	200,000	
	accounts payable control		200,000
D.	Accounts payable control	200,000	
	overhead control		200,000

6. XYZ Manufacturing Company incurred manufacturing overhead costs of $130,000 for February. Repairs and maintenance were $20,000,

accumulated depreciation was $50,000, indirect labor was $40,000, and utilities were $20,000. Which of the following entries is correct?

A.	Manufacturing overhead control	60,000	
	accounts payable control		60,000
B.	Accumulated depreciation	50,000	
	Accounts payable control	80,000	
	manufacturing overhead control		130,000
C.	Manufacturing overhead control	130,000	
	accounts payable control		130,000
D.	Manufacturing overhead control	130,000	
	accumulated depreciation		50,000
	accounts payable control		80,000

Chapter 3

Use the following information for questions 7 through 9.

James and Son is a local CPA firm that employs 10 full-time professionals. The budgeted compensation per employee is $125,000. The annual maximum chargeable time to each client is 1,250 hours. Clients always receive their full amount of time. All professional labor costs are included in a single direct-cost category and are traced to jobs on a per-hour basis. Any other costs are included in a single indirect-cost pool and allocated according to professional labor-hours. Budgeted indirect costs for the year are $1,500,000 and the firm expects to have 20 clients during the coming year. A partner spent 500 hours on Client A during the year.

7. What is the budgeted unit direct-cost rate for professional labor?

   A. $52.50 per hour

   B. $50.00 per hour

   C. $42.48 per hour

   D. $43.33 per hour

8. What is the budgeted unit indirect allocation rate per hour?

   A. $80

   B. $60

   C. $20

   D. $100

9. What is the amount of cost charged to Client A for the year?

    A. $55,000

    B. $73,330

    C. $26,665

    D. $71,665

The following information pertains to questions 10 through 12.
    Computer Components Inc. manufactures hard drives for computers. The company uses a plantwide predetermined overhead rate to allocate manufacturing overhead. Overhead is allocated based on machine hours. In 20XX the company budgeted 50,000 machine hours. The budgeted manufacturing overhead for the year was $400,000. The actual costs incurred by the manufacturing facility are shown below.

Cost Item	Total Costs
Raw materials purchased on account	$50,000
Raw materials used	25,000
Direct manufacturing labor	30,000
Indirect manufacturing labor	8,000
Indirect materials used	6,000
Lease on factory equipment	7,000
Utilities in factory	1,000

Job 201 incurred 700 machine hours during its production.

10. What is the budgeted manufacturing overhead rate for the year?

    A. $5.20 per hour

    B. $5.00 per hour

    C. $4.20 per hour

    D. $8.00 per hour

11. What is the total actual overhead for the year?

    A. $210,000

    B. $620,000

    C. $260,000

    D. $360,000

12. What is the total cost of Job 201?

   A. $101,800

   B. $60,600

   C. $80,800

   D. $79,800

Chapter 4

The following information pertains to questions 13 through 17.

The XYZ Manufacturing Company has two production departments, Cutting and Molding, and two service departments, Buildings & Grounds and Repair & Maintenance. Overhead costs for each department and the allocation bases for the respective departments are shown below for the month of July:

	Buildings & Grounds	Repairs & Maintenance	Cutting	Molding
Departmental overhead	$40,000	$60,000	$70,000	$60,000
Number of square feet occupied by departments		500	1,500	2,000
Direct labor hours			5,000	3,000

13. Under the direct method of cost allocation, the amount of building and grounds allocated to repair and maintenance would be:

   A. $35,000

   B. $30,000

   C. $5,000

   D. $0

14. Under the direct method of cost allocation, the amount of building and grounds allocated to the Molding Department would be:

   A. $22,857

   B. $20,000

   C. $30,000

   D. $31,250

15. Under the direct method of cost allocation, the amount of building and grounds allocated to the Repair & Maintenance Department would be:

    A. $20,000

    B. $17,143

    C. $15,000

    D. $31,250

16. Under the step method of cost allocation, the amount of repair and maintenance costs allocated to Cutting would be:

    A. $42,000

    B. $37,500

    C. $40,625

    D $35,000

17. Under the step method of allocation, the total amount of service costs allocated to the Cutting *and* Molding Departments would be:

    A. $105,000

    B. $100,000

    C. $60,000

    D. $40,000

Chapter 5

18. Laser Company uses the FIFO method in its process costing system. During the period, 30,000 units were completed by the assembly department and transferred to the next department. The total conversion costs that were added during the period were $1,600,000. The beginning inventory in the assembly department consisted of 10,000 whole units, 50% complete for conversion costs. The total costs in the beginning inventory were $550,000. The ending work in process inventory consisted of 8,000 whole units, 60% complete with respect to conversion costs. The equivalent units for conversion costs would be:

    A. 29,800 units

    B. 34,800 units

    C. 39,800 units

    D. 48,800 units

19. Refer to the data in problem 18. What would be the unit conversion cost for costing the completed and transferred units? (Round to four decimals.)

    A. $72.1477

    B. $35.2350

    C. $53.6913

    D. $18.4564

The information below pertains to questions 20 through 24.

The Hart Company produces heart rate monitors for sale to distributors. The company uses a process cost system with an assembly and testing department. The system has two cost categories: raw materials and conversion costs. Raw materials are added at the beginning of the process in the assembly department and conversion costs are added evenly throughout the process. Hart uses the weighted average cost approach. Production and accounting reports for the assembly department showed the information below for December 20XX.

Production Data	
Work in process, beginning inventory	4,000 units
Raw materials (100% complete)	
Conversion (50% complete)	
Units started during December	20,000 units
Work in process, ending inventory	6,000 units
Raw materials (100% complete)	
Conversion costs (60% complete)	
Cost Data:	
Work in process, beginning inventory	
Raw materials	$25,000
Conversion	$30,000
Raw materials costs added during December	$85,000
Conversion costs added during December	$160,000

20. The equivalent units of production for raw materials *and* conversion for work done to date would be:

    A. 20,000 and 19,600

    B. 22,000 and 20,600

    C. 24,000 and 21,600

    D. 26,000 and 23,600

21. The conversion cost per equivalent unit would be:
   A. $7.4074
   B. $8.7963
   C. $13.8889
   D. $5.0926

22. The raw material cost per equivalent unit would be:
   A. $3.5417
   B. $8.7963
   C. $13.8889
   D. $4.5833

23. The amount of raw material costs assigned to ending work in process would be:
   A. $98,999
   B. $95,667
   C. $27,500
   D. $102,667

24. The amount of conversion costs assigned to units completed and transferred is:
   A. $140,741
   B. $158,333
   C. $193,519
   D. $201,818

Chapter 6

The information below pertains to questions 25 through 28.

Allmart is a distributor of auto parts and uses an activity-based costing system. It has two major activities to which it assigns its overhead costs: order filling and delivery, and customer support. The accountant has aggregated the data in the following exhibits concerning its projected annual overhead costs activity data. Listed below are the overhead costs:

Overhead Costs	
Wages and salaries	$400,000
Other overhead costs	$200,000
Total	$600,000

Listed below are the resource consumption rates:

	Resource Allocation Rates		
	Activity Cost Pools		
Overhead Costs	Order Filling & Delivery	Customer Support	Total
Wages and salaries	60%	40%	100%
Other expenses	65%	35%	100%

Listed below are the volume of activity drivers and related volume used to allocate activity costs:

Activity Driver Volume	
Activity	Activity Driver and Volume
Order Filling & Delivery	4,000 orders
Customer support	80 customers

25. The amount of overhead costs allocated to the order filling and delivery activity would be:

   A. $240,000

   B. $130,000

   C. $180,000

   D. $370,000

26. The activity driver rate for the allocation of the order filling and delivery costs to the order cost object would be:

   A. $60.00 per order

   B. $92.50 per order

   C. $32.50 per order

   D. $45.00 per order

27. Assume that 300 orders were processed during the month of January. The total amount of order filling and delivery costs allocated to the 300 orders would be:

    A. $18,000

    B. $9,750

    C. $27,750

    D. $13,500

28. The activity driver rate for the customer support activity would be:

    A. $2,750 per customer

    B. $3,000 per customer

    C. $7,400 per customer

    D. $2,857 per customer

29. Which of the following would be a facility-level resource and activity?

    A.   Materials used assembling fasteners

    B.   Cost to set up a job

    C.   Costs to design a mold

    D.   Costs to occupy floor space in a building

Chapter 7

30. Playful Toy Company makes expensive toys. Playful has fixed costs of $200,000. The average toy sells for $60 and has a unit variable cost of $45. What is its break-even point in sales dollars?

    A. $266,667

    B. $13,333

    C. $600,000

    D. $800,000

31. Peters Company sells one product for $80. Variable costs are $60 per unit. At the current volume of 40,000 units sold per year, the company is just breaking even. Compute the total fixed costs based on this information.

    A. $800,000

    B. $600,000

C. $106,667

D. $1,500,000

The following information pertains to questions 32 through 33.

The Genome Company uses the high-low method to estimate its cost function. The accountant has estimated the following information for the coming year.

	Finished Products	Total Costs
Highest level of observation within the relevant range	3,000	$40,000
Lowest level of observation within the relevant range	1,000	$22,000

32. What is the unit variable cost per unit per product?

    A. $6 per unit

    B $8 per unit

    C. $5 per unit

    D. $9 per unit

33. What is the total fixed cost for the cost function?

    A. $15,000

    B. $13,000

    C. $12,000

    D. $10,000

34. How many units would have to be sold to attain a target operating income (before taxes) of $25,000 if the unit selling price is $50, the unit variable cost is $35, and total fixed costs are $15,000?

    A. 1,000 units

    B. 2,667 units

    C. 667 units

    D. 500 units

35. The accountant in the Dawson Company provided the following.

	Sales Price per Unit	Variable Cost per Unit
Product G1	$10	$8
Product G2	$9	$6
Total fixed costs		$30,000

What is the break-even point for G1, assuming the sales mix consists of three units of G1 and one unit of G2?

A.   3,333 units of G1

B.   9,999 units of G1

B.   4,444 units of G1

D.   6,666 units of G1

Chapter 8

Use the following information for questions 36 and 37.

Easy Mow manufactures lawn mowers for sale to large retailers. It presently manufactures the carburetors for its lawn mowers in the company's main plant. Easy Mow estimates that it needs 26,000 carburetors per year. A company has offered to sell Easy Mow the part for $65 each. If Easy Mow buys the part from outside the company instead of making it, it will not use the excess capacity for another manufacturing activity. Since other manufacturing activities are in the plant, Easy Mow estimates that 30% of the fixed overhead can be avoided.

The following list shows the cost if Easy Mow manufactures the carburetors.

Raw materials (per unit)	$30
Direct labor (per unit)	$20
Total fixed overhead	$500,000

36. In deciding whether to make or buy the part, the total relevant costs to make the part are:

A. $1,300,000

B. $1,600,000

C. $1,500,000

D. $1,450,000

37. What is the best decision for Easy Mow and what is the total cost advantage that would result?

A.   Make, $240,000

B.   Make, $390,000

C. Buy, $110,000

D. Buy, $120,000

Use the following information for questions 38 through 41.

The Collier Company management proposes to invest in equipment that will add solar energy to a building. The new equipment costs $300,000, including installation; it would have a useful life of 5 years with no salvage value and would be depreciated using straight-line depreciation. It would replace an asset with a book value and tax basis of $50,000 and a disposal value of $20,000. Management estimates that the new machine will generate annual cost savings of $70,000 after offsetting operating costs. Collier has a tax rate of 40%. The purchase qualifies for an investment tax credit of 7%.

38. The net cash outflow at the time of purchase of the machine, including tax considerations, would be:

A. $300,000

B. $247,000

C. $259,000

D. $268,000

39. The net cash flow for the end of year 2 would be:

A. $70,000

B. $10,000

C. $66,000

D. $74,000

40. The net present value of cash flows in year 5 would be:

A. $41,976

B. $66,000

C. $46,992

D. $37,422

41. What is the net present value of the entire project and what should the decision be, based on the quantitative data?

A. ($9,070)—Do not undertake

B. $9,070—Undertake

C. ($7,009)—Do not undertake

D. $10,500—Undertake

Chapter 9

The following information pertains to questions 42 and 43.

Enriched Lime Company manufactures lime for lawn applications. It produces the lime in 50-lb. bags and sells to retail nurseries. It presently has capacity for manufacturing 4,000 bags of lime per month and is selling all of its capacity at $10 per bag. It has total variable costs of $5 per bag and fixed costs of $2 per bag. A large home retailer made a special offer to Enriched Lime for 2,000 bags of lime per month at a price of $8 per bag during the summer months. It did not propose any purchases beyond the coming summer.

42. What is the minimum price that Enriched Lime should ask for the special order?

    A. $5

    B. $10

    C. $7

    D. $8

43. What qualitative factors could make a difference in the company's decision?

    A. The home retailer might consider buying an additional 1,000 for a total of 3,000 bags of lime at $8 per bag and pay for the $1.50 per bag shipping charges.

    B. The home retailer suggests that it is interested in offering a long-term contract to purchase all of Enriched Lime's capacity at $8 per bag and pay for the shipping cost of $1.50 per bag, if they are satisfied with the quality of the lime that they are purchasing for this summer.

    C. The president of the home retailer offers the CEO of Enriched Lime a place on its board of directors.

    D. None of the above.

44. Fish and Tackle Company manufactures and sells 10,000 fishing rods for $36 per unit each year. It has $400,000 invested in total assets. Manufacturing costs are $100,000 per year and selling and administrative expenses are $200,000 per year. Using the cost-plus pricing method, what would be the required markup, if the company desires a 15% ROI?

    A. 15%

    B. 10.2%

C. 8.3%

D. 20%

The following information pertains to questions 45 and 46.

ABC Manufacturing is considering adding product C to its present product line. The company is in a very competitive market and analysis has revealed that the new product must be priced at $50 or less. The company requires a minimum return of 20% on its investment in any new product or project. To design and develop and bring the product to production would require an investment of $1,000,000. The annual costs after the product goes on the market are expected to be $850,000 per year based on current operations. Sales of product C are expected to be 20,000 units per year.

45. What is the target cost per unit?

A. $42.50

B. $45.00

C. $40.00

D. None of the above

46. What is the cost reduction target?

A. $50,000

B. $150,000

C. $30,000

D. None of the above

Chapter 10

Use the following information for questions 47 through 49.

The All Rite Company accountant has developed the sales budget for the first two quarters of 20X5:

January	$300,000	April	$270,000
February	$250,000	May	$300,000
March	$280,000	June	$200,000

Cash collections have been determined to be according to the following pattern.

- 60% of sales collected in month of sales
- 30% of sales collected in month after sale
- 7% of sales collected two months after sale
- 3% of sales are uncollectible

Uncollectible receivables are written off on the first day of the third month after sale.

47. Cash collections for March are:
    A. $294,000
    B. $252,400
    C. $260,400
    D. $264,000

48. What is the amount of receivables written off in June?
    A. $8,100
    B. $8,400
    C. $8,300
    D. $7,500

49. What is the ending balance of accounts receivable for the end of May?
    A $147,000
    B. $155,400
    C. $140,000
    D. $144,000

Use the following information for questions 50 and 51.
    Jones Easy Shoes manufactures sandals for beach wear. The following table displays the production budget for one of its shoe lines for the third quarter of the year:

Month	Production
July	20,000
August	21,000
September	18,000

Each unit takes two units of raw material A, which costs $2.50 each. Jones has 2,000 units of material A on hand June 30 and requires a minimum inventory of material to be at 10% of the next month's production. Production in October is expected to be 16,000 units.

50. How much material of A needs to be purchased in September?

    A.   36,400 units

    B.   36,000 units

    C.   35,600 units

    D.   34,000 units

51. What is the cost of the purchases for September?

    A. $106,800

    B. $53,400

    C. $109,200

    D. $108,000

52. The following trial balances were taken from the Riley Company at the end of the period:

Accounts receivable	Dr. 100,000
Allowance for uncollectable accounts	Cr. 5,000
Sales discounts	Cr. 6,000

Riley made adjustments to write off $1,500 in bad-debt expense after the above trial balances were taken. What are the balances in accounts receivable, allowance for uncollectible accounts, and sales discounts accounts after this adjustment, respectively?

    A.   100,000, 3,500, and 4,500

    B.   98,500, 5,000, and 4,500

    C.   98,500, 3,500, and 4,500

    D.   98,500, 3,500, and 6,000

Chapter 11

Use the following information for questions 53 and 54.

The Rubber Storage Company produces plastic and rubber-based storage bins for sale to a large home improvement retailer on a long-term contract. The storage boxes sell for an average price of $20.00 each. The average box has an estimated raw material cost of $7.00 and labor cost of $3.00 per box. Unit variable cost is estimated to be $1.25 per finished unit. The company expects to produce 4,000 units during the coming month and 45,000 during the coming year. The company has a highly automated production process. Manufacturing fixed overhead costs are expected to be $17,500 for the next month and $216,000 for the next year and are allocated based on the finished units' expected long-term capacity. Since the company has a contract to sell all of its capacity, it has minimal selling expenses.

53. What is the budgeted manufacturing overhead rate?

    A. $10.00 per unit

    B. $6.05 per unit

    C. $5.63 per unit

    D. None of the above

54. What is the total flexible budget for 3,800 units, 4,000 units, and 4,100 units, respectively?

    A. $33,250, $35,000, $35,875

    B. $16,750, $18,500, $18,375

    C. $15,750, $17,500, $18,375

    D. None of the above

55. What is the flexible budget formula for predicting the month and annual manufacturing overhead?

    A. TC = $216,000 + $11.25X

    B. TC = $17,500 + $11.25X

    C. TC = $216,000 + $8.75X

    D. None of the above

56. Assume that Rubber Storage sold 44,500 units during the year. Further assume that total variable costs were $495,000 and that total fixed costs were $217,000. What is the flexible budget variance for total costs?

A. $4,625U

B. $9,250U

C. $3,950F

D. $4,625F

Use the following information for questions 57 and 58.

Roma City Hospital uses activity-based budgeting (ABB). One of its activities in the hospital laboratory is individual testing. After allocation of overhead costs to the laboratory using resource drivers, the budget for the activity was estimated to be $145,000 for 20X4. The cost driver to charge costs to a patient was number of patient procedures.

It was estimated that 5,000 procedures would be performed by the testing activity for 20X4. At the end of 20X4 the actual number of procedures was 5,100 and the actual cost for the activity was $151,000.

57. What was the budgeted cost driver rate for 20X4?

A. $29.60

B. $29.00

C. $28.43

D. None of the above

58. What was the activity variance?

A. $2,961U

B. $6,000U

C. $3,100U

D. None of the above

Chapter 12

Use the following information for questions 59 through 62.

The Gastonia Company manufactures fertilizer distributors. The company uses a standard cost system and allocates overhead based on machine hours. The following information relates to the company's assembly department manufacturing overhead for the current year:

Standard Cost for One Unit:	
Variable overhead rate	Two hours @ $3 per machine hour (MH)
Fixed overhead rate	Two hours @ $4 per machine hour (MH)
Budget Data:	
Budgeted output units	30,000
Budgeted machine hours	60,000
Budgeted variable manufacturing overhead	$180,000
Budgeted fixed manufacturing overhead	$240,000
Actual Data:	
Actual output units produced	33,000
Actual machine hours	63,000
Actual variable manufacturing overhead	$188,000
Actual fixed manufacturing overhead	$231,000

59. What is the variable manufacturing overhead flexible budget variance?

    A. $10,000F

    B. $8,000U

    C. $9,000U

    D.   None of the above

60. What is the variable manufacturing overhead spending variance?

    A. $8,000U

    B. $1,000F

    C. $7,000U

    D. $1,000U

61. What is the fixed manufacturing overhead spending variance?

    A. $33,000F

    B. $9,000F

    C. $9,000U

    D.   None of the above

62. What is the fixed manufacturing overhead production volume variance?

    A. $12,000F

    B. $24,000F

    C. $18,000F

    D. $24,000U

Chapter 13

The following information pertains to questions 63 through 65:

The Clear Glass Company sells two types of insulated window panes to window installers: Tinted and Low Tint. The company had the following budgeted and actual data for the month of April:

	Budgeted		Actual	
	Tinted	Low Tint	Tinted	Low Tint
Selling price per pane	$25	$20	$26	$19
Variable cost per pane	15	10	14	10
Contribution margin per pane	$10	$10	$12	$9
Unit sales	2,400	2,000	2,300	2,100
Fixed costs		$8,000		$6,000

63. What is the total sales volume variance based on contribution margin?

    A. $300U

    B. $8,300U

    C. $0

    D. $8,000U

64. What is the total sales mix variance based on contribution margin?

    A. $301U

    B. $0

    C. $602U

    D. None of the above

65. What is the total sales quantity variance based on contribution margin?

    A. $301U

    B. $301F

    C. $602F

    D. $0

Chapter 14

The following information pertains to questions 68 through 70:

The Multinational Company has two divisions, X and Y. Division X sells a component part to Division Y. Both divisions are autonomous and make their own decisions with respect to sales and sourcing. The Multinational controller has provided the following data:

	Division X	Division Y
Market price of finished component	$160	
Variable cost of finished component	100	
Contribution margin	$60	
Market price of final product		$250
Variable cost:		
Division X (1 component @ $100)	$100	
Division Y	$75	$175
Contribution margin		$75

The variable cost of Division Y will be incurred regardless of where it purchases the components, internally or externally.

66. Assume that X has been selling Y the part at $160 each. Demand for the part has been reduced and there is excess capacity throughout the market, including in Division X. An outside vendor has offered to sell Y the part for $120, if it purchases 3,000 units. Division X refuses to meet this price. What is the effect on the overall company profit, if Y accepts the offer?

    A. $60,000 loss to overall company

    B. No effect on overall company profit, since each division is autonomous.

    C. $120,000 loss to overall company

    D. $120,000 profit to overall company

67. If Division X wants to transfer the component to Division Y at a $160 transfer price, what is the likely outcome, if there are no overall company constraints?

A. The two divisions would negotiate and arrive at the transfer price that is in the best interests of the company as a whole.

B. Division Y would buy from Division X at the $160 price, since it should keep the production within the company.

C. Division Y would not want to buy from Division X since the component could be purchased in the market for $120.

D. Division Y would buy at the $160 price, so long as Division X agrees to supply all the quantity it needs to make a profit.

68. Division X is operating at full capacity and has backorders for the component part. What is the minimum price that Division X should accept from Division Y?

    A. $160

    B. $100

    C. $175

    D. $75

The following information pertains to problems 71 through 72.

    The following data were constructed from the Sycamore Company for its Southern Division for 20X5:

Sales revenue	$6,000,000
Accounts receivable	600,000
Total assets	4,000,000
Current liabilities	200,000
Net operating income	600,000
Land held for future use	200,000
Net income	420,000
Income tax rate	30%
Minimum return on capital	15%

69. What is the return on investment for the investment center?

    A. 10.000%

    B. 10.500%

    C. 18.875%

    D. 10.400%

70. What is the residual income for the investment center?

    A. $120,000

    B. $30,000

    C. $90,000

    D. $240,000

Solutions

1.   A   ($3,000,000/500,000) = $6

2.   C   (500,000 − 400,000) × $6 = $600,000

3.   A $6 × 400,000 = $2,400,000

4.   D

5.   C

6.   D

7.   B $125,000 × 10 = $1,250,000; 1,250 × 20 = 25,000 hours; $1,250,000 ÷ 25,000 = $50.00 per hour, rounded

8.   B $1,500,000/25,000 hours = $60 per hour

9.   A   (500 × $60.00) + (500 × $60.00) = $55,000

10.   D $400,000/50,000 hours = $8.00 per hour

11.   C $120,000 + 40,000 + 50,000 + 50,000 = $260,000

12.   B $25,000 + $30,000 + ($8 × 700 hours) = $60,600 (See answer in # 10 for rate).

13.   D (Under the direct method, no support costs are allocated to another support department)

14.   A $\left(\dfrac{2,000}{1,500 + 2,000} \right) \times \$40,000 = \$22,857$

15.   B $\left(\dfrac{1,500}{1,500 + 2,000} \right) \times \$40,000 = \$17,143$

16.   C   First, compute the allocation of Buildings & Grounds to Repairs & Maintenance: $\left(\dfrac{500}{500 + 1,500 + 2,000} \right) \times \$40,000 = \$5,000$

Next, compute allocation of Repairs & Maintenance to Cutting:

$$(\$5,000 + \$60,000) \times \left(\frac{5,000}{5,000 + 3,000} \right) = \$40,625$$

17. B ($60,000 + $40,000) = $100,000 (All service department costs would be allocated.)

18. A

To complete the beginning inventory: $10,000 \times 0.5 = 5,000$ units

Completed this period: $30,000 - 10,000 = 20,000$ units

Work done ending work in process this period: $8,000 \times 0.6 = 4,800$ units

Equivalent units under FIFO = $5,000 + 20,000 + 4,800 = 29,800$

19. C $1,600,000/29,800 = $53.6913

20. C

First, compute units completed and transferred: $4,000 + 20,000 - 6,000 = 18,000$

Raw materials = $18,000 + 6,000 = 24,000$ equivalent units

Conversion = $18,000 + (6,000 \times 0.60) = 21,600$

21. B $\left(\dfrac{\$30,000 + \$160,000}{21,600} \right) = \$8.7963$

22. D $\left(\dfrac{\$25,000 + \$85,000}{24,000} \right) = \$4.5833$

23. C $6,000 \times \$4.5833 = \$27,500$

24. B $(4,000 + 20,000 - 6,000) \times \$8.7963 = \$158,333$

25. D $(\$400,000 \times 0.6) + (\$200,000 \times 0.65) = \$370,000$

26. B $370,000/4,000 = $92.50 per order

27. C 300 orders $\times$ $92.50 = $27,750

28. D $(\$400,000 \times 0.4) + (\$200,000 \times 0.35) = \$230,000$

$230,000/80 = $2,875 per customer

29. D

30. D $\$200,000 \div \left(\dfrac{\$60 - \$45}{\$60} \right) = \$800,000$

31. A Let TFC = Total fixed costs

$$\left(\frac{TFC}{\$80-60}\right)=40{,}000 \text{ units}$$

TFC = \$800,000

32. D $UVC=\left(\dfrac{\$40{,}000-22{,}000}{3{,}000-1{,}000}\right)=\$9$

33. B TFC = \$40,000 – (\$9 × 3,000) = \$40,000 – \$27,000 = \$13,000

34. B \$50Q – 35Q – \$15,000 = \$25,000

\$15Q = \$40,000

Q = 2,667 units

35. B 3Q(\$10 – 8) + Q(\$9 – 6) – \$30,000 = 0

6Q + 3Q = \$30,000

9Q = \$30,000

Q = 3,333 units of G2

3Q = 9,999 units of G1

36. D (\$30 × 26,000) + (\$20 × 26,000) + (\$500,000 × 0.30) = \$1,450,000

37. A \$65 × 26,000 = \$1,690,000 to buy

From # 36: \$1,450,000 to make

\$240,000 advantage to make

38. B (Note a complete solution is shown in the table below # 41.)

\$21,000 Investment tax credit + 20,000 Sale of old asset + 12,000 Tax savings from sale of old asset (see note 4 in table below) – \$300,000 purchase of machine

39. C $\$70{,}000-[\$70{,}000 \text{ annual savings} -\left(\dfrac{\$300{,}000}{5}\right)\text{ depreciation}\times 0.40]$ = \$66,000

40. D \$66,000 × 0.567 = \$37,422

41. A [(\$66,000 × 0.893) + (\$66,000 × 0.797) + (\$66,000 × 0.712) + (\$66,000 × 0.636) + (\$66,000 × 0.567)] – \$247,000 = (\$9,070)

The project yields a negative cash outflow of \$9,070 and should not be undertaken, unless there are overriding corporate qualitative goals that would persuade management to accept it.

		Schedule of Cash Flows for Collier Company					
		Investment in Project	Cash Flows at End of Each Year				
		0	1	2	3	4	5
1.	Cost of equipment and installation	($300,000)	0	0	0	0	0
2.	Investment tax credit savings	21,000	0	0	0	0	0
3.	Proceeds from sale of old asset	20,000	0	0	0	0	0
4.	Tax savings from sale of old asset	12,000	0	0	0	0	0
5.	Annual cash flows before taxes	0	70,000	70,000	70,000	70,000	70,000
6.	Taxes on annual cash flows	0	(4,000)	(4,000)	(4,000)	(4,000)	(4,000)
7.	Net cash flows for each period	($247,000)	$66,000	$66,000	$66,000	$66,000	$66,000
8.	Present value factor at 12%	1.00	0.893	0.797	0.712	0.636	0.567
9.	Present value of cash flows	($247,000)	$58,938	$52,602	$46,992	$41,976	$37,422
10.	Net present value of the project	($9,070)					

Explanations relating to specific entry numbers in the table:

2. $300,000 \times 0.07 = \$21,000$

4. $50,000 tax basis – $20,000 sale of old asset = $30,000 loss $\times 0.40 = \$12,000$

5. $70,000 annual savings before taxes

6. $70,000 annual savings $- \left(\frac{\$300,000}{5}\right) \times 0.40 = \$4,000$

8. Present value factors are taken from the table in the appendix at the end of Chapter 8

9. Row 9 × Row 10

10. The cash outflows at the time of the investment less the sum of cash savings from years 1–5

42. B   The company is at full capacity and should not accept an offer less than the $10 selling price it is presently receiving.

43. B

44. D $\text{Markup} = \left(\dfrac{\$400,000 \times .015}{10,000}\right) = \$6$

$\text{Cost} = \left(\dfrac{\$100,000 + 200,000}{10,000}\right) = \$30$

$\text{Markup \%} = \$6 \div \$30 = 20\%$

45. C $\text{Target cost} = \$50.00 - \left(\dfrac{\$1,000,000 \times .20}{20,000 \text{ units}}\right) = \$40$

46. A Cost reduction target = Expected cost – Total target costs

Cost reduction target = $850,000 – (20,000 × $40) = $50,000

The costs based on current operations, exceed the target costs by $50,000 requiring the company to perform value reengineering to design the product and underlying operations to meet the cost reduction target.

47. D ($0.6 × $280,000) + (0.3 × $250,000) + (0.07 × $300,000) = $264,000

48. B $280,000 × 0.03 = $8,400

49. B [(1.0 – 0.6) × $300,000] + [(1.0 – 0.6 – 0.3) × $270,000] + [(1.0 – 0.6 – 0.3 – 0.07) × $280,000] = $155,400

50. C [(18,000 × 2) + (16,000 × 0.10 × 2) – (18,000 × 0.10 × 2)] = 35,600 units

51. A [(18,000 × 2) + (16,000 × 0.10 × 2) – (18,000 × 0.10 × 2) × $3.50] = $106,800

52. D The accounts receivable is credited for $1,500 and the allowance for uncollectible accounts is debited for $1,500 and the sales discount account is unaffected.

53. B Fixed overhead rate = ($216,000/45,000) = $4.80

Total overhead rate = $4.80 + $1.25 (variable) = $6.05

The rate would be based on an annual production to smooth out any variations during the year.

54. C (See the table below.)

55. B (See the table below.)

Number of units sold	3,800	4,000	4,100
Revenues @ $20 per unit	$76,000	$80,000	$82,000
Less: Variable costs:			
Raw materials @ $7.00 per finished unit	26,600	28,000	28,700
Direct labor @ $3.00/per finished unit	11,400	12,000	12,300
Variable manufacturing overhead @$1.25/unit	4,750	5,000	5,125
Total variable costs @ $11.25 per finished unit	$42,750	$45,000	46,125
Contribution margin	$33,250	$35,000	$35,875
Less: Total fixed costs	17,500	17,500	17,500
Net operating income	$15,750	$17,500	$18,375

56. **D** Flexible budget = $216,000 + $11.25(44,500) = $716,625

Actual costs = $495,000 + $217,000 = $712,000

Flexible cost variance = $716,625 − 712,000 = $4,625F

57. **B** $145,000/5,000 = $29.00

58. **C** $(5,100 \times \$29) − \$151,000 = \$3,100U$

59. **D** (Actual variable OH) − (std hours allowed for finished units × BVOHR)

$\$188,000 − (33,000 \times 2 \times \$3) = \$8,000F$

60. **D** (Actual variable OH) − (Actual quantity of MH × BVOHR)

$\$188,000 − (63,000 \times \$3) = \$1,000U$

61. **C** (Actual fixed OH) − (Budgeted fixed OH)

$\$231,000 − \$240,000 = \$9,000U$

Or $\$231,000 − (60,000 \text{ hrs} \times \$4) = \$9,000U$

62. **B** (BQ × BFOHR) − (SQ allowed × BFOHR = (BQ − SQ allowed) BFOHR

$(60,000 − (33,000 \times 2))\$4 = \$24,000F$

This is a favorable variance since there were 6,000 more productive machine hours used than budgeted; thus, the facilities were better utilized than expected.

63. **C** Sales volume variance (SVV) = (ASV − BSV) BCM, where:

ASV = Actual sales volume

BSV = Budgeted sales volume

BCM = Budgeted contribution margin

Tinted (2,300 − 2,400)$10 = $1,000U

Low Tint (2,100 − 2,000)$10 = $1,000F

Total SVV = $0

64. **B** First, compute the sales mix proportion for each product:

	Actual Volume	Proportion	Budgeted Volume	Proportion
Tinted	2,300	52.27%	2,400	54.550%
Low Tint	2,100	47.73%	2,000	45.450%
Total	4,400	100.000%	4,400	100.000%

$SMV^a = BCM^a \times (ASM^a − BSM^a) \times ASV^a$, where:

SMV^a = Sales mix variance for product A

BCM^a = Budgeted contribution margin for product A

BSM^a = Budgeted sales mix for product A

ASM^a = Actual sales mix for product A

ASV^t = Actual sales volume for *all* products

Tinted SMV = 4,400(0.5227 − 0.5455)$10 = $1,003U

Low Tint SMV = 4,400(0.4773 − 0.4545)$10 = $1,003F

Total SMV = $0

65. D   SQV^a = BCM^a × (ASQ^t − BSQ^t) × BSM, where:

SQV^a = Sales quantity variance for product A

BCM^a = Budgeted contribution margin for product A

ASQ^t = Actual sales quantity for all products

BSV^t = Budgeted sales quantity for all products

BSM^a = Budgeted sales mix for product A

Tinted SQV = $10(4,400 − 4,400)0.5455 = $0

Low Tint SQV = $10(4,400 − 4,400)0.4545 = $0

66. A   Transfer price should be $100, the variable cost to Division X

Therefore, the loss is: ($120 − $100) × 3,000 units = $60,000

67. C

68. A

69. A

ROI = Profit margin × Investment asset turnover

$$ROI = \frac{Operating\ Income}{Revenue} \times \frac{Revenue}{Investment\ Center\ Assets}$$

$$ROI = \frac{\$600,000}{\$6,000,000} \times \frac{\$6,000,000}{\$4,000,000 - \$200,000 - \$600,000}$$

ROI = 10.0% × 1.875 times = 18.75%

70. A

RI = Divisional operating income − (Divisional investment base × Minimum capital charge)

RI = $600,000 − [($4,000,000 − 600,000 − 200,000) × 0.15] = $600,000 − $480,000 = $120,000

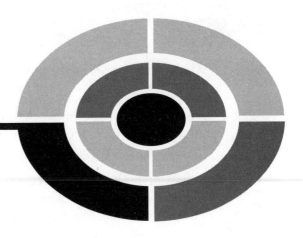

Glossary

A

Absorption costing is a method of inventory costing in which total manufacturing (raw materials, labor, and overhead) costs are included in the inventoriable cost; also referred to as *full absorption costing*.

Absorption pricing method uses as the base the full manufacturing costs of an item to set a price and adds a markup to cover selling and administrative costs and ensure a reasonable profit.

Account analysis method is a subjective method of cost estimation that analyzes each account in the general ledger and classifies each as a variable or fixed cost.

Activity is a repetitive set of tasks performed for a specific business purpose.

Activity-based costing (ABC) is a costing system that assigns all costs to the activity that produces the object or service and then assigns the cost of these activities to the object as it consumes the activity costs. (See also *Activity-based management*.)

Activity-based flexible budget is a flexible budget of an activity that is required to produce and sell products or services.

Activity-based management (ABM) is a system that uses activity-based costing to make decisions concerning customer service and customer profitability. (See also *Activity-based costing.*)

Activity driver is a measure of the frequency and intensity with which a cost object influences activity levels. An example of an activity driver is the number of setups in a furniture production department. (See also *Resource driver.*)

Asset cost is an expended resource or the incurring of liabilities to acquire assets.

Asset turnover is a measure of the investment center manager's ability to generate revenue for each dollar of assets invested in the center, or how many sales dollars are generated by each dollar in capital asset investment. It is computed by dividing the segment's revenue by its investment base.

B

Balanced scorecard is a comprehensive measurement system that "balances" non-financial measures with financial measures to assist executives in managing strategy creation, execution, and evaluation.

Batch-level costs are consumed based on a batch of products being processed through the activity. That is, the groups of products involved are all processed together, regardless of the number of items in the batch. The best example of this level of costs is setup costs.

Benchmarking is a measure that is used to compare the performance of a company's products, services, and activities. The measure is usually that of a best-practice segment within the company or an external best-practice company. (See also *Best-practice performance measures.*)

Best-practice performance measures are process or system measures identified by research or experience in a business, nonprofit, or governmental organization that represent exceptional performance and have been widely recognized as "best" by peer organizations. (See also *Benchmarking.*)

Bill of materials is a document that contains information on product materials based on specifications of the quality and quantity needed in production.

Breakeven point is the volume point where total revenue equals total cost.

Budget is a financial plan of revenues and/or costs of an overall organization or segments of an organization.

Budget slack is the intentional overestimation of cost or the underestimation of revenue for purpose of "beating" the budget by making the targets more easily achieved.

Business process is a set of activities and methodologies used to perform or enable the work needed to achieve a business objective or output.

C

Capacity See *Expected, Normal, Practical, Productive*, and *Theoretical capacity*.

Capital budgeting is long-term capital expenditure analysis for planning the levels of investment in capital assets.

Capitalized cost is the present value of a uniform series of periodic costs that continue for a long period of time.

Cash budget is a budget of the cash balance at the beginning of the period, the projected cash receipts, the projected cash payments, and the ending cash balance at the end of the period.

Certified management accountant (CMA) is a designation given to accountants who have met the educational requirements and the professional competence in management accounting established by the Institute of Management Accountants (IMA). The IMA issues a CMA certificate to those meeting these requirements.

Certified public accountant (CPA) is a designation given to accountants who have passed a qualifying examination and met certain educational and public accounting experience requirements established by a state licensing authority. They are licensed by a state authority to attest to the accuracy of organizational financial statements issued to parties external by a business or non-profit entity.

Chief financial officer (CFO) is the senior executive who is responsible for all the financing and accounting functions of a business.

CMA See *Certified Management Accountant*.

Common cost is a cost incurred by a function, facility, activity, or cost object that is shared by two or more users, such as different segments of a business.

Contribution margin is the difference between sales and variable cost, measured on a total or unit basis.

Contribution margin approach to pricing is a short-term approach to pricing that computes the impact on profit of different levels of volume, starting with variable cost. The variable cost is set at the lowest possible short-term price.

Contribution margin ratio is the unit contribution margin or total contribution margin divided by the unit sales price or total sales, respectively. (It is sometimes called a *contribution margin percentage.*)

Contribution margin statement is an income statement that lists total revenues and deducts variable costs (in total or by individual variable costs) to arrive at a total contribution margin.

Controllable cost is a cost affected directly by the decision of a responsibility center manager.

Controllable revenue is revenue that is partly affected by the decision of a responsibility center manager.

Controller is the chief accounting officer of the business who is responsible for all accounting functions in the corporation. The Controller normally reports to the CFO. In some businesses, the title "Comptroller" is used instead of "Controller."

Cost is a general term that means the sacrifice of resources for a specific purpose. Usually, an accompanying adjective clarifies the type of cost.

Cost allocation is a process of assigned indirect costs to a cost object and is sometimes called *cost assignment.*

Cost behavior refers to a change in total costs between two different levels of activity.

Cost driver is a level of activity or a factor that causes or drives the costs of an object or activity.

Cost estimation is the estimation of costs based on the relationship between past cost behaviors at different levels of activity. (See also *Cost prediction.*)

Cost hierarchy is the classification of costs under levels of cost pools based on the relation of costs to cost drivers. The various levels are unit-level, batch-level, product-level, and facility-level.

Cost object is the purpose for which a cost is incurred.

Cost prediction is the prediction of future costs from predicted relationships. (See also *Cost estimation.*)

Cost variance is a variance between the actual price and a budget or standard price, or a variance between the actual quantity and the budget or standard quantity.

Cost-volume-profit analysis is method for studying the interrelationship between total revenues, total costs, operating income, and total volume. Specifically, it analyzes the impact on profit of changes in the sales price, unit variable cost, total fixed costs, or total volume, or a combination thereof.

CPA See *Certified Public Accountant.*

Cross-functional teams involve all functions in the delivery chain, including product design, engineering, manufacturing, purchasing, suppliers, sales, and accounting.

D

Decentralization is a means of more widely distributing decision making to bring it closer to the point of service or action. While decentralization is usually associated with a large multiple-division, often multinational, company, it really occurs any time higher management assigns the responsibility for managing any size of organizational subunit.

Decision model is a defined method for choosing between alternative decision outcomes.

Decision tree is a graphic representation of various decision alternatives and their outcomes and related probabilities (risks) that are visually available to the decision maker.

Depreciation is a charge against revenue to write off the cost, less salvage value, of an asset over its estimated useful life. There are different methods of depreciating assets.

Depreciation tax shield is used in a capital budgeting analysis and estimates the amount of depreciation that could be deducted from future benefits from an investment in a capital asset.

Differential cost is a cost that differs between two alternatives.

Differential revenue is revenue that differs between two alternatives.

Direct allocation method is used to allocate a support department's costs directly to a production department without including services rendered to other support departments.

Direct cost is a cost directly traceable to a cost object.

Discount rate is a rate used to discount the estimated future cash flows from a capital investment decision. The rate incorporates the projected inflation rate and the amount of estimated risk. This is sometimes called the *opportunity cost* of capital.

Discounted cash flow method is a capital budgeting method for estimating the projected cash inflows, discounting them to the year 0, estimating the cash outflow for an investment at year 0, and comparing the net cash flows in making a capital expenditure decision.

Discretionary cost center is usually an administrative or staff function in an organization that provides services and incurs expenses in which there is no input–output relationship. In a large company these centers would include units such as advertising, legal, public relations, research and development, and accounting.

E

Economic value added (EVA) = Net operating profit after taxes less a capital charge on investment.

Employee time sheet is a record of the time charged to a specific job.

Equivalent unit is the percentage of completion of whole units that are in process during the various stages of production. The equivalent units of production are used to compute an average cost in a process costing system. (See also *Whole unit.*)

Expected capacity is a level of capacity based on the forecasted sales and production levels for the next operating period, usually 1 year. This is a short-run concept and is not used for the planning of long-range fixed asset needs.

Expense is the expenditure of resources to generate revenue during a specific period of time.

F

Facility-level costs are consumed to run a production facility, an organization, or a business as a whole, regardless of the product or service mix, how many products are produced, or how much of the products or services are sold. Some examples of facility-level costs are administration, occupancy costs (such as depreciation, utilities), and computer systems.

Favorable variance is the amount that raises income compared to the budgeted amount.

Financial accounting is a major branch of accounting involving the collecting, recording, and periodical reporting of financial transactions in summary form on an income statement, a balance sheet, or a cash flow statement in accordance with legal, professional, and capital market requirements.

FIFO (first in–first out) method is an inventory method that assumes the beginning inventory will be completed first during the current period and transferred out to another department or to finished goods. In process costing, it separates the beginning inventory costs from the current period's production and assigns them to the first units completed. It then assigns current period costs to equivalent units required to complete the beginning inventory, next it assigns current costs to units started and completed this period, and then it assigns current costs to units in ending working process.

Fixed costs are usually referred to as total costs that do not vary with changes in a given level of activity within the relevant range. They relate to the capacity to produce or to sell the product or services of the business. On the other hand, unit-fixed costs decrease in proportion to the increase in activity.

Fixed overhead production volume variance is the difference between budgeted fixed overhead and allocated fixed overhead.

Fixed overhead spending variance is how much actual fixed costs exceeded the master or static budget.

Flexible budget is a tool for planning and controlling overhead costs in manufacturing, merchandising, and service organizations. It is flexible in that it adjusts the revenues and costs to the various levels of projected or actual activity.

Full absorption costing is the same as absorption costing. (See *Absorption costing*.)

G

Goal congruence is when an individual, members of a group, and the management team have common goals that match those of the organization.

Gross margin is the difference between revenues and manufacturing costs in a manufacturing company or revenues, less cost of merchandise sold in a merchandising company.

H

High-low method is a simple method for estimating cost relationships and thereby separating mixed costs into variable and fixed costs. This method is useful when the cost patterns between costs and volumes can be described with a straight-line function and there is a small amount of variance between the points scattered around the line and the line itself.

Hybrid cost systems are cost systems that incorporate some aspects of a job order costing and process costing. (See also *Operational costing system.*)

I

Incremental cost is the additional cost incurred from the production or delivery of an additional unit of product or service. It is similar to a differential cost.

Incremental revenue is the additional revenue generated from the production, delivery, or sale of an additional unit of product or service. It is similar to differential revenue.

Indirect cost is a cost that is not easily traceable to a cost object. It is also called *overhead cost.*

Indirect manufacturing cost is a cost that is not easily or economically traceable to a cost object in the factory. It is also called *factory overhead cost.*

Industrial-engineering method is a cost estimation method that breaks down processes into repetitive operations or repetitive steps and then determines the relationships between inputs and outputs. It is a "bottoms up" approach to estimating variable costs and fixed costs.

Inventoriable costs include all costs to purchase or manufacture items of inventory.

Investment is the total resources used by a company or a segment to generate income.

Investment center is a responsibility center in which the manager is responsible for revenues, costs, and its investment in assets. Investment centers are often called *divisions.*

Investment tax credit is dollar-for-deduction on the company's tax return when the United States Congress (and some states) has passed tax legislation that allows an investment tax credit on the purchase of certain assets. Refer to the tax law to determine if such a credit is in effect at any given period of time.

J

Job cost record is a source document for entering all costs of a batch or job.

Job order cost system is a costing system in which the costs are traced to an individual batch or job. The job can be for production of products or for a bundle of services.

Just-in-time (JIT) is a process of purchasing, receiving, and placing inventory into production just when it is needed. This cuts the amount of inventory in stock, thus reducing inventory investment and storage costs.

K

Kaizen budgeting incorporates continuous improvement in the budgeting process. (See also *Kaizen costing*.)

Kaizen costing is a Japanese methodology of achieving continuous improvement through small steps. (See also *Kaizen budgeting*.)

L

Lag indicators are measures—usually financial—of the final results of an earlier plan.

Lead indicators are measures that identify future outcomes or predictors of the organization's ability to meet its future strategic goals. Also called *key factors of success*.

Life cycle costs are costs incurred for a new product or service from its research and development, design, purchase, and production, to its maintenance, distribution costs, customer service, and customer support.

Linear cost function is a mathematical equation where, when depicted on a graph, the total costs versus volume of an activity is a single line within the relevant range.

Long-range planning involves developing the broad steps to achieve the business's strategic long-range growth goals.

Loss is an expired cost that was usually unintentional and does not relate to the generation of revenues.

M

Management accounting involves the measuring, analyzing, reporting, and interpreting of financial and non-financial information for managers within organizations to assist them in their decision making and management control roles.

Managerial evaluation involves evaluating the personal performance of a segment manager.

Manufacturing company is a business that purchases raw materials and converts them into finished products.

Manufacturing overhead is all indirect labor, indirect materials, and any other indirect expenses related to producing a product. It refers to any manufacturing cost that is not directly traceable to a product.

Margin of safety is used in conjunction with cost-volume-profit analysis and is the expected sales less break-even sales.

Master budget is a comprehensive company profit plan for the coming year.

Material requisition is an authorization form to request and receive materials from a storeroom into production (work in process). It is the source document for entering the transaction into the accounting journal.

Material requisition form is an authorization and a record of the cost of materials charged to a job or a department.

Materiality is a financial omission, nondisclosure, or misstatement that would cause the financial statements to mislead users of the statements when making evaluations or decisions.

Merchandising company is a business selling goods that were purchased in a finished form.

Mixed variable cost is a cost that contains both variable and fixed elements. Also called *semivariable cost*.

N

Normal capacity is a level of production (represented by productive assets) based on long-range plans for company growth, market forces, and the like. The period of time ranges from 5 to 10 years and considers the capacity needs during this span of time. Thus, this definition of capacity will likely be similar to or less than practical capacity at times, due to normal business cycles.

O

Operational costing system is a type of hybrid costing system that determines costs of batches of products that have standardized production methods but different raw materials in each batch. For example, the production of clothing requires several standardized operations but different materials may be input in any of the operations.

Opportunity costs are the potential benefits (cost savings or profit) foregone by selecting one alternative over another.

Outsourcing means that the overall company or a segment of the company purchases goods and services from outside the company rather than producing the same goods or services within the company.

Overallocated indirect (overhead) cost is the excess of allocated costs over the actual overhead costs for a given period.

Overhead is a general term that refers to indirect costs and expenses not directly related to selling or producing of a product or service. (See also *Manufacturing overhead.*)

P

Payback method is a capital budgeting method that measures the estimated time it will take to recover—in terms of cash inflow—a capital asset expenditure.

Performance computer "dashboards" report, on a real-time basis, a key set of performance metrics (6 to 10) that provide a "quick-look" summary of mission-critical information to management.

Period expenses are periodic expenses charged against periodic revenue to determine net income.

Practical capacity is a level of production that allows for the effects of normal interruptions such as idle time, breakdowns, and holidays. This is essentially an engineering definition in that it is defined using the engineering capabilities of the fixed facilities involved.

Predetermined overhead rate is used to allocate overhead costs to cost objects. It is determined by dividing the estimated overhead costs for a future period by the total estimated overhead allocation base for the same period.

Process cost system is a type of cost accounting system that accumulates costs by a process that produces homogeneous units within a manufacturing facility. The costs of each process are divided by the number of units produced to obtain an average unit cost.

Product cost is all direct material, direct labor, and manufacturing overhead costs required to produce a product and make it part of inventory.

Product-level costs are consumed based on activities that provide services for an entire product line regardless of how many items are eventually produced. For example, original product design and design modifications are product-level activities.

Production capacity normally refers to the ability to produce based on the level of production represented by productive assets, which are primarily capital long-term assets.

Production volume variance is the difference between budgeted fixed overhead and allocated fixed overhead. (See also *Fixed overhead production volume variance.*)

Profit center is a decentralized unit in which the manager has the responsibility and the authority to make decisions that affect both costs and revenues that in turn affect the profitability of the assigned center. Profit centers are sometimes loosely called *business centers* and are found in all types of organizations, such as banks, restaurants, divisions, and any organization where the manager has responsibility for making decisions that affect both profit and expenses.

Profit margin is a measure of the divisional manager's ability to generate revenues at the lowest cost, or how much of each revenue dollar goes to income. The manager will be motivated to increase sales and decrease expenses. It is computed by dividing the operating income of a segment by the total sales of the segment.

R

Regression analysis a quantitative tool for estimating cost relationships between variables in a cost estimation function.

Relevant costs are those predicted costs that differ among two or more alternative courses of action.

Relevant range is the range or band of activity for a specified period in which the proportional relationship between the levels of activity and the total costs is assumed to remain valid.

Relevant revenues are those predicted revenues that differ among two or more alternative courses of action.

Residual income is the amount of operating income left over after deducting a minimum capital charge based on the firm's investment base. The minimum capital charge is the minimum rate of return set by senior management based on risk and other investment opportunities foregone.

Resource driver in an activity-based costing system is a measure of the actual resources used by an activity (it drives the consumption of resources). An example of a resource driver is the percentage of time a production supervisor spends on one activity among the several activities that he or she supervises. (See also *Activity driver.*)

Responsibility accounting system is both a process and a structure. As a *process* it is a system of measuring, collecting, and reporting data by responsibility center. As a *structure*, a responsibility accounting system involves creating responsibility centers. (See also *Responsibility center.*)

Responsibility center is an organizational unit in which the manager is held directly responsible for the performance of the unit.

Return on investment (ROI) is widely used to evaluate investment center managers on whether they have generated a target rate of return on the company's investment in the division. The ROI is computed by dividing the operating income by the company's investment base. It is composed of the profit margin and the asset turnover.

Revenue centers are usually sales departments or sales regions responsible for marketing and selling a product or service.

Rolling budget is a budget that is kept relatively current by adding a new month or quarter and dropping the most recent past month or quarter. (See also *Responsibility center*.)

S

Sales budget variance is the difference between the total sales budget (budgeted sales price × budgeted volume) and the total actual sales (actual sales price × actual volume).

Sales market share variance is the difference between the actual company market share proportion and the budgeted company market share proportion times the actual market size in sales units, times the budgeted weighted average sales price.

Sales market size variance is the difference between the actual total area market size in volume minus the budgeted total area market size in volume times the budgeted weighted average sales price, times the budgeted market share proportion.

Sales mix variance is very useful in evaluating whether the company is meeting its market niche target as stated in its strategic goals. It is computed as the budgeted sales price times the actual volume, times the difference between the budgeted sales mix and the actual sales mix.

Sales orice variance is the difference between the budgeted sales price and the actual sales price times the actual sales volume.

Sales quantity variance is the difference between the sales units of all products in the master budget and the actual sales units sold of all products sold times the budgeted sales price of an individual product, times the budgeted sales proportion for the same product.

Sales volume variance is the difference between the budgeted sales volume in the master budget and the actual sales volume times the budgeted sales price.

Scatter diagram method is a rough cost estimation method that plots costs of past activity levels and is roughly used to separate mixed costs into variable and fixed costs. (This method is sometimes called the *scatter graph method*.)

Semivariable cost. See *Mixed variable cost*.

Service company is a company that sells services or some other intangible product to customers.

Service department. See *Support department*.

Short-term planning involves breaking down the long-range plans into smaller steps for the coming year or the coming quarter. The master budget is an example of a short-term plan.

Six Sigma is a quality improvement methodology whose objective is to eliminate defects in any aspect that affects customer satisfaction.

Standard is a predetermined criterion or benchmark against which actual performance can be compared.

Standard cost is the cost of one unit of product output for materials, labor, and overhead usually determined by an engineering study. Thus, it is a unit concept as compared to a budget benchmark, which is a total concept.

Standard cost system is a system of accounting under which the cost of products is determined using standard costs instead of actual costs.

Static budget is a detailed plan of revenue and expense projections based on one level of activity only.

Stepped fixed cost is a cost that increases in steps. It is sometimes called a *stepped cost*.

Step-down allocation method (sometimes called *the step-down method*) gives partial consideration to reciprocal services provided by other support departments when allocating support department costs. It requires that support departments be sequenced or ranked in a predetermined order before the allocation process can begin. The most common approach to determining this ranking is to use the highest percentage of services provided to other supported departments.

Strategic analysis is scanning the business' competitive environment to ascertain the major influences, opportunities, and factors that will determine the success of the organization and identifying the strengths and weaknesses of the organization in managing these opportunities and influences.

Strategy is a plan of action resulting from scanning the business environment (potential markets, customers, products and services, and competitors) for opportunities to meet its overall goals.

Sunk costs are expenditures made in the past that cannot be avoided or changed by any future decision.

Support department is a department that provides support to other internal departments within an organization. It is also called *service department*.

T

Target costing involves setting a competitive market price for a product based on market analysis, computing the maximum costs that will be allowed, and working out cost reductions made possible by the improvement of technologies and processes.

Theoretical capacity is a level of production that requires the perfect utilization of fixed assets. There are no machine breakdowns, no inefficiency, and no breaks or holidays.

Transfer price is the price of a product or service that is transferred to other internal divisions or they can be sold either internally or externally on the open market. When sales are made to other divisions, they become revenue to the selling division and purchases to the buying division.

Treasurer is an officer responsible for cash and other financial resources of the company, such as maintaining bank relations, managing investments, handling cash receipts, and similar operations. The Treasurer normally reports to the CFO.

U

Underallocated overhead cost is the amount of allocated overhead that is lower than the actual amount of overhead for a given period.

Unfavorable variance is the amount that reduces income compared to the budgeted amount.

Unit cost is a cost determined by dividing total cost by total units of some measure.

Unit-level costs are consumed each time a unit of output is completed by an activity. That is, the quantity of usage relates to the volume of output of production. This output may be a product or a service.

V

Value-added activities are activities in the value chain that, from the perspective of the customer, add value to a product or service.

Value-added costs are costs that, from the customer's perspective, do not add utility or value to the product or service.

Value chain is a linked sequence of operations or processes that add value or usefulness to a product or service from the start of the chain through each link to the end delivery to the customer. For example, in a manufacturing company the chain would contain all the stages of research and development, design, physical resource acquisition, production, marketing, distribution, and customer service.

Value engineering consists of breaking down the product into its design elements or functions and challenging each element to determine if it adds value to the customer at the lowest cost.

Variable costs are total costs that vary in direct proportion to changes in the level of some measure of activity. However, unit variable costs remain constant as volume of activity changes.

Variable overhead efficiency variance is the difference between the flexible budget based on actual input of the cost driver and the flexible budget based on standard units allowed of the cost driver times the budgeted variable overhead rate per unit.

Variable overhead flexible budget variance is the difference between the total flexible variable overhead budget and the total actual variable overhead.

Variable overhead spending variance is the difference between the actual variable overhead and the budgeted variable overhead based on the actual quantity of the cost driver times the budgeted variable overhead rate.

W

Weighted average method is a method of process costing that assumes an average use of resources in each process and computes an *average* cost per unit of beginning inventory and the current period's production (cost done to date). The total costs of work done to date are divided by the equivalent units of production done to date.

Whole unit is physical unit that is started into production and when finished will be a complete unit. (See also *Equivalent unit*.)

INDEX

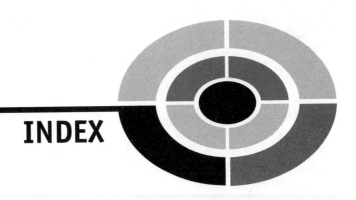